# HR – The Business Partner

## Second Edition

# HR Series Preface

*The HR Series* is edited by *Julie Beardwell*, Associate Dean, Leeds Business School, and *Linda Holbeche*, Director of Research and Policy at CIPD, and is designed to plug the gap between theory and implementation. The books draw on real-life examples of strategic HR in practice and offer practical insights into how HR can add value to the business through transforming individual and functional delivery. Intended for serious HR professionals who aspire to make a real difference within their organization, *The HR Series* provides resources to inform, empower and inspire the HR leaders of the future.

# HR – The Business Partner

## Furthering the Journey

Second Edition

Barbara Kenton and Jane Yarnall

AMSTERDAM • BOSTON • HEIDELBERG • LONDON • NEW YORK • OXFORD
PARIS • SAN DIEGO • SAN FRANCISCO • SINGAPORE • SYDNEY • TOKYO

Butterworth-Heinemann is an Imprint of Elsevier

Butterworth-Heinemann is an imprint of Elsevier
Linacre House, Jordan Hill, Oxford OX2 8DP, UK
30 Corporate Drive, Suite 400, Burlington, MA 01803, USA

Second Edition 2010

**British Library Cataloguing in Publication Data**
A catalogue record for this book is available from the British Library

**Library of Congress Cataloging-in-Publication Data**
A catalog record for this book is available from the Library of Congress

ISBN: 978-1-85617-847-1

For information on all Butterworth-Heinemann publications
visit our website at elsevierdirect.com

Printed and bound in Great Britain
09 10 11 12   10 9 8 7 6 5 4 3 2 1

Working together to grow
libraries in developing countries

www.elsevier.com | www.bookaid.org | www.sabre.org

ELSEVIER    BOOK AID
            International    Sabre Foundation

# Contents

Contents

# List of Figures

# List of Tables

# Foreword

Whilst much has been written about strategic HR management and its contribution to organisational performance, real life examples of what works are pretty thin on the ground. The books within this series draw on live examples of strategic HR in practice and offer practical insights, tools and frameworks that will help transform the individual and functional delivery of HR within a variety of organisational contexts.

The concept of Business Partnering has been one of the most problematic in terms of its implementation since Dave Ulrich first introduced and popularised the approach in the 1990s. The 'Ulrich model' has been widely adopted as an approach for structuring the HR function, especially in large organisations. According to this, Business Partners, a small corporate centre, centres of excellence or expertise and shared services, in-house or outsourced, are the principal delivery channels for functional excellence. Business Partnering as an approach underpins the original Ulrich functional roles model.

As practice informs theory, the concept of Business Partnering has continued to evolve and become a dominant way of thinking about how HR can provide value-adding solutions to meet real business needs. When Barbara Kenton and Jane Yarnall produced the first edition of this book in 2006 they provided an excellent 'state of the nation' on HR Business Partnering. In this new edition they have gone a step further – providing not only a progress report on the evolution of the Business Partner role but also an intensely practical slant on how to carry out this multi-faceted role effectively.

There can be little doubt that the Business Partner role is evolving rapidly. In many organisations, the role of strategic Business Partner is now separated out from Business Partnering in general. What is particularly helpful about Jane and Barbara's approach is that they recognise the contingent nature of the Business Partnering, and therefore the importance of situational relevance and 'fit'. They therefore stop sort of providing an idealised and potentially impractical blueprint. At the same time they have deduced from a variety of sources some key Business Partnering trends and commonalities which are now emerging irrespective of the nature or sector of the organisation. These will form a very useful checklist for any HR practitioner seeking to introduce Business Partnering, or improve its current effectiveness. As the authors point out, successful Business Partnering occurs when as much thought has gone into preparing line managers for their partnership role as into preparing HR professionals to become Business Partners.

The authors make good use of their research amongst practitioners. As they say, they have drawn on theory where appropriate but have focused more on practice – which is where many practitioners experience the real challenges and are looking for inspiration. They have added new chapters on the skills such as project management which experience suggests are ever more needed to be effective in a BP role. They have updated all the chapters and provide helpful pointers on where they see the role evolving to next. The authors point out that Business Partnering is both a mindset and a skill set – especially the ability to build and maintain effective value-adding business relationships. In a very real sense they are helping to move the field of Business Partnering forward by describing not just the 'what' and the 'why' of Business Partnering but also the 'how'. This new edition therefore makes a very welcome addition to this series and will be an invaluable source of guidance to HR and other professionals who are seeking to become truly effective Business Partners.

# Acknowledgements

There are so many people who have contributed to this book either overtly or indirectly that sadly it is impossible to give credit to them all.

We are particularly grateful to the organisations and people working as Business Partners who contributed their time and energy in talking to us about the research. We also want to acknowledge the many other authors whose work we have drawn on to bring you this book. They have helped to stretch our thinking and widened the circle of knowledge by their generosity in allowing us to use their work here.

In addition, we would like to thank our colleagues at Roffey Park and elsewhere, who have supported our writing and provided inspiration through their own work. In particular, we would like to thank the clients who have provided case studies for this book.

Thanks must go to the whole team at Elsevier publishing for their continued support and encouragement in making this book possible and finally, we would like to thank our friends and partners for supporting us along the way and providing both encouragement and tolerance at just the right times.

# The Authors

**BARBARA KENTON** FCIPD, MSc, DTM, Dip Gestalt is a freelance consultant and Director of WHooSH *The Change and Conflict Consultancy* which supports individuals, teams and organisations through the challenges of change. With over 20 years experience in training, development and consultancy at both operational and strategic levels, she has particularly supported HR functions in their transitional journey by helping them to develop the key process skills needed to work more strategically with the line. Prior to working freelance in 2004, Barbara worked as a senior consultant at both Roffey Park Institute and the Civil Service College and has a background in the public sector. She has worked internationally in Poland, Holland, South Africa, United States, France, Germany and Northern Asia and is the co-author of Change, Conflict and Community with Suzanne Penn (also published by Elsevier). In a voluntary capacity she works as a community mediator. Barbara can be contacted on: barbara@whoosh.uk.com and details of WHooSH can be found at www.whoosh.uk.com.

**JANE YARNALL** PhD, BA (Hons), FCIPD is Director of Skills Evolution Ltd, a company specialising in organisational development and training. Her expertise includes work on HR Business Partners, career frameworks, competency development, assessment and development centres, as well as design and delivery on a broad range of bespoke training and development programmes.

Jane has over 20 years experience in Human Resources, both within corporations and as an independent consultant. She received a doctorate for her research into the impact of organisational self-development programmes on career satisfaction and organisational commitment. She has also published articles on the role of line managers and the current status of training evaluation; as well as, more recently "Strategic career management: developing your talent" published by Elsevier. Jane can be contacted via Jane@skillsevolution.co.uk and details of Skills Evolution can be found at www.skillsevolution.co.uk.

# 1

# Introduction

*You do not need to navigate a company to a pre-defined destination you take steps – one at a time into an unknowable future. There are not paths, no roads ahead of us. In the final analysis, it is the walking that beats the path – it is not the path that makes the walk*

Poet Machada in the 5th Discipline – Senge (1990)

At the time of writing the original book, one job title that seemed to be on the increase for people in HR was that of "Business Partner". Since our first publication in 2005, the title Business Partner has become commonplace although still not widely introduced in all organisations. Certainly some of the challenges that existed around that time are still significant today. We decided now was the time to write a revised edition as the thinking and practice of Business Partnering has moved on. Having said that, many of the themes in the original book remain constant, particularly around the skills to develop and the challenges to overcome. We have made the following specific additions to the book with the aim of bringing it up to date:

- A new part on project management skills;
- A new part on thinking styles;
- A chapter with case studies based on practitioner experience;
- A resource list and recommended further reading; and
- General updates to all chapters, including recent research and information on the value triangle as a way of assessing your contribution to the business.

In this chapter, we examine the history of the role of the Business Partner and the drivers for the changing role of HR. We also look at what it means to be a Business Partner in broad terms and how this differs from the role of both the internal and external consultant. We look at how thinking about Business Partner practice has evolved since 2005 and draw on more recent research to highlight what seems to be useful now in considering the Business Partner role. Ultimately, organisations and those of you working in HR will still need to think carefully about the drivers for any change in the way you work and what makes most sense for you in your own organisational context.

We start by looking at the title in more detail – what do the terms "Business" and "Partner" imply? – "Business" implies a level of strategic intervention, which goes beyond the individual. This differentiates a historic role of HR as being just about people and working at an operational level. It also implies that those in the role will have a good understanding of the nature of the business and therefore be in a good position to advise others in this respect. "Business" also conjures up a level of professionalism and credibility, a matter of factness, which sets people in this role apart from those in more traditional and operational HR roles.

Therefore, the role of the Business Partner includes having a good understanding of strategy and/or the ability to think strategically about the business needs. We recognise that Business Partners will not always be working at a strategic level in the organisation and come on to this later. At whatever level of working, the elements of supporting the business and helping turn strategy into action remain important aspects. "Partner" and what this title conjures up is something very different. "Partnership" implies working alongside, equal responsibility and shared skills and expertise, supporting clients within the business including providing an expert perspective when appropriate. Put these two together and you get an idea of the role of the Business Partner. Our definition from 2006 still seems relevant for this revised edition: "someone who maintains a strong connection with employees and the operational side of the business, while focusing on strategic goals and influencing through others" (Kenton & Yarnall, 2006).

## A little of the history of business partnering

Dave Ulrich has long championed the role of strategic Business Partner, linking it to a business imperative for a more pro-active approach from HR with less reliance on operational expertise.

Ulrich's thinking (1997) was that HR needed to transform itself with a focus on adding value through four key roles, each of which needed to work as a "Business Partner" with a specific outcome or deliverable in focus (Figure 1.1).

Ulrich described the four roles as follows:

■ Strategic Partners – with a focus on strategy execution and meeting customer needs through aligning HR priorities;

**Figure 1.1**  Ulrich's matrix.

- Administrative Experts – ensuring efficiency in the infrastructure; supporting the business and improving organisational efficiency by reengineering the HR function and other work processes;
- Employee Champions – paying attention to increasing employees commitment and capability through listening and responding to their needs; and
- Change Agents – delivering organisational transformation and culture change.

The aspirational role of the Business Partner since this model was introduced has perhaps been to deliver strategic objectives in line with all of the above. Most would agree that to achieve and maintain this high level of strategic intervention is challenging. Those truly skilled in one or more of the roles can command a high salary and with that goes a high expectation of what they can deliver. Certainly the emerging role over the years has become more, rather than less complex, and in our discussions with HR practitioners it would seem that people are providing a whole host of services without neat boundaries or role distinction.

In recognition of the mismatch between theory and practice, Ulrich and Brockbank (2005) revised the roles previously identified and included a new role of "HR Leader" to separate out the responsibilities of more senior HR Partners. The model on the next page (Figure 1.2) shows the separate and connected role of HR Leader signalling the importance of leadership throughout all roles.

Ulrich and Brockbank emphasise the need to tailor the model to the needs of the organisation and this would reflect our own views on the importance of working with a model which best fits the requirements.

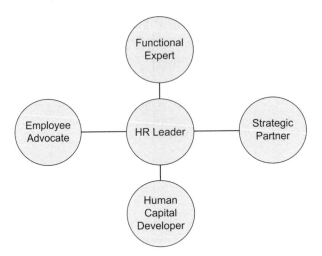

**Figure 1.2** Revised partner roles.

Although Ulrich is the most quoted of authors on the topic of Business Partnering, many others have compared the traditional role of HR with an emerging need for a more strategic function. The model on the next page (Table 1.1) highlights some of the comparitors between the transactional and strategic functions.

Traditionally, the role of HR has included a fair percentage of administrative work, which in many organisations has now either been outsourced, substituted for advanced IT programmes or in some way re-organised within the overall structure of HR. The purpose of these moves has been to create a more responsive client-centred service, which is proactive in its approach to developing the business. In theory, these changes should also create more space for HR professionals to work at a strategic level within the organisation. So rather than being driven by a need within HR for greater power (although this undoubtedly is a spin off) the changes are needed to keep apace with the fast pace of organisational life and demands now placed on organisations.

These include legislative changes (e.g. equal opportunities legislation, Government modernisation agenda), financial changes and increases in mergers and partnerships across organisations; shifts in employee expectations and needs and increased opportunities from advanced IT capabilities.

Roffey Park Research (2009) highlights the significant factors given by their respondents for implementing HR Business Partnering with 73% (from a research population of 305) citing support of business strategy as a factor. Other factors rated highly by respondents included improving organisational performance and improving HR performance.

**Table 1.1**   HR Roles Compared: Transactional vs Strategic

| Role of the HR Professional | Transactional Approach | Strategic Approach |
| --- | --- | --- |
| Areas of interest | Recruiting, training, pay, work relations | Strategy and culture of the organisation and policy |
| View of the organisation | Micro | Macro |
| Client | Employees | Managers and the organisation as a whole |
| Status in the organisation | Rather weak | Rather strong |
| Educational requirements | Specialist in human resource management | General HR education with management experience or general manager with HR experience |
| Time range for activities | Short range | Medium- to long-term range |
| Business based on | Transactions | Change/transformations |

M. Green, Public Personnel Management, Spring (2002).

Interestingly "reducing HR headcount", which those in HR might suspect as a reason for change was only mentioned by 28%.

## What does the role involve?

We have already established that the role of Business Partner is both complex and evolving. However, most would agree that the role in theory at least is strategic in nature and has a focus on aligning HR with business strategy. In reality not all Business Partners will be working with senior managers but where the role is applied at more junior levels, challenges manifest which are discussed in more detail throughout the book.

The definition of the role depends largely on the paradigm or lens through which we view it. For example as:

■ A strategic role with underpinning assumptions;
■ A practice aligned with the role of the internal consultant; *or*
■ A formal set of skills associated with different roles.

## Business partnering as a strategic role

Viewed as a role: what would a strategic business partner be doing that someone in a more traditional HR role might not? and how would we notice?

Some assumptions about effective Business Partnering practice that seem to be around through our discussions with HR include:

- Influence comes through having a seat at the Executive table;
- Value added contributions come from intervening at a strategic level and are likely to include activities such as organisational design, talent management, strategy development and planning and organisational change; and
- Transactional activities, e.g. hands on recruitment, maintaining services and records and performance management get in the way of successful Business Partnering.

If these assumptions are believed either explicitly or implicitly within the HR function then the journey of transformation might be a very frustrating one. The reality in organisations is that depending on the size and culture, HR may or may not have a seat on the Executive Board. HR will need to work within the reality of "what is" as well as influencing any future way of working. Part of the influencing agenda of HR may be to get into a position of influence with senior managers in the organisation. The concept of value added work goes far beyond organisational design and strategy and in our view, work continues to be needed by HR to define added value in the eyes of the external and internal customers. So-called "transactional" activities (often those most closely aligned to meeting the direct needs of people in the organisation) need to be valued as much as the more strategic elements of the HR role, so that people know the organisation cares about its people as well as the business overall. Where Business Partnering has perhaps failed in organisations is where there has been a loss of focus in relation to taking care of some of the fundamental work of HR. Having said all of that, we differentiate between strategy initiation/development and strategic thinking in Chapter 6, seeing the ability to do the latter as fundamental to the role at any level.

From this paradigm some of the activities aligned to Business Partnering practice might include:

- Strategic planning;
- Organisational development and design;
- Improving organisational productivity and quality;
- Facilitating mergers, acquisitions and partnerships;
- Scanning the environment for new products/potential new partnerships;

- Recruitment and selection – strategy rather than implementation;
- Employee development – training/education, management development, performance appraisal, career planning, competency/talent assessment – again strategy and advice on these areas rather than carrying out the strategy;
- Compensation and benefits – reward and recognition initiatives, retirement programmes and redundancy programmes;
- HR information systems – management of;
- Overseeing Trade Union negotiations; and
- Responsibility for legal and regulatory requirements – equal opportunities policy and practice, employee record keeping.

## Business partnering as a practice

### How does business partner practice compare to that of a consultant?

In this introduction, we wanted to pay some attention to similarities and differences between how people do what they habitually do in the role of Business Partner compared to internal and external consultants.

Whilst most writing on consultancy draws upon the external consultant as an example, writers accept that there are particular issues faced by consultants operating from within.

It is recognised that internal consultants possess many of the skills deployed by their external counterparts (Armstrong, 1992; Duncan & Nixon, 1999; Laabs, 1997). They have the additional advantage of knowing the business – its systems, language and culture, from the inside. However, the internal consultant works within a complex contractual environment where reporting lines may be the same as that of their client. They will typically not hold budgetary or other power to enforce change and may be perceived as agents of a broader corporate agenda rather than true client helpers. As Armstrong (1997) states:

> *" Internal consultants may have just as much expertise, although as employees it may be more difficult for them to be – or to be seen to be – as independent as those from outside the organisation. They have to demonstrate that they are able to deliver truly objective advice. "*

If the role of the internal consultant is to facilitate change, then particular challenges exist over and above those facing consultants from outside. The skills and attributes they bring to the role are often overlooked when line managers look for support to achieve change so internal consultants can find themselves busy with mundane operational tasks whilst external consultants get the more challenging, strategic projects. This sidelining is a function of many factors: the credibility of the consultants themselves, their ability to market their offerings, the micropolitical landscape, status and value issues connected to consultancy use.

Typically the internal consultant is drawn from one of the teams of professional service providers such as HR, IT or finance where there is a history of supporting internal customers with specific problems.

Writers agree (Laabs, 1997; Armstrong 1992; Duncan & Nixon, 1999) that the internal consultant's role is to lead and influence change through supporting clients to learn and apply new skills. In this sense, there is a tension in the internal consultant's role; how to help the client, where the best help that can be given may not be aligned to the organisation's agenda.

Block (2001) recognises these tensions, *"Because you work for the same organisation, line managers can see you as being captured by the same forces and madness that impinge on them. Thus they may be a little slower to trust you and recognise that you have something special to offer them".*

The main differentiating factors between internal and external consultants are summarised in Table 1.2 below.

**Table 1.2**   Internal/External Consultants: Key Differences in Role

| External | Internal |
|---|---|
| Credibility through brand status and previous experience | Credibility through history of interactions within the business |
| Broad business perspective – bringing new ideas | Deep organisational perspective |
| Limited organisation-specific knowledge, possibly at content level only – 'Not made here' | Understands its culture, language and deeper symbolic actions |
| Perceived as objective | Perceived as an organisational 'agent' |
| Special | The same |
| Low investment in final success | High investment in final success |
| Meets client's agenda | Meets corporate agenda – which may not be client's |
| Needs time to understand the people – may misinterpret actions and interpersonal dynamics | Knows the people, but may have preconceptions |
| 'On the clock' – timed, expensive, rare and rationed | Free, accessible, and available |

There are many similarities between the list on the right-hand side and the Business Partner role. The topic of whose agenda you are meeting is discussed in more detail throughout the book and in Chapter 4 we explore the different roles consultants might adopt and the implications for working inside the organisation.

**Challenges and tensions**

In Kenton and Moody's (2003) research internal consultants were asked about their biggest challenges in the role. By far the most frequently mentioned were:

■ Lack of understanding of the role within the business;
■ Lack of trust;
■ Lack of senior management support; and
■ Lack of power to action projects/proposals.

These issues also link to research and discussions around challenges for those in the role of Business Partner. For example, Roffey Park Research (2009) compares the understanding of the role by people in HR and Business Partners with that of line managers. Forty-four percent of managers included in the survey were either unclear or somewhat unclear of the roles of those in HR Business Partnering.

If we view Business Partnering as a practice, then generic competencies might lend themselves to ways of working at the different levels within HR. We have suggested some competencies that might be used for the development of roles, at the end of this chapter.

## Business partnering as a formal set of skills associated with different roles

The concept of Business Partnering goes beyond changing traditional operational HR job descriptions to looking more carefully at the skills required and the capacity for individuals to influence change.

In Part 2 of this book we focus on skills which we still consider fundamental to the role of Business Partner at whatever level of the organisation this sits. These core skills include: self and organisational awareness, relationship skills, consultancy skills, thinking skills, project management skills and skills in leading and influencing change.

## Links to culture and level of maturity of the organisation

As well as how we define Business Partnering, we also need to consider the level of development and culture of the organisation. We consider this a key factor if

HR is to successfully move from a more transactional role to something more strategic. This is a challenge to say the least where HR operates as a function distinct and separate from initiatives aimed at people and organisational development (OD or HRD). If the growth and placement of HR do not sit alongside our understanding of the organisation, we are bound to find frustrations and challenges – working against the prevailing culture rather than with it.

Models of the shifting HR role could helpfully take account of models of organisational development. For example, Harung and Reiber (1995) highlight some useful descriptions of organisational development, which reflect the level of maturity of an organisation.

| | | |
|---|---|---|
| Reactive | → | Proactive and preventive |
| Partial perspective | → | Holistic overview |
| Command and control | → | Collaboration and empowerment |
| Short-term perspective | → | Long-term perspective |
| Task oriented | → | People oriented |
| Ambivalent to feedback | → | Welcoming feedback |
| Resistance to change | → | Innovation and entrepreneurship |
| Conventional | → | Path finding |
| Significant component of struggle | → | Joyful self-expression and dynamism |
| Stereotype | → | Plays many roles successfully |
| First-order learning | → | Second order- (learning to learn) |
| Efficiency (doing things right) | → | Effectiveness (doing right things) |
| "Win-lose" | → | Towards "win" |

Harung and Reiber point out that in the earlier stages of development an organisation might only demonstrate the features shown on the left-hand side of the diagram, while organisations in more advanced stages of development would more likely demonstrate those on both sides.

In our experience, when significant change is happening in organisations, responses to change on both an individual and organisational level can vary between reactive (left-hand side) and proactive or creative (right-hand side). The temptation can be to manage or control change by taking a firmer, more entrenched stance, rather than taking a helicopter perspective and applying a more flexible and responsive approach.

Senior managers increasingly need prompts to think strategically from those with knowledge in HR to help them understand the impact of changes on the organisation and how to best make use of the people employed to make the business a success. Part of the role of the Business Partner is to help the organisation see where it currently is, the implications that follow from the present culture and the options needed for moving to where it needs to be.

The HR function could also usefully pay attention to this when thinking about the organisation's readiness to change to support Business Partnering practice. More about this in Chapter 4.

Our view is that there will be a number of people working inside the organisation, who may be called Business Partner or HR Advisor, Change Agent, Internal Consultant or variations on these themes. Whilst the roles may differ in the level of authority and specific remit, there will be some common challenges to all. This book aims to provide useful advice and considerations for anyone in an internal consultancy position.

## Background to our research approach and framework for this book

Our research for the book was carried out in the following ways:

- Informal interviews on the telephone and in person with HR practitioners;
- Gathering stories over a number of years from consultancy programmes including the Roffey Park residential programmes (Consultancy skills and HR Business Partner);
- Data from Roffey Park's Management Agenda and more recent Business Partnering Research;
- Desk research – reading and research from books and articles on consultancy, HR practice, OD and change;
- Questionnaires and interviews towards "The Role of the Internal Consultant" by Barbara Kenton and Diane Moody; and
- On-going discussions with colleagues working in a similar field.

Some of the assumptions which underpin this work are:

- Those in the role of Business Partner or aspiring to this way of working are in demanding roles and working in challenging times;
- Many people in HR working in this way are already highly skilled;
- Learning comes through sharing ideas and experiences;
- Learning can come through challenge and success;
- Noticing what works well is as helpful as noticing what does not;

- It helps to look outside our own organisation at practice elsewhere to see what might work for our own organisations; and
- The more Business Partners can understand the systems they are working in and with, the more effective they are likely to be.

We have adopted the model by Harung and Reiber, described earlier in this chapter, to provide a framework reflecting Business Partnership behaviours. You may want to compare this with any existing competency frameworks you have in place or use it to define new ones.

We should stress that this includes generic behaviours, more aligned to the *process* of Business Partnering. Specific behaviours for example around organisational design or talent management might need to be added in, although we would warn against making the list too long or complex.

Part 2 of this book focuses specifically on key competencies as shown below and a more detailed guide of what is covered in each chapter is outlined at the beginning of each part. For example "delivering to the business" is reflected in the chapters on key consultancy skills, managing projects and reviewing performance. In addition this competence area is covered in Part 1.

## Behavioural framework for business partners

## Delivering to the business

### Holistic overview
- Understands systems thinking and uses this to consider impact of interventions;
- Understands the bigger organisational context and future vision and strategy of the company;
- Demonstrates a good understanding of the business environment;
- Encourages discussions which help identify things stopping the organisation from moving forward; and
- Strategic thinker – takes a helicopter view on business needs.

### Plays many roles successfully
- Is able to flex their skill and experience to suit a wide variety of business needs;
- Able to provide both expert advice and support and guidance appropriately; and
- Identifies and uses appropriate specialists where boundaries of role end.

### Long-term perspective
- Avoids getter bogged down in the operational side of HR work;
- Delegates appropriately to others;

- Keeps up to date with trends inside and outside the sector which may have business implications; and
- Helps to shape the direction of the business in line with strategic priorities.

## Working alongside managers in the business

### Collaboration and empowerment

- Develops good internal networks across their defined area of the business;
- Builds and maintains effective relationships with people outside their functional area;
- Engages relevant key stakeholders and sponsors;
- Actively involves others in the decision-making process; and
- Ensures that clients are confident and competent to carry on after any intervention.

### People oriented

- Builds strong relationships with clients quickly;
- Able to build and maintain rapport with a wide range of people;
- Demonstrates empathy and understanding in challenging times;
- Builds trust by getting to know clients and their needs well;
- Identifies and works with the strengths of others in the team;
- Shares knowledge and information with others

### Towards "win"

- Ensures that contracts are in place for specific areas of work which meet the needs of the client and the business;
- Monitors contracts at both the content and process levels;
- Clarifies the boundaries of both their role and the work to be carried out;
- Avoids creating unrealistic expectations by their clients; and
- Acts with political sensitivity towards "win" situations for individuals and the business.

## Self-awareness and impact

### Focused on learning

- Questions basic assumptions about self and others in order to heighten learning;
- Continually seeks self-improvement;
- Demonstrates a good awareness of strengths and areas for development;

- Uses learning as a basis for future development;
- Seeks opportunities to move out of comfort zone;
- Shares learning about the organisation and business issues with others; and
- Chooses self-development opportunities which are appropriate to needs.

## Self-expression

- Actively promotes the business of the organisation through deeds and words;
- Demonstrates credibility by understanding the business and the range of issues facing managers;
- Resilient – able to cope with the day-to-day pressures;
- Able to maintain an appropriate work life balance; and
- Presents information in a confident and clear way which meets the needs of the audience.

## Dynamism

- Is regarded as someone who "walks the talk";
- Acts as a role model for others in the organisation;
- Engages others by showing a real interest in them as individuals;
- Approachable and visible; and
- Brings visible energy and drive to the role.

## Creating and leading change

### Proactive and preventive

- Proactively seeks opportunities within the business to support strategy;
- Anticipates likely obstacles to implementing business change;
- Applies knowledge and understanding of change theory to implement changes successfully;
- Strikes an appropriate balance between achieving the business goals and managing emotional reactions to change; and
- Able to use influence to engage others in the change process.

### Innovation and entrepreneurship

- Finds creative ways to work with managers, drawing on a range of methodologies to support business needs;
- Able to work independently and make strategic decisions aimed at business improvement; and
- Looks for and identifies solutions beyond the obvious.

## Path finding

- Able to cope with ambiguity and complexity;
- Role models working on the edge of own comfort zones; and
- Identifies new possibilities to take the business forward and create competitive advantage.

## Delivering a business-focused service

### Prioritising

- Places the right priority on business needs in the light of longer term goals;
- Recognises the need to withdraw from a piece of work and moves on without impacting relationships;
- Demonstrates an understanding of the difference between urgent and important;
- Utilises business data to help shape the direction of the business; and
- Able to challenge appropriately and say no when necessary.

### Utilising feedback

- Actively seeks and reviews feedback as the basis for insight and learning;
- Demonstrates learning from feedback by applying new ways of working;
- Looks for ways to improve the service of the Business Partner provision; and
- Seeks to enhance relationships and actions by thorough questioning during reviews.

### Demonstrating effectiveness

- Sets appropriate measures at the start of any project;
- Ensures buy-in from the business to the evaluation process; and
- Utilises evaluation data to demonstrate the added value of interventions and the impact on business strategy.

We have included a checklist and a list of references at the end of each chapter as a resource for continuing professional development. At the end of this book you will find further resources to help with your continuing professional development.

This book aims to be a practical guide, which draws on theory rather than an academic piece, which may draw on practice. Whether or not we have struck the right balance here is for the reader to decide. We also acknowledge that we have drawn on the work of many others to bring you this book, including our own colleagues and participants on programmes.

Throughout this book we use the terms Business Partner and internal consultant intermittently as in our view the Business Partner also needs to be an internal consultant, although depending on definitions, the internal consultant will not necessarily need to be a Business Partner! We also use the terms "client", "sponsor" and stakeholders" and these terms are explored in more detail in Part 1.

We live in a time when there is so much knowledge available to us that it is hard to know where the boundaries are. This in a way parallels the challenges for the Business Partner whose role is becoming increasingly complex. We wish you luck in the challenges, but more importantly we wish you well in your role in delivering a meaningful service to your organisation and its people.

## References

Armstrong, M. (1992). How to be an internal consultant. *Human Resources, Winter*(1992/3): 26–29.

Block, P. (2001). *Flawless consulting* (2nd ed.). San Francisco: Jossey Bass/ Pfeiffer.

Duncan, J. R., & Nixon, M. (1999). From watchdog to consultant. *Strategic Finance, 80*(10), 42–46.

Green, M. E. (2002). Human resource consulting: why doesn't your staff get it? *Public Personnel Management, 31*(1), pp. 111–120, IPMA International Personnel Management Association.

Harung, H. C., & Reiber, P. C. (1995). Core values behind 115 years of development: a case study of GC. Reiber & Co., Bergen, Norway. *The TQM Magazine, 7*(6), 17–24. MCB University Press. ISSN 0945-478X.

Kenton, B., & Moody, D. (2003). *The role of the internal consultant.* Roffey Park Institute.

Kenton, B., & Yarnall, J. (2006). *HR – The business partner, shaping a new direction.* Elsevier.

Laabs, J. J. (October 1997). *Stay a step ahead with 5 key skills. Workforce, 76*(10), 56–58.

Senge, P. M. (1998). *The fifth discipline – The art and practice of the learning organisation.* London: Century Business.

Ulrich, D. (1997). *Human resource champions.* Boston: Harvard University Press.

Ulrich, D., & Brockbank, W. (2005). *The HR value proposition.* Harvard Business School Press.

# Part 1

## Shaping the Business Partnership

The transition from Operational HR to Strategic Business Partnership is a difficult one. Whether you are already working as a Business Partner and are reviewing your effectiveness, or whether your HR function is considering a move to a Partnership model, this part is likely to be of use to you. This part is aimed at helping you think through how to position the Partnership, both from an organisational perspective and as an individual working as a Partner. The chapters focus on how to position and market the Partnership, how to structure and staff the function to suit your organisation and how to target your approach towards your clients.

Chapter 2 examines how Business Partnerships can position themselves to suit both the business strategy and culture. Partnerships need to begin from a starting point of assessing what they are seeking to achieve and influence before they can build their brand image and develop an appropriate marketing plan. The chapter covers how to gain an understanding of the current perceptions of the function and then work to gain clarity on the gap between those perceptions and the desired position of the function. A staged process is presented to help understand the existing client needs and the service provided and advice is given on how to promote the success of the Business Partnership Function by building on value-added case histories.

Chapter 3 examines the various options for structuring a Business Partnership Function depending on the service it chooses to deliver. It examines some of the more practical issues such as what background and qualifications do Business Partners need? How should the Business Partnership be funded? and What information systems are needed? In addition, the chapter focuses on what organisations are doing to develop and enhance the skills of their Business Partners.

Finally in Chapter 4, we cover how you position yourself as a Business Partner from an individual perspective. The chapter includes topics such as getting established with clients, creating early impressions and how to review the relationships you already have. The notion of different Business Partner roles is explored in more depth and the advantages and disadvantages of working as experts, process consultants or just a pair of hands are discussed. The chapter also presents the CONSULT framework as a way of focusing on the relevant issues when first working with a client.

Some of the key behaviours concerned with delivery to the business (outlined in Chapter 1) will be demonstrated by Business Partners in setting up and positioning themselves in the organisation. Having a holistic overview and long-term perspective are both critical to success in this area, and specific behaviours include 'seeking opportunities within the business to support strategy' and 'having an understanding of the bigger organisational context and future vision of the company'.

# 2

# Positioning the Partnership

Over the last 10 years or so, many organisations have taken the step of making changes to the HR function through the introduction of Business Partners, either in name or principle or both. What has become clear is that definitions, understanding of the role and ways of working are many and varied.

It is unlikely that any Business Partnership can succeed unless the function has spent time analysing what it is seeking to achieve and how it can add value to the business. While this may seem obvious, it can be easy to re-brand HR without giving sufficient thought to the reasons for doing so. There is also a further step required, which is to promote the aims and benefits of the role within the business. This is a step, which, in our experience, is often neglected in organisations and can lead to a lack of understanding and even, at times, resistance from internal clients towards the new Business Partners.

For some organisations, there will be no specific launch of the Business Partnership Function. The new roles might come into existence as part of a wider change programme and may evolve through a restructuring exercise, with some Partners continuing to support old transactional roles during a transition period. For other organisations, launching the new Partnership role and communicating the changes may be the first consultancy project the new service undertakes.

Whether it is a big bang approach or a subtle transition, consideration will need to be given to what the new function is aiming to achieve and how the Business Partnership can promote the work it undertakes and the value it brings to the organisation. To do this, there is a need to understand the perceptions of the people within the organisation, the image and direction the function wants to project and the opportunities there are for developing credibility.

## What are you seeking to achieve?

Positioning a Business Partnership Function is not a straightforward process. There is undoubted value in having 'inside' agents who understand what is going on, who have strong, established relationships, and who are skilled in their interventions. But there are also disadvantages in operating internally and potential consequences to launching a big bang approach to a function if the organisation is not ready for it.

As a first step, it is important to clarify your aims and understand what value you are trying to add by introducing Business Partners. Questions you might ask yourself are:

- Is it just a title change or are there pressing business needs that you hope the Partners will address?
- Why would a consultancy approach be better than other approaches in this situation? (e.g. using external consultants or continuing with the existing service).
- What was missing from previous approaches?
- If the Partnership already exists, what are the current perceptions and what needs does it currently meet?

New Business Partnerships need to be very clear about the business case for moving into this arena. If the Business Partners are not able to articulate the value they can bring, or the priorities for the Partners are unclear, then the Partnership is unlikely to be successful.

From the Business Partners we spoke to, the following were cited as business drivers for a move towards Business Partnership:

- Strategic alignment
  - to improve the alignment of people management practice with business goals
  - to help managers understand their people in the context of the organisation
- Service
  - to provide an accessible point of contact for clients
  - to improve overall service levels
- Financial
  - to provide improved services at no extra cost
  - to control burgeoning costs on externals.

Most Business Partners felt they were able to offer as good a service as or sometimes better than that of the people working externally and felt frustrated that their clients did not always see them in this light. A possible reason for this might be that the Business Partners do not always spend the time marketing themselves in the same way as do the external providers. External consultants usually present themselves as a packaged product, with a clear process for achieving results for the organisation. Often with internal consultants, the work begins before the potential value is "sold" to the client.

As a Business Partner you need to be continually viewing your services from the client's perspective and assessing whether you are offering what the client wants. For a Business Partner this may be in the form of:

- Adding measurable value to the business: This might be in terms of enhanced customer satisfaction, reduced costs, improved efficiencies, profits, etc. Tangible improvements in these areas will get clients interested, so presenting your services in this way can be a strong marketing lever.
- Having a real understanding of the business and the business priorities: It is important to clients that you show an understanding of their problems and issues. If they need to spend time and effort getting you up to speed on how their area of the business operates, this is likely to reduce their willingness to share their more complex business needs.
- Focusing on the business critical activities or hot spots: If you are able to bring some energy and commitment to solving business critical issues, it is likely that a client will be interested in your ideas.
- Having a strong process for addressing problems: Knowledge of tools and techniques that can be used to gather data or diagnose a problem is likely to impress a client and reassure them that you know what you are doing. You need to be careful however not to use off-the-shelf tools which do not fit the circumstances you are facing and instead develop your own processes that target the issues.

The Business Partnership needs to have a clear focus on what it is offering to the business and the value that brings. You need to be asking yourself "would I want to buy the service I am offering if I was the client?" and "What am I bringing to the client that they don't already have?"

## What are the cultural considerations?

Whether your title is that of Business Partner, Internal Consultant, Change Agent or HR Consultant, in our view, your understanding of the culture of the organisation and ability to take a big picture approach to working alongside your internal clients will be key to your success. Knowing the organisational culture and how systems and processes work within that context will help determine the priorities for the Business Partnership and the readiness of the organisation for the changed nature of the role.

Before looking in more detail at how the culture might influence the purpose of the Business Partnership, it may be worth reminding ourselves of what culture and systems thinking are about.

The culture of the organisation is often described as "the way things are done around here". It includes both the overt behaviours of people in the organisation and the set of beliefs that govern those behaviours. It is important to distinguish the differences (where they exist) between the espoused culture (usually reflected in the marketing material on display to the external customer or client) and the actual culture as experienced by people working in the organisation.

For example, in the *Toyota* plant in Cincinnati the work processes are clearly displayed for both employees and visitors to see. Everything is in its right place. The chinos and comfortable but smart clothing give an impression about how people work with each other and the cars. The values also show through in the "Toyota way", which means employees on the assembly line have the right to stop production if they have concerns over how things are progressing. There is a visible pull cord, which is described to visitors during the factory tour. The values in the organisation need to be demonstrated in action as well as words if they are truly to support the overt culture.

Roffey Park Research makes the link between cultural characteristics of organisations and the success of the Business Partnering role using a model of culture devised by Goffee and Jones (Griffin et al, 2009).

In brief, the findings point to a direct relationship between successful Business Partnering and what is described as a "communal" culture by Goffe and Jones. In these organisations, the espoused and actual cultures of the organisation are closely aligned and the behaviours are more closely linked to that of an "open system" with greater readiness to work in a Partnership.

## Systems theory and thinking

In the section above, we have touched on the idea of systems thinking. Here we differentiate between open, living systems and closed systems:

*Closed systems*: A system which operates in isolation from its surrounding environment. This assumes that there are clear boundaries that can be managed or controlled. HR can sometimes operate as a closed system through either a lack of conscious awareness or an unwillingness to listen and observe how it is impacting on other areas of the organisation.

*Open, living systems:* Open, living systems take account of the symbiotic relationship between different parts of the whole. For example, if the HR function is operating as an open system it would continually be taking in information about the needs of the organisation and how HR needs to shape itself to match emerging needs.

A basic, if not in-depth understanding of systems theory and thinking is, in our view, essential for those working as consultants within organisations to understand how the interconnecting parts of the business work together and function as a whole. The functioning of the separate parts and the interconnection of these parts are important. An easily available although complex system to understand is that of the human body.

The body is a healthy system if the individual parts are functioning properly and work together effectively. So, for example, someone may have a healthy heart, but their kidneys do not function well. Their total health is therefore hampered by one part of the body dysfunctioning and while the heart may be healthy now, because the functioning of the kidneys is vital to overall health, the heart will eventually be affected too along with other organs. Anyone with diabetes will know how fluctuating blood sugar levels can affect more than one area of the body.

If we go to our G.P. with constant headaches, a number of things might happen: We may be asked a series of questions to try to find out what the root cause of the headaches is; we might be given a prescription to stop the headaches; both might happen. The underlying cause of the headaches could be a huge range of things from dehydration to deterioration of eyesight to a dysfunctioning liver, or a combination of all three.

> *"Systems have emergent properties that are not found in their parts. You cannot predict the properties of a complete system by taking it to pieces and analysing its parts"*
>
> (O'Conner & McDermott, 1997)

The health and well-being of an organisation is an example of something that is not easily defined. We may know when it is absent – people often talk about low morale in a department or organisation. It may be a combination of many other factors such as changing work structures, high turnover, decreased profits, hostile bids, etc. When the whole system is functioning well and we can see it in action, we will have a better idea of what is going on. Methods such as Appreciative Inquiry (Cooperrider, Sorensen, Whitney, & Yaeger et al., 1999) are aimed at teasing out what works well in a system so that this can be taken forward into the future. By breaking down the component parts and analysing them, we only have a better understanding of the particular part, which in itself is useful, but it will not necessarily aid our understanding of the system as a whole.

Carrying out a cultural and systems analysis will help the Business Partnership to gain a greater understanding of the organisation as a whole and highlight priorities for change.

The role of the Business Partner will be to understand how the organisational system works as a whole and where attention needs to be paid to ensure healthy growth for the future.

The following are some pointers for working with the culture of your own organisation:

- What are the overt signs that tell you what the organisation is like? – e.g. environment, layout of rooms, positioning of individuals within the rooms, decorations, what's displayed on the walls, etc.
- How do people treat each other? – are conversations spontaneous and open or are people cautious about what they say and to whom? If someone new comes into the organisation how are they treated?
- What formal and informal processes are in place? For example, are meetings used as a way of communicating? And if so – how formal or informal are they? What gets discussed? What would not ever appear on the agenda?
- What groups or cliques exist in the organisation? Is there a real "golf club" or its equivalent?
- How do decisions get made? And who by?
- What's valued in the organisation? – getting the work done even if it means staying late? or having a healthy work life balance?
- Think of a metaphor to describe your organisation and explore this further – for example if it is like a runaway train, who is driving it? And who are the passengers? What will stop it? Where is it going?
- What happens if we change one part of the overall system? What impact might it have elsewhere in the organisation?
- What would the current situation look like from different system perspectives?

By asking these questions of others in the organisation through your informal networks you can build up a good picture of what the culture of the organisation might be. The culture tends to be determined by the informal rather than the formal processes so don't be fooled by the policies and value statements that are readily available, rather look below the surface.

The model adopted for the Partnership will vary depending on the strategic business objectives of the organisation and the culture needed to support those objectives. Freeman (1997) highlights different ways in which Business Partners can align themselves to the business depending on the strategic objective of the company (Table 2.1).

Each of these role biases will require a different style and set of skills and competencies from the Business Partners. Understanding the contribution the Business Partner is making to the business and the cultural needs stemming from the strategy is essential in ensuring that the role is focused on areas that add value to the organisation. Many of the Business Partners we spoke to were able to articulate what they were doing (e.g. "we're trying to facilitate two parts of the business to communicate more effectively with one another"), but were less clear as to whether or not this would make a difference to the strategic objectives. Unless the links between strategy and approach are clear, it is unlikely that the Business Partner will be adding value, and they will certainly not have the basis on which to evaluate their success (a topic which is explored in more detail in Chapter 10).

**Table 2.1**  Aligning Business Partnership to the Strategy

| Strategic objective | Cultural issues | Business partner focus |
|---|---|---|
| Customer focus | Service levels | Group dynamics |
| | Team-working | Cross-functional working |
| | Communication | Team building |
| | | Clarifying roles/objectives |
| | | Achieving consensus |
| Quality/Reliability | Security | Technical consistency |
| | Professional expertise | Technological improvements |
| | Attention to detail | Effective procedures |
| | | Creating new solutions |
| | | Knowledge management |
| Speed of growth | Personal achievement | Complex influencing |
| | Project based | Strong project management |
| | Recognising contributors | High flexibility |
| | Initiative | Responding to stakeholders |
| Flexibility/Adaptation | Reputation | Network building |
| | Freedom to operate | Establishing reputation |
| | Creativity and risk | Partnerships |
| | Relationship building | Encouraging risk |

Adapted from Freeman (1997).

## Understand current perceptions

Our research suggests that where an Internal Consultancy group exists – particularly where its focus is HR – the members are most likely to identify themselves as junior or middle managers (through pay or grading levels). Usually the consultants are former HR or training specialists who have now been asked to operate under a different business model. Although we found examples of organisations externally recruiting for specific consultancy skill sets, there were only a limited number of organisations taking this approach. The visibility of the internal consultants is consequently often based on their hierarchical status, together with their historical position and therefore presents huge challenges in influencing decision makers (often the clients) at more senior levels. Increasing visibility through effective marketing and self-promotion is a key lever in overcoming this hurdle.

If you are already working as part of a Business Partnership Group within the organisation offering a consultancy service, you will need to consider:

- What reputation already exists about your group?
- What value do you currently bring?
- If you were offering a service under another guise, how might that impact on your credibility for the new service?

If your reputation appears to be based on the people staffing the function, then this might suggest that you need to move away from promoting "heroes" to promoting a strong process that adds value to the business. If individuals as opposed to the process become branded within your group, then building credibility is down to individuals and is likely to be an uphill battle for HR managers moving across from traditional HR roles.

As much time, effort and resource need to be put into marketing an internal consultancy as would be needed to establish one providing for an external client base.

To quote from Schein (1987):

> *"Consultants are typically thought of as outsiders. Even so called internal consultants who work full time for a given company are typically thought of as outsiders to the particular department they are working in at any given time. They are thought of as being free to negotiate their areas of responsibility with others who are defined as clients; they work on a contract basis; they have the power that derives from being an independent outsider and being perceived as an expert in certain areas and they have the freedom to leave a difficult situation except where professional responsibility dictates hanging in".*

Reconciling this view of the role of consultants with how you are currently perceived is a critical milestone on the road to establishing a successful internal consultancy. If you are currently seen as providers of administrative services, however good you are, prospective clients may not consider you for consultancy assignments, as operational credibility may not be a transportable commodity.

*Airbus* is one company where they "had to fight really hard to not just become do-ers", particularly as the culture gave credibility to people who implemented change and the other elements of consultancy were not seen as proactive and, as a consequence, did not build the Partner's credibility. Another Partner in *Zurich Financial* told us, "*the main challenge is acceptance by our customers who know us already that we provide more than just an additional pair of hands. We need to constantly ensure that we continue to operate as consultants and not get pulled into the everyday operational needs. This can be difficult when starting from scratch in an organisation that has a 'just do it!' mentality".*

## Assess your brand image

The advantage that internal consultants can be said to have is that they know the business inside out. Members of the consultancy team will most likely have lived and breathed the products, financing, staffing issues and business strategies and be well tuned into the hopes, fears, likes and dislikes of the movers and shakers within the business. Paradoxically, the disadvantage for the internal consultancy will also be that they know the business inside out! The external consultant may appear to offer something new from another world, whereas the internal consultancy may be associated only with the service they formerly provided. The internal consultancy may also seem to be too entwined with the host organisation's culture and therefore lacks the independence and objectivity of the outsider.

A useful first step in marketing Partnership functions is to carry out some diagnostic work to assess the brand image. *Severn Trent Water*, which is part of Severn Trent plc made the move to becoming Business Partners in response to managers saying that they wanted a more strategic contribution from HR. To assess their brand image and focus, they invited in an external consultant from the CIPD to give them an idea of how they stacked up against other organisations. Work was also carried out internally with line managers, which gave them positive feedback about the current service and what people wanted.

An internal consultancy needs to plan intentional activity to ensure that they align with their brand objectives. This includes how they interact with the business culture – if this is based on status and hierarchy, do they mirror this or make a statement of their independence and freedom by operating in a way that reflects their own values and beliefs about consultancy. If the brand objective is to be seen as independent and objective, the brand statement and action might be "that we use the most appropriate person to do the job based on their expertise and experience."

## Developing your marketing plan

Positioning the Partnership requires a clear understanding of the business needs and how the service you are offering can meet those needs. There needs to be a clear value in the process you are offering as well as the individuals servicing the Partnership. Often Business Partnerships make the mistake of focusing on *individual* value, at the expense of the value of the *process*, which can impact the perceptions of the function as a whole. Research by Roffey Park (Griffin, Finney, Hennessey, & Boury, 2009) worryingly found that only a third of HR Business Partnerships thought they had buy in from line managers to the new ways of working. So, whilst a focus on line readiness is important to factor into any launch, there is also a vital need to communicate and market the new approach effectively.

Taking a marketing approach to repackaging and re-branding a Business Partnership can be a useful way forward and needs to follow a number of steps:

1. Assess the need
2. Define the service
3. Test the market
4. Deliver the service
5. "Brand" the resulting case study

### Step 1: Assess the need

There is no point starting a Business Partnership function without a clear view of the specific business tasks that require help from HR consultants. All too often it is HR themselves who push for change in their function, before they have even assessed whether the change is right for their organisation. Research suggests that some HR departments have taken the move to Business Partnership purely because of external influences ("everyone is doing it") or under a directive from their HR Director, without any clear indication that it will support the business strategy or improve organisational performance (Giffen et al., 2009). HR departments need to prove to themselves that there is a sizeable need for their service. How big is the need? How many business tasks need help? Where are they located in the business? What are the benefits of doing things your way? As a team you need to have the confidence that you are focused on the needs of your internal customers and not just the HR agenda.

Meislin (1997) offers a checklist for internal consultants to use in identifying the help they can provide to their clients.

**What do your clients need from you?**
1. Client's Name/Business Unit?
2. Who is your client's customer?
3. What type of product or service does your client provide?
4. What is your client's long-term mission or strategic direction? How is it marketing this?
5. Over the next one to two years, what will be your client's biggest marketplace challenge?
6. What kind of help will your client need to face this challenge?
7. How can you help your client to reach short- and long-term business goals?
8. How can you give your client more than standard help? What value-added benefit do you offer above and beyond your role?
9. If you're already working with this person, how does he/she rate you in satisfaction terms? What kind of feedback has she/he given to you?
10. What important points do you need to keep in mind for future work with this client?

You need to discover what the key buying criteria are for your clients and what they value, which means really getting inside the mindset of your clients and understanding them from the outside in.

One of the difficulties Business Partners often face at this stage is deciding who the client is. This topic is covered in more detail in Chapter 3. If the Business Partnerships view their client as predominantly "the organisation", then it should come as no surprise that individual line managers seek the services of external consultants in preference to the internal Business Partners. However, if the Partnership has an over-riding aim to impact the culture and strategy of the company, then working solely on line managers agendas is unlikely to lead to success either. Consequently, it is important that the Partnership comes to some agreement about whose agenda it is serving. For example, is a high-level HR need to move the organisation to a more collaborative culture more important than helping your local manager create a smooth transition for a new policy?

Conflicting agendas between the strategy of the Partnership as a whole and the needs of operational line managers need to be raised and discussed. Successful Partnerships will spend time exploring how they can achieve their clients' needs whilst also moving them towards a more strategic vision of what the Partnership is seeking to achieve. This role clarity is at the heart of the success of many Business Partnerships. Research from Roffey Park (Griffin et al., 2009) found that the greater the role clarity, the higher the reported success of HR Business Partnering.

## Step 2: Define the service

In order to successfully promote the Partnership unit, you need to be clear on the strategy and direction it is taking. It is a mistake to try and reconfigure an existing in-company service provider into one offering consultancy without addressing the following fundamental business planning issues. Particular issues that are likely needed to be discussed and debated are:

**Client issues**
- Who are our clients?
- How well do we understand their area of the business?
- What is our current brand image with our clients?
- What are their needs?
- Are they working with us because they think they should or because they value us?

**Customer issues**
- How are our customers segmented?
- Are there policies and practices that make it difficult for them to be successful?
- What are we offering both individually and collectively?

**Products**
- How do our current product offerings impact the business?
- Where can we add most value to the business?
- What is the level of demand?
- Have we got a clear idea of where the greatest need is?

**Goals**
- What are we aiming to achieve with the Business Partnership unit?
- What brand image do we need to support these objectives?
- Who are our competitors and what do they offer?

Having drawn some conclusions to these questions, you can then begin to frame an overall strategy to enable the unit to be successful. It may be that in discussing these questions the focus of attention shifts away from certain clients and/or services to others as the priorities become clearer.

A Partnership unit may decide, for example, to focus on upper-middle to senior managers as its clients as it believes that they can add the most value at this level and have a stronger influence on the organisation. However, the impact of these decisions needs to be carefully managed if the credibility of the function is to be maintained. If, for example, the unit decides it is no longer providing development centres as the service is too costly and time-consuming, the rationale for this needs to be effectively communicated to the business and an alternative supplier source if necessary. The alternative is that the team agree among themselves when a development centre is next in demand they lose credibility by not being able to deliver or offer a means of delivering a solution. Word can soon spread within a company that a business unit is not able to help meet people's needs.

It is important that the Business Partnership documents the service it will provide. This avoids a Business Partner turning up to their first client meeting with just a big smile and a blank piece of paper. If the Partnership function has developed a clear process that is proven to add value to the business, then both Business Partners and their clients will feel confident that working together on a consulting project will add value. Workshops, focus groups, awareness sessions and in-house meetings and magazines are all useful ways of explaining and communicating the service.

*The Body Shop* is an example of a company who spent a lot of time considering how to market themselves internally. They worked as a team to develop a service and then positioned it as led by senior managers.

They came up with the name "The LADS" which stood for Leadership And Development Section and was catchy enough to get them known within the organisation and signal that a change had taken place. As a team they saw themselves on a continuum from dependency to independence to interdependency or Partnership. They mapped this out as a way of plotting their relationship with Line Managers and this eventually became the path they took holistically with the organisation as a whole.

They received extensive external and internal marketing advice and established a brand image – and used the power of metaphor to capture the passion and imagination of their learners. The following is an extract from their write-up of the experience (Inside Outreach, 2002).

---

*"To build a common sense of what we were trying to achieve we created the image of the learner as an independent explorer and traveler, not a passive spectator. Our slogan was 'Learning is for Life… not just for courses' and we used this extensively in our materials and marketing literature.*

*When we were clear about our offering, we mounted a campaign for learning and we used a lot of visual imagery which fitted into the Body Shop culture and visual environment - with quotations like E M Forster's: "Spoon feeding teaches you nothing but the shape of the spoon" strategically placed over the canteen servery. Plus we had the Board Directors team giving out Passports to Learning at the factory gates at 6.00 a.m. on a cold January morning!!*

---

*(Continued)*

*The care we put into our image alongside delivering the goods really paid off. We had some clear messages about our offer and what we were doing to disseminate within the organisation and beyond and we were well published in the internal communications and external press. There was a great motivation and enthusiasm amongst the team – success bred success. All the work we did had a positive impact and got reinforced. We particularly impacted through the design and delivery of a suite of management development programmes – with the innovative approaches moving the thinking more towards a learning culture."*

## Step 3: Test the market

Once you have assessed the need and clearly defined a service to meet that need, then you can test the market and refine your service as appropriate. An initial high-profile project can be a good way to develop a proven case study, which can then be used as a solid foundation for gaining credibility and further work.

The approach you can take to marketing your function will be influenced to a large degree by the culture of the organisation and the readiness of the clients. It is likely that your internal clients will have a wide range of reactions to your role as Business Partner. Figure 2.1 illustrates how clients progress in terms of their perceptions of the role:

Awareness of the products and services

Expressing an interest

Raising an issue which may require your services

Recognising competence

Trusting you to do the job

**Figure 2.1** Client perceptions of the business partnership role.

Your marketing approach will obviously need to be targeted at the appropriate level. Initially, this may mean a focus on raising awareness on the role and what service you can provide. Case studies and presentations targeted towards their critical business issues will be a way forward here. If, however, a client is already beginning to question you and raise issues of importance to them, then the approach will need to be quite different and you can start to use consultancy skills to draw out the client and demonstrate your process expertise.

*Pfizer* are an example of one company who has successfully marketed the transition of the HR role to that of internal consultants. They used Ulrich's (1997) matrix, which was described in Chapter 1, as a basis for charting their progress. Starting from a strong operational focus where the HR section worked as employee champion and focusing on quality policies and processes to support this, they began by gaining a greater understanding of the business and its goals and drivers and started to build relationships and credibility with key players. This enabled them to move to a more strategic focus where they could challenge thinking and help facilitate discussions on the future of the organisation. Having achieved this, they then moved on to concentrate on the senior leaders in the organisation and focus on culture change. The move was not without resistance and the team drew in external consultants to help take the pressure off the internals and enhance their credibility by using others to reinforce their approach.

## Step 4: Deliver the service

The service you deliver will vary hugely depending on your role and remit. We pay more attention to the interventions you might be involved in Chapter 8.

## Step 5: "Brand" the resulting case study

The importance of branding in terms of business success has increased in recent years and it is unlikely that the Business Partners operating at a strategic level will have escaped being involved in discussions about how to increase the brand profile of the company in order to win more business and attract essential resources. It is imperative that the HR function develops its own brand image that aligns closely to that of the business as a whole.

If your market testing is successful, then you will have a successful case study to launch your new brand image. Ideally, you will want to choose a case study that is seen as a hot topic or critical to the business. Thereafter, the Partnership needs a constant and relevant message to the business to maintain a successful profile.

Tapping into existing promotional opportunities is essential in this activity and numerous avenues are available which should be used as building blocks for communication.

**Written marketing materials**
Brochures, report presentations, past case studies and articles in company newsletters are all useful in raising the profile of the Business Partnership. Stories of your success are particularly valuable in developing your credibility with the business.

**Workshops/breakfast meetings**
These can be used to brief managers on the services on offer and help raise awareness on the role of the Business Partner.

**Conferences and seminars**
Talking at slots on management conferences about work. Presenting alongside and external speaker can also help raise your profile.

**Networking events**
It is essential that Business Partners get out into the business and get seen. This means taking advantage of all opportunities to informally network across the organisation. Professional institutes such as the CIPD and Institute of Management Consultants also hold events, which provide an ideal opportunity to network externally with other Business Partners and gain useful insights into your work.

**Web**
Intranet sites can be particularly useful as a marketing tool, especially when the department is being set up or where potential clients are not aware of the capabilities on offer. This can sometimes be the case where an organisation works across different locations. The *Immigration Authority* uses the intranet for managers to download HR policies and also to access interactive training, where managers self-select HR issues and receive question and answer support.

**Logos and brand names**
Logos can be useful to create a brand for the function, but you need to be careful that they symbolize what the function does. There may also be trademarks, such as Investors in People, which are important to include. A distinct identity can be useful in informing the organisation about what you stand for or what you offer.

    *Coca-Cola* found that the credibility of their Partnership function could be influenced by something as simple as the name given to a particular project. As a result of this, they ensured that they selected unique and unambiguous names and had a clearly identified leader for each piece of work.

**Testimonials**

Make sure you get positive testimonials for your work. Word-of-mouth referrals are one of the best ways to get new business. Where you are seeking to get a start in a new market, it can be useful to hold a pilot in an area that you know will be successful and use this as a stepping-stone to other areas of the business.

**Gifts**

Items that symbolize or remind managers and employees about the work you are trying to achieve are a useful way of raising awareness. *Nortel*, for example, gave out a wooden puzzle with a core competency on each piece at the end of a briefing programme, to symbolize that each employee has at least one strength and that each piece is important. The puzzle was cheap to produce and kept the model in the forefront of people's minds (Morris, 1996).

## Balancing organisational and individual needs

We have touched already on some of the challenges faced by the Business Partners as they seek to position themselves within the business. At an organisational level, cultural influences and historic perceptions of HR around the business will have an enormous impact on what can be achieved. Establishing a strong marketing approach which establishes the service requirements and tests the approach is a good starting point. In the next chapter we will build on this by going on to look at different structural options for setting up a Partnership.

However, it is worth highlighting at this point that the Partnership also needs to be positioned at an individual level with clients. Lack of capability or desire to change at an individual level by line managers can be a big obstacle to success. This is a topic we will address in more detail in Chapter 4. It is achieving the balance between these two aspects which will lead to effective positioning.

## Summary

Positioning the Business Partnership Function requires a clear understanding of the business needs and how the service you are offering can meet those needs. Whilst the move to a Partnership model may be driven by financial, service or strategic imperatives, the value the Partnership brings will depend on whether the priorities it establishes are correct and whether the Business Partners themselves are able to influence change.

Gaining a thorough understanding of the culture and systems of the organisation is essential, not only because Business Partners need to understand how they can influence strategic change, but also because the cultural dynamics of the organisation will have an impact on the shape of the role the Business Partner plays. Fast growing companies focused on flexibility and personal achievement, for example, will require a stronger project management focus and more complex relationship management skills, whereas companies with a more established, quality-driven culture are more likely to value a focus on procedural improvements.

Our experience shows that internal consultancies rarely put in as much time and effort into promoting themselves to their clients as external providers, and yet often there is confusion about what the function is seeking to accomplish and the process for achieving it. Partnerships can benefit from taking time to understand the existing perceptions of their function within the business and examining the brand image they are promoting. The gap between this image and the service they are seeking to deliver can then be established.

The starting point for any marketing plan needs to be an analysis of the clients needs. With Business Partners this is often not straightforward, as they frequently have split loyalties between line management needs and the needs of the business as a whole. Balancing those needs and setting clear priorities is the first step in defining what the Partnership is about and what it is aiming to achieve.

A strong brand image can then be built by offering a service which meets the business needs and uses case study examples and promotional opportunities within the business to reinforce simple messages about the Business Partnership function.

## Checklist

Key considerations for positioning the Partnership:

- What are the business drivers for moving to a Partnership model?
- What are the strategic objectives you need to align with?
- How well does the Partnership role support the cultural aims of the business?
- Can you articulate what you can offer your clients?
- What are your client's perceptions of you and your role?
- What brand image are you seeking to achieve?
- What service do you provide?
- How clear is your marketing strategy?
- Where is your client positioned in terms of your role?
- What successes can you market as case studies?
- How effectively do you leverage the promotional opportunities open to you?

# References

Cooperrider, D. L., Sorensen, P. F., Whitney, D., & Yaeger, T. F. (1999). *Appreciative Inquiry: rethinking human organization toward a positive theory of change*. Champaign Illinois: Stipes.

Freeman, C. (May 1997). Training your HR Pros to fit your culture. *HR Focus, 74*(5), 9–10.

Griffin, E., Finney, L., Hennessey, J., & Boury, D. (2009). *Maximising the value of HR business partnering*. Roffey Park Research Guide. Roffey Park: Horsham.

Inside Outreach Ltd. (2002). See www.inside-outreach.co.uk.

Meislin, M. (1997). *The internal consultant: Drawing on inside expertise*. Menlo Park: Crisp Publications.

Morris, D. (1996). Using competency development tools as a strategy for change in Human Resource function: a case study. *Human Resource Management, 35*(1), 35–51.

O'Conner, J., & MCDermott, I. (1997). *The art of systems thinking. Essential skills for creativity and problem solving*. Thorson.

Schein, E. H. (1987). *Process consultation, Vol. II*. Cambridge, MA: Addison Wesley.

Ulrich, D. (1997). *Human resource champions*. Boston: Harvard University Press.

# 3

# Setting Up the Partnership Function

Within any organisation there will be choices to be made about how to structure and staff the Business Partnership. If the business drivers and client needs discussed in the previous chapter are clear, then this may already provide an indication of how best to set up the function. However, often structures and staffing issues emerge from the existing shape of the organisation, rather than being designed to meet a particular need. This chapter is aimed at exploring the implications of different structural models as well as highlighting what is happening in practice within organisations.

This chapter seeks to address questions such as:

- What do Business Partners do day-to-day?
- What are the advantages and disadvantages of different structural models?
- Where should the Business Partnership be located?
- What role do information systems and Shared Service Centres play?
- How should the department be funded?
- What background do Business Partners need?
- What development might be needed?
- What reporting structures work best?
- Are external consultants still of value?

## What do business partners actually do?

In the introductory chapter, we defined what we mean by the term Business Partner and made mention of the complexity of the role. Having worked with many HR teams working towards or working as Business Partners, it is increasingly clear that the question of what a Business Partner actually does is not a straightforward one to answer! Whilst you can get answers such as "I operate more strategically" or "I act as an internal consultant and coach to managers in the business", often when you probe further, the role is neither clear to the organisation nor to the individuals themselves. Part of the reason for this, is that the way the role is positioned in the company and the cultural and historical influences vary enormously between organisations – so one company's Business Partners may be sitting at the top table discussing the implications of a merger or acquisition, whilst in another company, they may be still fire-fighting transactional tasks and taking on a few more strategic projects, such as talent management.

Whilst there is no "ideal" model to follow, it is worth expanding on the potential scope of the role in order to help clarify where you want and need to focus. To do this, the role definitions from a sample of adverts for HR Business Partners was used and positioned in Ulrich's (1997, 2005) HR framework, which was explained in the introductory chapter. This framework separates out activities that are more concerned with process or people issue on one axis and the day-to-day operational activities through to longer term change issues on the other axis. Whilst all of these roles need to act in partnership with the business, it is generally recognised that those with a future strategic focus are more in line with the Business Partner roles HR teams are trying to shape for themselves (see Table 3.1).

Whilst some of the categorisation may be up for debate, what is striking from this analysis is that the HR Business Partner role most definitely straddles all four quadrants of the matrix and is rarely exclusively future focused. It is this complexity that leads organisations to put considerable thought into how best to structure the HR function.

## What are the options on how partnerships should be structured?

### What service do you deliver?

In our work with HR teams, one of the constant challenges that arise for HR Business Partners is how to move to a more strategic position which adds greater value, whilst also maintaining a high quality of service for the transactional HR work. Lawler and Mohrman (2003) first highlighted this obvious dilemma that HR functions face when they attempt to become more strategic, stating that "*HR is not in a position to abandon completely the basic transactional responsibilities associated with workforce management*". Mercer HR Consulting (Griffiths, 2004) also state that there is a general recognition that more business understanding is needed in HR, but suggest that HR need to prove that they can deliver effective and efficient service on the administrative functions before they are able to make the transition to supporting top priority business needs.

**Table 3.1**   Role Mapping the HR Business Partner onto the Ulrich framework

| *Future process-focused tasks* | *Future people-focused tasks* |
|---|---|
| **Develop effective resourcing strategies** | Coach and guide line management on performance management; |
| **Develop new initiatives, e.g. for talent management; attendance management** | Advise on restructures; |
| **Lead the role out of new procedures and policies** | Facilitate mergers, acquisitions and partnerships; |
| **Project manage change initiatives** | Work with Business Leaders to define new strategy; |
| **Benchmark against other organisation** | Project manage change initiatives |
| *Operational Process-Focused Tasks* | *Operational People-Focused Tasks* |
| **Co-ordinate selection and assessment processes** | Day-to-day advice and support to operational management; |
| **Manage the attendance policy** | Employee relations case work |
| **Analyse and report on HR trends** | Disciplinary and grievance guidance |
| **Manage HR information systems** | Trade Union negotiations |
| | Advice on TUPE and redundancy |

Consequently, to be effective a number of different aspects need to change and also be perceived to have changed by the organisation. These include not only the work that is being undertaken by HR, but also the skills of the individuals in the HR function; the way the function is structured and the way it promotes its services and interacts with the key stakeholders of the company.

Our work with HR teams transitioning to Business Partners has shown time and time again that in order to be successful companies need to first find a way to provide an effective transactional service. This may be through:

■ Outsourcing the day-to-day administrative functions;
■ More effective use of Information Technology;
■ Setting up a service centre;
■ Devolving responsibility to line management for HR processes.

This will then free up time for HR to participate in strategy development, change processes and implementation. However, if the transactional HR tasks are not adequately provided for, then it will be almost impossible for HR to break away from the more reactive nature of these tasks. Lawler and Mohman's (2003) longitudinal study of HR within organisations backed up this argument and found that where HR was a truly strategic Business Partner they had a far higher level of activity in areas of planning, organisational design and organisational development.

One of the first tasks in shifting to a Business Partnership model is therefore to establish the effective delivery of transactional HR activities. Increasingly, organisations are rushing into strategic HR partnerships at the expense of oper-ational, day-to-day HR services and as a result are instantly losing credibility (Pfau & Cundiff, 2002). As part of the research for this book one business manager told us that their move towards Business Partnership included re-branding the HR function as "Providing Excellence", but this was viewed as a joke within the organisation as they appeared unable to do something as simple as issue an accurate offer letter following a successful interview. Whilst many Partners will want to move away from the transactional HR, it is still essential that the basics are in place before the transition occurs.

Ulrich (1997) also warned against taking a fixed view of the role of HR and the dangers of focusing on the business value roles of strategic partner and change agent at the expense of the role of administrative expert and employee champion. He argued that even if the administrative role sits inside a service centre or operates as an outsourced function, it still needs to partner with the organisation in some respects.

However, if we are talking about Business Partners working as strategic partners, influencing change through process consulting, how should organisa-tions go about structuring their HR function to best effect? The nature of the company will play a key role in finding the answer to this question, but some of the more typical models we uncovered in our research are outlined below.

**Model 1: business partners as process consultants working alongside the line, with specialist and transactional HR provided centrally or outsourced**
In this model, the HR Business Partner does not have any day-to-day transactional duties, as these are either in a service centre or outsourced. They also have the ability to access specialist HR advisors, perhaps from a central function, to pro-vide advice in areas such as learning and development or pensions. This frees up the HR Business Partner to work at a more strategic level with the business, shaping and driving change alongside the operational managers. The type of activity this type of Business Partner might be involved in would include project managing a restructure or establishing a new mentoring scheme.

This model has the advantage that Business Partners are able to develop strong working relationships with line management and have a good knowledge of the business issues they are facing, as well as the resources at their disposal. The Business Partner adds value by working as a process consultant, coaching and mentoring managers and helping to diagnose business problems and develop solutions. Where specialist advice is needed, such as for employee relations or reward strategies, they are able to call in expertise from the centre.

If the centralised transactional HR function is efficient and effective then this model should work well. However it also relies on line managers recognising the value of process consultants and allowing the Business Partners to get involved in strategic issues when they don't have expert advice to give. As a result, the ability to make this model work can often lie in the individual Business Partners' credibility and their influencing skills – a topic we will return to later in this book.

*Barclays* was one company we spoke to which followed this model. They introduced a Business Partnership model for HR in the later part of 2001 as part of a move away from a decentralised HR set-up. The new model has three components:

1. A centralised HR Service Centre which carries out the transactional HR processes;
2. Centres of excellence, which are comprised of groups of specialist advisors working in two main areas, namely:
   (a) Resourcing and learning;
   (b) HR specialist practice which covers:
      – equality and diversity
      – talent management
      – pensions.
   These centres of excellence have evolved over the past few years. Their prime role is to develop policy and processes to support the business, but they also have a delivery capability.
3. The Business Partner team, who work alongside the business operation.

Of the 72,000 people in Barclays, approximately 1000 are in HR. Of these, roughly 400 are in the Service Centre and there are about 130 Business Partners.

Prudential are another organisation cited in People Management (2004) as following this model. They have Business Partners working as consultants and they draw on expertise from the centre, whilst a service centre deals with the administration. The Business Partners do not have their own budget, but use the advice of HR experts who do. A key part of the role is therefore to be able to influence others without budgetary power.

However, as the person on the ground, it can be difficult to separate yourself from the day-to-day HR activities. Even if this is achieved, one Business Partner from the Hyde Group highlighted to us that once they successfully managed to separate themselves from the transactional HR problems, they found that they were disadvantaged on occasions as they still needed to be in close contact with what was going on. Zurich Financial have overcome this to a certain extent by setting up a "Solutions Consultancy" where the Business Partners contract with transactional and specialist HR teams when they require assistance. This has the advantage of clarifying the role boundaries whilst ensuring communication is kept open when required.

Shared Service Centres are becoming increasingly attractive to large organisations and many are moving towards this approach to manage the transactional issues. For example, the *National Trust* recently moved to a shared service centre model to reduce the amount of time HR spent on routine queries. They have an intranet site containing information on employee benefits and a service centre to answer personal queries on benefits. If these are not answered they are referred to the regional HR Directors. Later in this chapter we will look at this aspect in more detail.

**Model 2: business partners as process and specialist providers working alongside the line, with transactional HR reporting in to them**
This model suggests that Business Partners work in an expert role as well as that of a process consultant – they may for example have expertise in mergers and acquisitions, or talent management, which they draw to influence strategy in those particular areas. This is likely to be an easier transition in companies not familiar with the benefits of process consulting, as the HR Business Partner will be perceived to be bringing something to the table. Typically in this model, the Business Partner has a higher status in HR and keeps in touch with the day-to-day activities by having the transactional HR roles reporting to them.

The *Immigration Office* have recently moved to this model of Business Partnership. They set up a service which provided more strategic alignment to the business, with expertise in areas such as organisational design, performance management, reward strategy and job evaluation. The response was very enthusiastic and positive and as a result an Interim Manager was brought in to trial the Business Partner approach. This was done in one of the most challenging areas of the organisation – National Asylum Support Services – which had a history of difficult HR challenges.

Despite preparing the Directors for what service might be on offer, the newly appointed Business Partner soon got pulled in to HR operational problems. So to counteract this, HR Advisors were appointed to work for the Business Partner and unblock the operational issues. The pilot ran for around six months with the Business Partner working on areas such as change strategy and workforce predictions and the HR Advisors providing back up on the operational issues. After the pilot period there were plenty of success stories and the Business Partnership role was expanded to other parts of the business.

Within the Immigration Authority, there are now eight operating Directorates each of which has a Business Partner with a Senior Advisor as well as other HR advisors reporting to them. The Business Partner has line management responsibility for the HR Advisors. The senior HR advisor role is to identify HR hot spots in the business and track records of HR and as such, it is more of a junior Business Partner.

One of the possible difficulties with this model, which was highlighted in the Immigration Office case, is that Business Partners may find it difficult to distance themselves from the transactional HR activities, particularly if they are perceived as the next level in command. In some procedures such as grievance for example, an investigation requires a more senior HR professional, which could lead to Business Partners becoming overloaded with transactional work. In addition, working as both expert and process roles may lead to unclear role boundaries and difficulties in setting expectations with clients.

**Model 3: business partners as process consultants working alongside the line, with specialist and transactional HR provided centrally and a local HR adviser as a focal point for transactional issues**

As in the first model, in this structure the Business Partner has no transactional duties or particular expertise and is free to operate strategically as there is a separate port of call locally for transactional HR issues. The two roles can also keep in close contact to familiarise each other with the key issues. Once again, this model relies on an effective central provision of HR services and a clear understanding by line management of the value a Business Partner can bring. Where it differs from model 1, however, is that it has the benefit of not leaving line managers feeling unsupported in terms of operational HR and not creating a hierarchy between Business Partners and Operational HR.

*Royal Bank of Scotland* is one company which had a similar approach to this model. They had a shared service centre for HR administration, but also had both HR consultants (Business Partners); HR technical experts in areas such as reward, resourcing and Organisational Development, and HR analysts working alongside line managers in the business. There was a close link between the two roles with the HR Analysts providing data on topics such as sick absence and turnover to help the consultants with their analysis of problems.

**Model 4: business partners working alongside the line on specialist and transactional issues using a process consulting approach**

Whilst some people react to this model by saying, "but that's not a Business Partner!" it is obvious both from our work with HR teams and by looking at the advertisements entitled HR Business Partner that have a range of duties from the transactional through to the more strategic, that this model exists – and is even commonplace! This model, where a senior HR professional takes an all encompassing role and works closely with line management is likely to be the way forward for smaller organisations which don't have a requirement for large HR service centres. The work differs little from that of more traditional HR Managers and what changes there are have come about in the way of working with managers, whereby the Business Partners are more facilitative and aim to develop self-sufficiency amongst the line by using a coaching approach.

*Canon Europe* have taken a similar approach to this. They do not have a separate HR service centre and instead each country has an HR Director/Manager; Senior Business Partner; Business Partner; HR Specialist and administrators.

The model has the advantage that all the HR functions are closely in touch with the business. However, the role definitions may be much less clear as a result. In several of the larger organisations we talked to it was hard to see a clear transition towards Business Partner, despite the change in job title. In those cases, the HR professionals were struggling to make time to be proactive with the business due to their heavy operational workload. This suggested to us that whilst this model may work in smaller organisations, or in companies with small business units, it is unlikely to generate change or be perceived as adding strategic value in a larger company unless the individuals themselves are very assertive about their role.

## Choosing an appropriate structure

An analysis of the different structural models in operation is useful in that it helps to indicate some of the underlying principles of the role that HR Business Partners should ideally be seeking. These are:

- A strong working relationship with the line;
- Good knowledge of local business issues;
- Intelligent clients who understand the value of process consulting;
- The ability to access strategic issues;
- Clear role boundaries with transactional HR;
- The ability to pull in expertise when required.

Not all of these factors are likely to be in place however. So choosing an appropriate structure will depend on the existing perceptions of HR and the experience of line managers in working in a process consulting style with HR. Table 3.2 gives a rough indication of the characteristics that need to be in place for each of the models to work.

## Location

The location of the Business Partnership will obviously depend on the structure of the company. *Coca-Cola*, for example, decided initially that it was important to get as close as possible to the business and it operated in a decentralised way out of more than 23 sites in the UK each of which has a local HR resource. Interestingly, the company has now re-structured its current Partnership to align it more closely with functions rather than locations (Personnel Today, 2007). The *Immigration Authority* however are geographically spread across the UK, but are

**Table 3.2**  Structuring the Business Partnership

| Model | Factors which need to be in place | Benefits |
|---|---|---|
| Model 1 | | |
| Business Partners as process consultants, with specialist and transactional HR provided centrally or outsourced | ■ Effective central or outsourced provision of transactional HR <br><br> ■ Line managers understand and value process consulting <br><br> ■ Business Partners able to access strategic issues | ■ Ability to build strong working relationships <br><br> ■ Gains an in-depth understanding of the business issues <br><br> ■ Ideally positioned to influence change without distractions |
| Model 2 | | |
| Business Partners as process and specialist providers, with transactional HR reporting in to them | ■ Effective provision of transactional HR is close to the line <br><br> ■ Line managers value specialist input along with process consulting <br><br> ■ Business Partners establish clear role boundaries with transactional HR | ■ In touch with the day-to-day HR issues <br><br> ■ Ability to tailor the specialist advice directly to the client <br><br> ■ Ability to build strong working relationships <br><br> ■ Gains an in-depth understanding of the business issues |

*(Continued)*

47

**Table 3.2** Structuring the Business Partnership—Cont'd

| Model | Factors which need to be in place | Benefits |
|---|---|---|
| **Model 3** | | |
| Business Partners as process consultants, with specialist and transactional HR provided centrally and a local HR Adviser as a focal point for transactional issues | ■ Line managers understand and value process consulting<br>■ Effective central provision of specialist services<br>■ Business Partners able to access strategic issues<br>■ Status issues are clarified | ■ Line managers feel supported on transactional issues<br>■ Ability to build strong working relationships<br>■ Gain an in-depth understanding of the business issues |
| **Model 4** | | |
| Business Partners working alongside the line on specialist and transactional issues using a process consulting approach | ■ Line managers need a one-stop service<br>■ Transactional issues are inter-linked with specialist advice and strategic intent | ■ Suited to a smaller organisation<br>■ Involvement in all areas gives a greater understanding of the whole |

divided up functionally rather than regionally as the differing functions have very different needs. As a consequence, they may have two Business Partners quite close together regionally but who offer services to two very different directorates.

When deciding on the optimum location, it is important to consider where everyone in the marketplace is located, including:

- internal clients
- internal customers
- external customers
- key stakeholders
- Suppliers.

To be effective, Business Partnerships need to find an appropriate balance between the centralised functions of the business and the strategic business units. The best location will depend on what your customers need from you, how close you need to be to the key stakeholders to have an influence and where you can best add value to the business.

*Cargill* are an example of one company who have changed the location of their Business Partners to enable them to focus more on their HR strategy. Cargill employ around 110,000 people globally and the HR function is currently structured along the lines of Model 1 above. It is split into three broad areas:

1. Shared service provision – a global unit with a regional person based in Europe.
2. HR in Europe – HR Business Partners embedded in the business who work on the strategic business agenda.
3. Specialists – who provide expertise in core areas.

They have been operating the above structure for four years, but previously they were working by country. Whilst some countries still have a country HR provision, Cargill found that this model did not drive into the key HR issues and people ended up providing the day-to-day shared service functions. The transition has not been easy and there are still some areas of the business where people are hanging onto their old jobs, refusing to give up what they see as power. As a consequence, turnover has been high in the last three years and they have moved people so that they can make the changes they want to see. However, they now have a structure where expertise is used well. The Business Partners work in true partnership with the specialists and they are able to sell a more holistic service to the business.

## Shared service centres

Increasingly Shared Service Centres are being established by organisations as a way of making the transactional HR activities more efficient and effective. The argument is that economies of scale can be achieved by centralising core services. Informational Technology is often at the heart of this approach – with intranet sites and call centres often used to support the function.

Aside from helping to speed up the transactional HR activities, advanced Information systems have also been found to be a key lever in becoming a Strategic Partner. Good IT systems enable HR to gather strategic data and analyse information in different ways. As a result Business Partners can explore issues and contribute to finding solutions in a more informed and business-focused way. Lawler and Mohrman's (2003) study found a strong correlation between a completely integrated HR Information System and a strategic partnership role. This was echoed in the study by Pfau and Cundiff (2002), which also found that an e-HR strategy focused on improving accuracy, upgrading services and transactional interrogation was of more value to the bottom line than one focused on enhancing communications or promoting culture change.

In an effective Service Centre, the customers define the level of service they require, which in HR terms usually means aspects such as pay and benefits, relocation services, selection and recruitment administration, training and development administration, employee changes (such as maternity and retirement) and attendance management.

A report by the Institute of Employment Studies (Reilly, 2000) found that the three principal drivers for the introduction of a shared service centre were cost, quality and organisational change. Cost savings often come from reducing staff numbers as well as the efficiencies through streamlining processes. Whereas quality is improved through greater accuracy and more professional customer service, which is targeted at their needs and supported by clear service level agreements.

However, the move to a Shared Service Centre can have serious implications. Some of the common problems that occur are:

- Line Managers feel unsupported by not having someone from HR close to them in the business, particularly if some of the HR tasks have been passed to them (such as interviewing) and they feel inexperienced;
- The loss of face-to-face contact can mean that the service becomes one of timely efficiency rather than depth of advice stemming from a real understanding of the issue;
- Creating HR roles in the centre which do not have a natural career progression into HR Business Partner roles, since they are not exposed to the role in order to build their experience;
- HR Business Partners lose sight of the type of issues being raised in the Service Centre and what is happening on the ground.

Despite these potential problems, a Chartered Institute of Personnel and Development (CIPD 2007) survey identified that some 28% of organisations have introduced centralised provision of shared administrative services. Of these 69% deliver them wholly in-house, 28% partially outsource them and 4% wholly outsource them. The CIPD provides some useful guidance on how to pilot and set up a service centre and make the transition, ensuring effective communication throughout.

*Surrey County Council* provides a good example of a shared service centre in action. Their HR Shared Services is responsible for carrying out the operational aspects of the HR life cycle for their staff and a number of external clients such as Surrey's schools. The Group has a customer base of approximately 30,000 individuals. There are four core areas within the Group: Payroll, Employee Services, Recruitment and Training Administration.

To overcome some of the difficulties of service centres, they also have a team which provides advice over the telephone and also travels around the county to various locations. This team helps with queries which need a face-to-face conversation like matters of a more confidential or difficult nature, e.g. helping managers with managing absence or with handling performance conversations.

## Funding

The way in which the partnership function is funded will have a big impact on the evaluation process. As a support function there are obvious choices between being centrally funded as an overhead or charging for the services across the organisation. Service level agreements, call-off contracts, project fees and pricing agreements are all possible ways in which the charging of the Business Partnership can take place. Some companies set their costs by estimating the number of consultancy days required and setting annual contracts.

Charging for services may seem a natural progression for HR activities where they are linked to the bottom line. It helps to show how the business can respond to competition from outside the organisation, as well as clearly demonstrating the value added by the function. *PowerGen*, for example, have a zero profit target HR centre, which charges at cost for its services across the organisation. The charges are set by examining the size of the business unit and the amount of change taking place. All of their customers are free to use other suppliers, and they have found themselves bidding against external providers for some services and occasionally losing the business (Hall, 1995).

Some partnership groups also undertake some fee-earning work outside the organisation with varying levels of success. *IBM* set up an external profit-making HR company called Workforce Solutions, which they found made them more innovative as a service provider. They eventually sold off the business despite its success as they found they were spending too much time costing solutions and marketing a cost-effective service rather than focusing on the service that would add most value to the business. Other organisations, such as *Xerox, Walt Disney Corporation* and *Pacific Bell*, have made more of a success of selling HR expertise externally. They found they were increasingly being asked to provide benchmarking information and this led to them selling their expertise. The value they have gained is not only professional recognition, but also an ability to learn from their customers (Laabs, 1995). Interestingly, for Xerox, the move meant that the HR function was re-aligned under sales and marketing as a product of the company.

Neubaum, Kellner, and Dawson-Shepherd (1997) suggests that if the function is not charged out then the work is often undervalued and perceived as a cost which can be cut. However, excessive charging can also lead to competition with external consultants, which can waste a lot of time and focus the work of the Business Partnership away from their core role. One large banking group changed their charging system when it became evident that their work was shifting towards areas of the business that had the budget to pay, away from parts of the business where they could really add value. As a consequence of these difficulties, Neubaum recommends that a cost should be charged to cover the overheads, but a profit element should not be included.

## Staffing issues

### Background and qualifications

The background and expertise needed to be a Business Partner vary enormously, depending on the business they are working in, the type of approach adopted (i.e. the balance between transactional and strategic work) and the readiness and capability of the line managers.

Mercer HR Consulting's survey of HR professionals (Griffiths, 2004) indicated that most organisations were more likely to invest in the HR staff that they currently employed and then develop business understanding and cross-functional experience amongst those staff. In our research, however, this seemed to be more the case for companies beginning the transition to Business Partner and as the function got more established, there appeared to be a trend towards broadening the background of Partners beyond HR and bringing in more consultancy expertise. This view appears to be backed up by research from Roffey Park (Giffin, Finney, Hennessey, & Boury, 2009) which indicates that HR Business Partner training programmes were implemented for 54% of Business Partners, but that financial skills, project management and consultancy experience were actively sought when selecting new Business Partners.

One reason for this may be that many HR professionals lack assertiveness and self-belief (People Management, 2004) and there is consequently a large gap between existing HR staff and the skills needed to be Business Partners. Indeed, Ulrich and Brockbank (2008) suggest that 20% of HR professionals will never be able to live up to the new expectations of the Business Partner role. In consultancy individuals need to be able to challenge the presenting problem and influence change and they need to have the confidence to do this without having the status to help them.

In some organisations we surveyed, such as *Seven Trent Water* and *Barclays*, the background of their Business Partners was mixed, with some coming from within the existing HR structure and some coming in from outside. A Business Partner we spoke to at Barclays had noticed an increasing trend to move away from the more traditional CIPD background which about 50% of the staff hold. The ability to diagnose, influence and coach was seen as equally, if not more, important than extensive HR knowledge. Seven Trent Water have appointed an HR Advisor with an engineering background who is "transitioning" into the

HR role, which signals to the business that Business Partners are not all pure HR people. They want to give the message out that they welcome people in from different backgrounds.

In other organisations, however, such as the *Immigration Authority*, CIPD qualifications are an important criteria. For them, transforming the role of the HR advisors was challenging and it was important that people were seen as credible with the relevant qualifications. Ideally they are aiming for all Business Partners to have CIPD qualifications and accreditation from the Institute of Management Consultants (IMC) following a course on consultancy practices.

The Business Partners must feel confident in their role and the power vested in them to be able to give difficult feedback to senior managers when appropriate. A lack of confidence or lack of position authority can lead to ineffective interventions, with the fear of credibility leading the consultant to make more expert judgements. There are particular issues for those moving from specialist functions such as training, personnel or operational management to consultancy. Business Partners do not always have positional power, particularly if their primary role is not that of internal consultant and they are performing this role as an additional function. The HR specialist who moves into the role must learn to deal with the ambiguity and frustration that will inevitably come from a lack of positional power.

In considering who is appropriate for the role, organisations should consider which people in their team would convince them to shift their thinking? If they wouldn't convince you, how will they convince others? As there is quite a different skill set required (which is discussed in more detail in Section 2), it is clear that not everyone in the "old" HR teams is always deemed suitable for the new business consultancy role. As a consequence, it is important to consider if the skills can be built internally or whether you will need to recruit people with an existing skill set, as in the case of the *Immigration Authority*. There may also be people in other areas of the organisation who have key skills/expertise that could be trained in the consultancy role and would benefit from being developed in this way.

## Experts or generalists?

Scanning through advertisements for HR Business Partners, it is again apparent that there is no clear skill requirement for the role, which is not surprising given the many different structural models in operation. Many companies state that they are seeking strong HR generalists, but often with the experience to do specific tasks – such as TUPE or Talent Management. However, the ability to manage and deliver projects and change programmes is certainly growing in importance for the role.

All Business Partners need to be expert in the skills needed to consult effectively with clients. The level of subject expertise needed will depend on the role the Business Partner is playing (see Chapter 4) and there are inherent dangers in setting yourself up as an expert in a particular field. However, it is likely that for most large partnership projects a mix of generalist skills and expert input will be required. Whether this expertise comes from the Business Partner or from elsewhere in the HR function is less critical and will depend on the structural model for the partnership.

Section 2 of this book explores the wider skill set in more detail.

## Reporting lines

Where Business Partner's report is also variable. Some organisations favour a dotted line to HR with a solid reporting line to the business unit, whilst in others it is the reverse – with a solid line to HR and dotted to the business manager. Whichever set-up is used, it is important to be clear on who is driving the priorities for the Business Partner and clearly establish where the priorities should lie.

Reporting lines for the Head of the Partnership function can also be critical. Ideally they would report directly into the Chief Executive or Chief Operating Officer. This will not only give the function more visibility and a higher level of sponsorship, but will also provide the function with more political pressure if required. Reporting through another HR Director or through the Business Unit Directors will create certain expectations about what will be delivered and will be a less influential position.

## Use of project teams

In order to address complex business issues, it is likely that for key projects there will be a need to bring together a combination of people with a mix of knowledge and skills. When working in teams, there is an added value in involving line management as well as the HR Partners, as this will provide a level of involvement and buy-in to assist in any implementation actions. However, teams bring with them inherent difficulties in terms of how business projects are managed. When working in teams, the Business Partners need to be clear on:

- Who does what;
- How you interact with the client;
- How you communicate with each other;
- How you monitor progress and update each other.

This issue of Project Management within the HR Business Partner role is becoming more prevalent and is a topic we will return to in the skills section of this book.

## Use of external suppliers

Effective partnerships have been found to make better use of external resources and will contract in specific capabilities or expertise as a way of strengthening their own position. Freelance consultants, Organisational Development (OD) Associates and Academics can all bring specialist skills and experience to a project that may not be present within the organisations. Effective Business Partners often hold a budget to enable them to bring in such people and they are not afraid of this damaging their own credibility.

If external resources are drawn in to work on a project, even when Business Partners are not the budget holder, it is critical that they are involved in the selection process and setting the scope of the external's work. Aside from this preventing misunderstandings or duplication of effort, it will also ensure that the Business Partner is more committed to making the contract a success.

*Fujitsu* are one company who draw on external partners to help them in their work. They undertook a recent project on talent management and used external suppliers to help them to profile the role. This resulted in a recruitment campaign plus an Academy for identifying internal talent, looking for "internal stand-alone leaders", which was all part of a strategy to get the right people in the right roles.

## Experience of the head

Studies have found that the Senior Executives in charge of an HR Business Partnership function are most effective if they have an HR background them-selves, as well as a good knowledge of the business. People who transfer into the role from the business often have difficulty in understanding how HR can con-tribute effectively to strategy development and implementation (Lawler & Mohrman, 2003). Interestingly though, many companies are beginning to specify leading change projects or strategic consulting as more useful backgrounds.

## Training and development

Many companies, such as *Shell*, have chosen to run tailored training in order to enhance their internal consultancy skills and develop more effective service providers. The staff in Shell People Services predominantly had HR generalist backgrounds, having worked in several operating environments both within and outside Shell. However, some had not had much prior experience of internal consultancy. To address this they developed a consultancy skills programme, covering the role of a consultant and the techniques and frameworks of effective consultancy. It also covered a range of issues such as influencing others, inter-personal awareness and personal presence. The modular course, designed and run by Roffey Park, allowed the participants to put theory into practice in the workplace and share experiences as a group.

Most companies also focus on increasing business awareness and understanding and some, such as *Royal Bank of Scotland*, provide financial training to help HR become more focused on the bottom line issues. University partnerships are also being used to support development. At the *Prudential*, Business partners are trained in strategic thinking at their own University and the *Civil Service* has linked with Kingston University to provide a masters degree in HR strategy and Change to help their transition to Business Partnership.

Companies with more established Business Partnership roles, such as *Royal Bank of Scotland* and *Shell,* have also carried out considerable work into defining roles and competency requirements. Halifax and Bank of Scotland (HBOS) has its own HR development centre and Shell have competencies and job profiles to help HR staff identify paths for career development.

In Section 2 we will focus on the key behaviours required for Business Partners. Core skills that we have identified include:

- Consultancy skills
- Project management
- Influencing
- Change Management and OD
- Interpersonal and Intra-personal effectiveness.

**Providing development opportunities**
It may be appropriate to rotate people through the function from the business, to provide not only a development opportunity for the individual, but also a new business insight into the project. Rotation of key managers from the business can have an added value in that it enhances the organisation's knowledge about what the Partnership function's role is and how it can have a positive impact on the business. However, there is a danger in this approach, as people new to the role are unlikely to be skilled in the consultant behaviours required to be most effective and as such may lack influence and credibility.

Longer term postings, typically one to three years, are a good compromise and have the benefit of bringing new skills and knowledge from the business into the partnership function, as well as broadening the consulting capabilities of the individuals. This is not easy to achieve, however, as line managers are often unwilling to take long-term secondments without the security of a post on their return to the business. It is imperative that any placements are not used as a way of "finding a hole" for managers who are surplus to requirements, and that the positions are viewed as a developmental step for high potential staff.

Depending on the size of the organisation, there may also be value in rotating HR staff through different aspects of HR and Operational Management, which is much easier to achieve. This will provide them with a more rounded picture of the different aspects of the business and a greater understanding of how different HR activities can add value.

In some more international companies, such as *Cargill*, there is a need to ensure that the Business Partners gain a broad cultural understanding of the different companies and gain more exposure to the acquisitions across Europe. They have developed the skills of their Business Partners in a number of ways:

■ Several people have moved to different countries;
■ HR have been given real responsibilities in the Business Units;
■ Using the London Business School;
■ Visiting sites, e.g. in Germany to get close to the customers
■ Young people are brought in and trained on new assignments;
■ Appointing a coach or mentor outside the own area, e.g. across shared services and HR Business Units.

Our own work with HR teams over the past few years has shown a need for a range of development opportunities from the initial understanding of the role and the process consulting approach, through to more in-depth skills and behaviours. The case study section at the end of this book illustrates one company's approach to training and developing its HR team in Business Partner competencies.

## Summary

A number of different models exist for structuring Business Partnerships. Some structures encourage stronger client relationships due to the close proximity and focus on the process of consulting, whilst others bring in more specialist advice and a closer relationship with transactional HR activities. The size of the organisation, the effectiveness of the existing transactional HR provision as well as the core business drivers and client needs will all be factors in deciding on an appropriate structure.

Business Partnerships need to be located where they can add most value to the business. This is likely to depend on where the key stakeholders are positioned and what your clients need from you. Reporting in to either the HR or Business Unit Director also has significant implications in terms of the expectations and priorities of the role.

Whilst some of the Partnership groups we came across charge for their services and even carry out work outside the organisation, it is more common for groups to work as an overhead in a traditional HR charging structure. This has implications for Business Partners in that it sends a message to the organisation about the value the function brings and may mean that Business Partners need to invest more time raising their profile and building credibility. Ironically, bringing in external suppliers with new expertise can often help Business Partners build their own credibility.

Information systems have been found to have a large impact on the ability of Business Partners to operate strategically and the move to Shared Service Centres in larger organisations is becoming more commonplace. Companies can use IT to speed up transactional activities and thus free up time for more strategic work, as well as enabling HR to gather and analyse strategic information in new ways.

Business Partners do not always start with positional power in organisations and as a consequence, the ability of the Business Partner to influence strategic change is often more likely to stem from individual confidence and interpersonal behaviours than a particular background or qualification. In our research we noted an increased trend to move away from more traditional HR qualifications to individuals skilled in a consultancy and project management approach. Much of the training and development being undertaken is also aimed at enhancing consulting skills as well as developing individual credibility and increased business understanding.

## Checklist

Key considerations for structuring and staffing the partnership:

- How effectively are transactional HR activities currently managed?
- What types of specialist expertise are required?
- How effectively do HR Information Systems support and capture data on the business?
- How strong are the relationships with the line?
- Where are the key clients and stakeholders located?
- Is process consulting understood and valued in the business?
- What level of experience does the existing HR team have?
- What particular expertise is required to assist the business?
- Are the existing team able to access strategic issues?
- How will project teams be managed?
- How will costs be charged?
- How strong are the external networks to key resources?
- How will the communication links with transactional HR be managed?

# References

CIPD. (2007). *The changing HR function.* Survey report. London: CIPD.

Freeman, C. (May 1997). Training your HR pros to fit your culture. *HR Focus, 74*(5), 9–10.

Giffin, E., Finney, L., Hennessey, J., & Boury, D. (2009). *Maximising the value of HR business partnering.* Roffey Park Research Guide. Horsham: Roffey Park.

Griffiths, J. (2004). Partnership drives worldwide change [Mercer HR Consulting]. *People Management, 10*(7), 12.

Hall, L. (18 July 1995). Pay your way. *Personnel Today.*

Herring, K. (October 2001). HR takes a hands-on approach. *Workforce, 80*(10), 42.

Laabs, J. J. (1995). HR for profit: selling expertise. *Personnel Journal, 74*(5), 84–88.

Lawler, E., & Mohrman, S. (2003). HR as a strategic partner: what does it take to make it happen? *Human Resource Planning, 26*(3), 15.

Neumann, J. E., Kellner, K., & Dawson-Shepherd, A. (1997). *Developing organisational consultancy.* London: Routledge.

People management. (June 2004). One step beyond. pp. 27–31.

Personnel Today. (May 2007). Coca-Cola plans to hire HR Business Partners to provide shared-service centres.

Pfau, B. N., & Cundiff, B. B. (November 2002). 7 Steps before strategy. *Workforce, 81*(12), 40–44.

Reilly, P. (July 2000). *HR shared services and the realignment of HR.* Report 368. Institute for Employment Studies.

Ulrich, D. (1997). *Human resource champions.* Boston: Harvard University Press.

Ulrich, D., & Brockbank, W. (2005). *The HR value proposition.* Harvard Business School Press.

Ulrich, D., & Brockbank, W. (Dec/Jan 2008). The business partnership model 10 years on: lessons learnt. *Human Resource Magazine.*

# 4

# Positioning Yourself with the Client

In the preceding two chapters we have focused on positioning the partner function and giving consideration to issues around how the function is structured, resourced and marketed. These could be considered to be at the hard edge of Business Partnering. Equally important in our view are the process issues around the relationships you need to build with your internal clients and the client system as a whole. The way each individual Business Partner positions themselves within the organisation is critical to the success of the function as a whole.

One of the key challenges facing those who go into the Business Partner role from an existing HR position is that of influencing stakeholders within the current culture of the organisation and on occasions, influencing a shift in culture through the interventions they make. Being part of the organisation brings both advantages and disadvantages: whilst having a strong understanding of prevailing cultural norms, internal agents may also be "blind" to them. With their own personal power and influence as the primary tools, those working internally may fail to account for the extent to which they contribute to sustaining the culture, which they hope to change. High self-awareness appears to be a key requirement for anyone working inside the organisation in this way.

Credibility comes in many forms. It can come with a good track record, which Business Partners who have been in HR in a previous role, may or may not have. Those recruited from outside the organisation may be at an advantage here in that there is no previous history. However, they will have to work harder at understanding the politics and culture of the organisation.

## Getting in!

The term "gaining entry" is commonly used when referring to the early stages of a consultant client relationship. It is equally valid if your title is Business Partner. The title as we have illustrated elsewhere does make a difference in that "Business Partner" infers a level of strategic intervention, so this is preferable to some other HR-related titles. The title is one way in which perceptions of people using the service can be influenced. If you have the title Strategic Business Partner with the backup of a seat at senior board meetings, you are already off to a good start for building relationships and credibility.

We refer to the term gaining entry here to examine the access that individuals have within the organisation, as well as the level to which they establish and maintain effective relationships with their internal clients. Gaining entry also means having a level of visibility within the organisation; being clear about what services you are offering and how you will work with your clients: specifically, the benefits of your service to them and the organisation.

Some key questions to gauge your existing level of influence:

■ Do people in the organisation know who you are?
■ What image comes to mind when they think about you or your group?
■ What services will you offer to your clients?
■ How do they know what's available?
■ What is the nature of the contract that you will have with them? – i.e. do you work to service-level agreements? Or what other standards can they expect?

Many of the people we have spoken to in organisations (apart from those with the title Business Partner) are still unfamiliar with the term and do not know what it means and how exactly it relates to the business.

At the gaining entry and relationship building stage (as well as at other stages in working with clients), it will be important for the internal Business Partner to act like an external. By this we mean approaching your clients as if you were selling your services to them. In some cases this will be exactly what happens under service level agreements. In others, the cost and time issues are less clear so it will be important to behave "as if" you were being paid directly by your client for the work that you do.

## Early impressions

The first impression you create with anyone, client or potential client (as they are all in that category), is of paramount importance. In the world of external consultancy, it is often the make or break time. If the client responds well to you on a personal level, you are more likely to "win" the work. Internally, you may be contracted to carry out work with a client, but if there is little rapport between you, you may find relationships becoming strained or non-existent. Rapport can be gained in a number of ways such as:

- Demonstrating knowledge and understanding of the client on a personal level;
- Demonstrating knowledge and understanding of the client's area of the organisation and business issues affecting their work;
- Mirroring aspects of body language;
- Matching verbal language, style and tone of the client;
- Matching other aspects of personality (e.g. level of directness, generalisations, attention to specifics and detail or concepts and ideas).

Some people feel uncomfortable about matching and mirroring as a way of gaining rapport. However, it is important to remember that you are not mimicking! – and intention is key. If you have respect for your clients and come from a belief that you will have a better relationship with them if they feel you are on their wavelength, you are more likely to do this in a way that feels congruent. Just notice how much you need to match and mirror so that the dialogue feels comfortable for you both.

## Client readiness and capability

The ability of the Business Partner to gain entry also depends on the client's readiness and capability for change (Beckhard & Harris, 1987). Often, a move into a consultancy role and away from operational support will mean a significant change for the internal client. For example, if managers have been used to personal contact with someone from HR to deal with personnel issues, which have now been transferred to a call centre, the shift in role will represent a significant change. Rather than a one-to-one meeting with someone to talk through problems/ organisational issues, the manager may now have two or three people to contact about different aspects. In addition, the manager might need to deal with personnel issues themselves, with little skill or capability to do this.

An example in one organisation we spoke to included the discomfort some managers had around dealing with "HR issues". Investigation by the HR team showed that there was a capability issue around the managers being able to deal confidently with poor performers. Unofficial HR teams had been set up locally to support managers but the advice they provided, which included options for how to proceed, did not deal with the underlying issue of the manager's lack of skill in dealing with poor performance consistently.

Beckhard and Harris's model for assessing the client's readiness and capability for change is useful here:

■ Assess the attitudes of key stakeholders towards the change – willingness, motives and aims = readiness;
■ Analyse the power sources, influence and authority issues, skills and information required = capability.

Some of the steps we recommended in the previous chapters will help you to determine both the levels of readiness and capability. If the Business Partnership function is to be successful some internal consultancy on your internal consultancy is necessary!

The readiness and capability equation can also be applied to those moving into the consultancy role as primary stakeholders in the change. It will be important to assess current levels of capability and skill amongst this group and find out what development needs they have at an early stage. Preferably skilling them up or recruiting suitable people in before services are offered.

As part of assessing the client's readiness and capability, the internal consultant can consider what else needs to happen towards successful change. Force-field analysis is a familiar change model, which can be applied to consider how to move from a present position to a desired future state.

An example of how this might look for the transition to Business Partnership is shown in Figure 4.1.

In this example some of the areas that appear as driving forces could be resisting forces; for example Senior Management commitment may not be present in your organisation.

It is usually easier to influence restraining forces, since when you increase the driving forces, people may feel pushed and become even more resistant. Having said that, some of the driving forces (particularly financial) can be so compelling that they help to force the changes needed.

Force field analysis can help at the early stages of establishing a Business Partnership in many ways:

■ It can help to uncover potential obstacles and reveal what is really blocking the proposed changes;
■ It can help anticipate special factors to take into account in preparing for implementation;
■ It helps to identify sources of support that you may not have previously considered.

After analysing the driving and resisting forces, it is important to think about actions for both minimising the resisting forces and increasing the driving forces.

| Current situation | Future goal |
|---|---|
| Operational HR services | Strategic Business Partnerships |
| Driving forces | Restraining forces |
| Dissatisfaction of internal clients with present service | Line Manager's capability and readiness |
| Pressure to drive down costs of HR | Reluctance by managers to take on 'HR' issues |
| Increased need for strategic HR advice | Lack of strategic skills in HR function |
| Commitment of senior managers | Pressure of increased operational issues |

**Figure 4.1** Transition to business partnership.

## Business partner roles re-visited

We touched on roles in Chapter 1. Another perspective on the roles you might find yourself taking is drawn from the world of consulting.

Many of you will be familiar with the Doctor–patient metaphor as a way of describing the consultant role. Where consultants have previously been regarded as an "expert" through his or her specialist role, they may find themselves inadvertently providing expert solutions to clients who still perceive them in this way.

## Expert or doctor–patient role

In the expert role, the client places the responsibility for identifying the root cause of the problem and subsequent solutions in the hands of the consultant or Business Partner. The client is likely to take a passive role and in this way the relationship can also take on parent–child like qualities in transactional analysis terms (Berne, 1993), with the client/child playing up from time to time. However, this role can have some advantages for both the consultant and client. It can be a good way to "gain entry" for the Business Partner. If you have been known for supplying a particular expert service and are seen to be credible, you have an added advantage with existing good relationships with clients who will have valued you for the service provided. For the client it can provide a huge sense of relief to know that someone is prepared to "take-on" your problem and sort it out for you. However, at either a conscious or sub-conscious level, clients may also think that if something does not work out, they have a ready-made scapegoat to protect their credibility and reputation. Once in this role, attempting to get the client to accept ownership and responsibility for the problem/issue can be tricky and attempts by the consultant to release themselves from this expert role can cause anxiety for both consultant and client.

Many people working inside the organisation in a consultancy capacity readily identify with the role of expert or Dr–Patient.

## Pair-of-hands or purchase–supply role

This is the role next most commonly identified by those people we have worked with inside the organisation. In research carried out by Roffey Park in 2003 (Kenton & Moody, 2003), we asked what the key challenges were facing those working internally, quotes included:

■ Being presented with the solution which someone thinks is right to implement rather than being allowed to research the issue/problem and complete a full consultancy process.
■ Actually being able to operate as consultants as opposed to project leaders.
■ We have to work hard to push our way in and work alongside them (managers) so we can create project plans, but we still have to squeeze our way into their diaries.

Working as a "pair of hands" usually means the power and responsibility lie with the client who invites you in to provide some solutions for which you have perceived expertise. Again, there are advantages and disadvantages, although many we spoke to would see this as an undesirable role. A clear disadvantage would be in creating an expectation within the client that you will always work with them in this way and not being included in the early and important discussions and decisions about organisational development. It is a transactional rather than a transformational role and those truly working at a strategic level in the organisation are less likely to be used in this way.

## Process consultation/collaborative role

This is the role many Business Partners will aspire towards, mainly because in this role, responsibility and ownership rest equally with you and your client. Each party sees that they have expertise and experience that will be of value in the relationship and they contract to work together in joint problem-solving and diagnosis. This clearly has some advantages, particularly in helping organisations to manage change. To be seen as an equal contributor in identifying organisational issues and likely ways forward, rather than expert or implementer means that the client is truly viewing you as a valued partner. If, however, you are to work in this way, certain competencies are key – including good self-awareness; skill in working with process issues; being comfortable with ambiguity and an ability to challenge clients constructively if you feel you are being enticed into other roles!

In order to work collaboratively, the client as well as the Business Partner must be capable and ready to work in this way. This, in turn, demands a set of values and behaviours for working which may be quite different from previous ways of working with internal service providers. If, for example, the client does not perceive a need for improvement, and/or the client does not have the appropriate problem-solving skills to engage in joint diagnosis, then working in this way will prove very difficult. In addition, some of the structural models for Business Partnerships outlined in the previous chapter will prove unworkable.

The extent to which cultural values of collaboration, open dialogue and self-awareness prevail has a key impact on positioning the client relationship within the intervention. So an important need exists for Business Partners to check out the client's readiness to "devote time, energy and the committed involvement of the appropriate people to a problem solving process" (Lippit & Lippit, 1986).

There are several factors, which may impact on the success of the Business Partner to work collaboratively with the client.

Internal Customer' values: On the face of it, it might seem that a strong "internal customer" value would align well with Business Partner activities. However, in practice this manifests itself through the tensions inherent in meeting the perceived need of the customer, framed as it often is by the customer's need for a speedy solution.

Relating this high customer-focused value to the consultant roles determined by Schein (1987) shows the challenges this can bring for an internal consultant:

| Consultant Role | High Internal Service Expectation |
|---|---|
| Expert | Deliver solution quickly without high client involvement |
| | Customer needs met early |
| | Lacks systemic approach to diagnosing. The presenting problem may not be real issue |

(*Continued*)

| Consultant Role | High Internal Service Expectation |
|---|---|
| Pair of hands | Reasonably aligned with high customer-focused values |
| | Focused on meeting customer needs |
| | Power lies with customer, though the customer's perception of the issue may be "wrong" |
| | Not possible to challenge customer's assumptions as customer is "right" |
| Process | Working collaboratively may be construed as "passing the buck" |
| | Customer expectations for solutions may not be met within the desired timeframe |

In some cases a clear distinction between the concept of "customer" and "client" has not been established when developing a Business Partner function: rather one approach has overlain the other, causing confusion in both the Business Partner's expectation of his/her role, and the client's expectation of the working relationships. One example highlighted this: in a large manufacturing company, an internal consultancy group had been established to provide HR interventions at divisional levels. As the group developed an awareness of their role, they began to understand where providing solutions (to what were often complex people issues) did not help the client in the long-term. In fact, these actions were helping to create a higher level of dependency – particularly once the client had built a strong relationship with the consultant and "knew where to go" with an issue. Whilst individual consultants recognised the need to move towards a process consultancy role, the message from their manager, a Director, was that the Internal Customer model of working should prevail. This leads to frustration and questions about the strategic relevance of creating the consultancy group.

## A framework for working collaboratively

At the beginning of any relationship, it will be important to identify some key areas to help provide a focus before taking more substantial steps.

The following framework can help Business Partners work together with their clients to establish what the issues are and what actions might need to be taken. In this way, it might provide a basis for a contracting discussion with the client. The beliefs that underpin this framework are closely aligned to those of process or collaborative consulting. The aim is to help the client think through the nature of the problem or issue she/he is facing and to find out if the client is truly committed to finding a way forward by asking questions and listening carefully to the response. The framework can be used as a mental checklist over the period of a project, as well as a checklist for a one-off conversation.

CONSULT stands for:

- Context
- Overview
- Needs of the Client
- Symptoms
- Underlying issues
- Long-term likely effects
- Tasks and timescales.

## Context

Here, the Business Partner finds out about the context of what is needed. Information is gathered about the area of the organisation in which the client works, so that the consultant has a clearer picture for going forward. Normally, you will already have a good or developing understanding of the business, however, it will be important not to make assumptions and rather let the client confirm the context from their own perspective. This is also a good opportunity to find out how this area of the business links to others. As well as a fact-finding discussion for your benefit, it can help to raise the client's awareness of the interface between their work and the work of other sections.

Questions for consideration:

- What is the main purpose of the team/unit?
- How many people are there?
- Where are people situated geographically?
- What are the differing sections/departments and how do they relate to one another?
- Who are the clients/customers? (as appropriate)
- What methods of communication are in place?
- What other processes and systems are used? (asking about areas of specific relevance).

## Overview

Get an overview of the situation as described by the client. This will be the first presentation of the "problem" as defined by the client and so it will be useful to pay attention to how the client describes what is happening. How open are they about what they understand to be happening? – What is unsaid? – What do you notice about their emotional level as they describe the situation to you? This overview will provide the bigger context before getting more detail.

Questions for consideration:

- What are the issues for discussion?
- What is happening at the moment?
- What has led up to this situation?
- Who is involved?
- How did this come about?

## Needs

The needs of the client should be identified. They may say that they want you to come up with the solution – in some way to "fix" the problem. Again, notice how they define their needs. What is said and what is implied will give you a good clue on their expectations of you and how they might want to work with you. They are also likely to have emotional needs of, for example, reassurance. If you pick this up at an early stage, it might be appropriate to give some reassurance in the form of empathy – "it sounds like this has been a difficult time for you" or "you've clearly put a lot of energy into this so far". This might sound obvious, but active listening and empathy are sometimes forgotten in either anxiety or enthusiasm to find out exactly what the problem is and how you are going to solve it! At this stage, you need to go slow to go fast. In other words, don't jump to conclusions about how this issue might be resolved.

Questions for consideration:

- What does the client need from you?
- What has already been thought about/tried out?
- What has prompted the client to take action now?
- What would make this situation better for the client and others?
- How might some of the explicit and implicit needs of the client be met by you?

## Symptoms

What are the overt symptoms the clients haves noticed that have brought them to asking you for your help? Examples might include customer complaints, arguments between staff, system failure, increased error rates/costs, reduction in quality, hostile competition, etc.

Symptoms are distinct from signs in that they tend to be more overt and identifiable results of problems or issues.

Questions for consideration:

- What has the client noticed specifically that is happening in relation to this issue?
- What examples are there of particular problems/issues?
- Specifically, what is causing this to be a cause for concern?
- Where is the problem? And where isn't it?
- How has it impacted on other areas of the business? – what have they noticed?

## Underlying issues

You will need to have an understanding of the issues that underlie the situation as outlined by the client. As these tend to be less obvious than the overt symptoms, the client may not know or fully understand these at this stage. Underlying issues may only emerge once work has begun, however it will be important to have a sense of the underlying issues as things progress and for both the client and the Business Partner to be fully appreciative of the full causes. For example, an issue of team morale may emerge to be more about the pay and reward system than conflicting relationships between team members. Having a diagnostic framework in mind, which encompasses soft and hard areas, will help at this stage.

Questions for consideration:

- What else is contributing to this problem or issue?
- What's the problem with the problem?
- What happened just before this became an issue?

## Long-term likely effect

How much of an issue is this for the client and the organisation? Paying some attention to this area will help you to establish the level of commitment the client has to engaging in the change process. If you sense at this stage that there is little engagement or little impact if the issue continues you will have some clues about the priority of this in the client's perception.

Questions for consideration:

- What is the likely impact if this issue continues?
- In what way do you see this as impacting on the business?
- If this continues? What is likely to happen?
- If we do nothing – what is the likely impact?
- How does this affect your bottom line?
- How is business likely to improve if this is tackled effectively?

## Tasks and timescales

What are the steps you agree to take next? This area is about being clear on the boundaries for the next stages of working and might include an initial contract between the consultant and client on further information-gathering/diagnostic activity.

Questions for consideration:

■ What needs to happen next?
■ What are the milestones to be agreed?
■ What activities will be important?
■ Who needs to do what and by when?
■ Who else needs to be involved?
■ What constraints do we need to aware of?

As with any framework, this needs to be applied flexibly. It will be rare for the client to follow the order this framework sets out and you will need to match where the client is and skillfully steer back to any areas, which you feel are missing. Don't feel you have to cover all these areas in one conversation. It may be more helpful to have these areas in mind as a backdrop to the longer term relationship with your client.

## Reviewing the relationship from different perspectives

There are four main themes to have in mind for reviewing your discussions with the client once the issue has been presented to you:

■ What do you know, think and feel about the issue?
■ How does the client see things from their perspective?
■ What would an organisational take on the issue be?
■ Given all the above, and acting as a consultant to yourself, how would you take this forward with the client?

You will invariably be starting from your own perspective. If you have received a letter, e-mail or phone call, you may already have some assumptions about the issue, more so when working inside the organisation. This can be a useful source of information to draw on for a better understanding of what is going on. *This is commonly known as the first person perspective.*

From your discussions with the client – how do they see things? – using CONSULT what have you found out about their hopes and fears and outcomes they want from working with you? Why is this issue important to them? *Looking at it from this angle is known as the second person perspective.*

Imagine now the organisation takes on a persona – what would he or she be saying about the issue? – bearing in mind what else is happening in the organisation. Here you are aiming to look at the issue from a more detached perspective rather than getting back into your own views and assumptions. Where does this view come from? And what is it based on? – how in touch are you with the organisation as distinct from perhaps one or two influential people on the Executive Board? *This is from a third person perspective.*

Finally, as an objective consultant to yourself, *from a fourth perspective*, what advice would you recommend to yourself for working with this client?

## Clients, sponsors and stakeholders

In the early stages of the relationship it will be important for Business Partners to establish the key players for the piece of work presented. An understanding of stakeholder management will be helpful here.

The client will normally be the person who has presented an issue to you. However, the client system will include everyone in the organisation potentially. So the question "who is the client?" is an interesting and important one. If the person who presents the issue to you is not at the most senior level of the organisation it is always worth considering his/her manager as another potential client who might need to be engaged in conversations about the issue at some stage.

## Sponsors

A sponsor will usually be someone at a senior level of the organisation who agrees or volunteers to "champion" a piece of work. In some organisations, the project planning approach requires each piece to have a sponsor. In our experience the role of the sponsor is not always clear. Again, the following questions might help to clarify the need for a sponsor and the role they would play.

- Does the issue impact on the organisation at every level?
- Does it impact significantly on the future of the organisation? – either the way work is carried out or the products offered?
- Will it require shifts in attitude or behaviours at the most senior levels?

■ Will it require support from senior managers, even if it does not affect them directly?

■ What are the risks of this project if there is no visible sponsor to support the work?

If a sponsor is named – either because if fits in with your company's approach to project planning or because you feel this would be useful, we would recommend a contracting discussion with the individual at an early stage. This ensures you are both clear about how the sponsor will actively support the work as it unfolds. Often sponsors are so in name only, with little clarity about how they should perform the role. Sponsors could be encouraged to be active in their role in the following ways:

■ Making a presentation to launch an initiative;

■ Holding open forums for question and answer sessions;

■ Attending planning meetings to give active support;

■ Adding their views on written communications such as updates on project progress;

■ Kicking off training and development programmes or attending for end of programme presentations.

## Stakeholders

A simple and useful way to determine the key stakeholders is to consider:

■ Who knows?

■ Who cares?

■ Who can?

These questions (Revans, 1980) make reference to stakeholder groups in terms of those who have information about the organisation, its history and current culture and/or about the presenting issue.

They include people who have been in the organisation for some time and could be at any level of authority. The priests and storytellers referred to by Deal and Kennedy (1982). These are the people "who know". Those stakeholders "who care" would include anyone with a vested interest in contributing to the work or with an interest in the outcomes. These people may or may not have power and influence – but it is worth asking yourself "what is the risk of leaving them out of the research/consultation process?" The final category are the people "who can" – which includes those with financial or position authority who have the potential to either help or hinder the progress of the work. A simple framework can be applied to analyse stakeholders and determine where you need to spend your energy as a Business Partner (Figure 4.2).

**Figure 4.2** Analysing your stakeholders.

Commitment and support will be evident by what people say about the project or issue you are trying to influence and also by their deeds. Are they prepared to commit time and energy to supporting this work?

Levels of influence in the organisation can be determined by some of the following:

- Is this person responsible for making strategic decisions in the organisation which affect the way the business is run?
- Does this person get listened to by people in the above category?
- Do they have a senior role in the organisation?
- Are they interpersonally persuasive and credible?
- Are they seen to be a good role model of management in the company?
- Do they have responsibility for a substantial budget linked to your project?
- Can they give this project the go ahead or put a block on action that might need to be taken?
- Do they "have the ear" of the Chief Executive or others on the Senior Management Board?

Based on levels of commitment, support and influence, you can decide on the priorities for stakeholder involvement. For example, where you have senior managers who are highly committed and in an influential position, how can they be used to support the changes that are needed? For example, a decision to go into partnership with another company clearly needs to have senior management support.

The influential supporters can be used to communicate positive messages about the benefits of the partnership to the organisation. Clearly, energy needs to be placed in the low commitment/high influence arena, as the drawbacks of either not getting support here or active opposition could be risky. If this is the case, it would be worth finding out the cause of the lack of commitment. These senior managers may have some very valid reasons for not supporting the changes more actively. How can you work to minimise the resistance or use it constructively?

You will probably not want to spend time and energy on those who have little commitment and little influence. However, those with commitment to the issue and low influence might usefully be used as a lever for others. Also, you will want to keep them engaged and involved, so in managing the work, you might want to consider if they can actively be engaged in running events or carrying out research.

## Relationship mapping

Another useful way to analyse the relationships you have with your internal clients is to spend some time in mapping the relationships. This can either be done for a specific project or for your internal relationships more generally. The example that follows is based on an NHS client seeking engagement of senior managers in the diversity action planning process.

Stage one: Map out the key people or groups who have a vested interest in the issue.

Stage two: Using the commitment and influence matrix, identify who is in which category (as far as you are able).

Stage three: Highlight in some way the degree to which you have an effective relationship with them – this can be done by showing solid or dotted lines to that

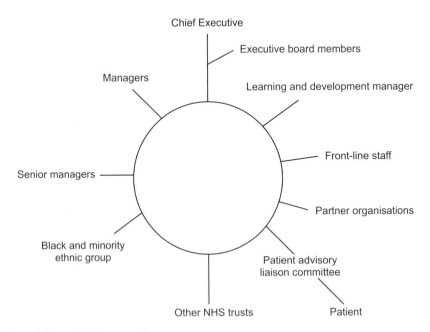

**Figure 4.3** Stakeholder mapping.

person or group of people. (Effective means are you getting what you need from them and vice versa. If you don't know what's needed, this could prompt a conversation to find out.)

Stage four: Finally, make an action plan to spend time on the relationships that are critical to the success of the project (Figure 4.3).

Another way to use the relationship map is to help you think about the relationships you have with your wider client system. Networking is another form of gaining entry, which is key to the success of the Business Partner role. Networks need to be built at an early stage and paid attention to throughout for effective practice. We return to the subject of networking in Chapter 5.

## Promoting yourself

Often marketing yourself is not considered to be an active part of the role of Business Partner. Your clients may be chosen for you and there may be little scope to influence the projects you work on. Whether it is perceived as part of your role or not, your ability to influence change in the organisation will be driven to a large extent by your ability to get involved in the right projects, with the right people. One Business Partner we spoke to commented that there was a vast difference between the effectiveness of the function and the way Business Partners carried out their role across the organisation. Where the perception of the individuals and their ability to access value-added projects is in question, they are less likely to be effective.

Business Partners who have moved internally into the role from a more traditional HR structure will find the need to market themselves and promote their own capability – a radical change to their previous role. However, if your organisation and the key managers within it are largely unaware of the change in role and what it means for them, it is highly unlikely you will be able to discuss problems and work in a collaborative way with clients. Your clients will need to understand what you can offer and have the confidence in your abilities to deliver.

Depending on the structure, there may be more or less of a need to market the services provided, but in some cases the internal partners will be competing on a level footing with external providers and will therefore need a more aggressive approach to marketing themselves. When the Business Partner has been recruited from a more traditional structure where there was a captive market for their services, this is even more of a significant change to their role and skill set.

One of the first steps in promoting yourself is to try to get a better understanding of your role and the contribution you bring. Key questions to reflect on are:

- What are your key skills?
- What is unique about you?

- How do you operate to best effect?
- What values and beliefs do you have that drive your work?
- What are your personal objectives as a Business Partner?

## Lift test!

Often you will be given a short opportunity to "sell" what you do to people you meet in the organisation. Thinking through an eloquent and informative response to the question "so what's your role?" will stand you in good stead. This is sometimes referred to as the "lift test".

The lift test is a good way of gauging if you are clear enough about what you do to be able to describe it to someone in the time it would take the lift to go from one floor to another. Write it down, practice it and test it out to make sure you can clearly "sell" what you offer within the business – clearly and succinctly. Does it say something about you and the way you like to work, as well as the outputs you deliver?

## Summary

The early stages of any relationship are key to its success. Whether we are talking about a lifetime partnership or an important business relationship, how you position yourself with the client and within the client system is a fundamentally important part of your overall role. The key things to consider here are: convincing yourself that you have something to offer; being clear about what that is and having the confidence to project that to others.

Gaining entry is not just about having the confidence to network and let people know who you are and what you do, it is also about having sufficient interest in all parts of the overall system (i.e. the organisation) to want to know how the interlinking parts connect and how individuals within the organisation work. It also means having a genuine interest in others and developing a curiosity about them as individuals as well as part of the overall system.

There is a difference between a client and a customer and if organisations have a culture and set of values in place which places the customer at the forefront of thinking, your internal clients might need to come to terms with accepting a balance between meeting their needs and the wider needs of the organisation. This means clear communication about the role of the Business Partner and the relationship between you and your internal clients.

Before jumping to conclusions about what needs to happen in any given situation presented by your clients it will be important to get the background information and find out "what is going on around here?" both in the way the client describes the situation to you and from your own take on what is happening. Utilising a framework, such as the CONSULT model described in this chapter, can help to ensure that the Business Partner digs deeper into the issues being presented.

This section has paid attention to the early stages of shaping the Business Partnership, which are crucial to its success. Paying attention to developing key relationships as well as the structural and positioning issues will help to make sure your internal clients are on board with the changes. Building good relationships with your clients is perhaps one of the most important skills of the internal consultant. Once trust and rapport are established, an effective working relationship can emerge.

## Checklist

- Are you providing expert advice only on those areas where you have sufficient expertise?
- Are your clients building their own knowledge and understanding through the process of working with you?
- Are any of your clients becoming overly dependent?
- Do the values of the organisation support your desired ways of working?
- Are you establishing the underlying cause for issues presented to you by clients?
- Are you identifying the key stakeholders – Who knows? Who cares? And who can?
- Have you contracted with sponsors about their role as well as your clients?
- How engaged are your clients at the outset of discussions?
- Are you involved in early discussions on business strategy with other senior managers?
- Have you identified all the key stakeholders in your current projects?
- Are you engaging stakeholders and using them to help influence others in the organisation?
- Have you built networks and are you maintaining them effectively?
- Are you networking with senior managers and those with influence in the organisation?
- Are you spending time finding out about people and who they are as individuals as well as what their business issues are?
- What else do you need to do to raise your profile and credibility within the organisation?

# References

Beckhard, R., & Harris, R. (1987). *Organisational transformations: Managing complex change*. Reading, MA: Addison-Wesley.

Berne, E. (1993). *What do you say after you say hello?* London: Transworld Publishers Ltd.

Deal, T., & Kennedy, A. (1982). *Corporate cultures – The rites and rituals of corporate life*. London: Penguin Books.

Kenton, B., & Moody, D. (2003). *The role of the internal consultant*. Roffey Park Institute.

Lippit, G., & Lippit, R. (1986). *The consulting process in action* (2nd ed.). San Francisco: Jossey-Bass/Pfeiffer.

Revans, R. W. (1980). *Action learning: New techniques for management*. London: Blond and Briggs.

Schein, E. H. (1987). *Process consultation, Vol. II*. Cambridge, MA: Addison Wesley.

# Part 2

## Developing a Professional Edge

The first section of this book has highlighted some of the challenges for HR teams in making the transition to Business Partners. Whilst there are often structural or strategic changes that take place, what is often more critical in the success of the move to Business Partnerships are the skills and abilities of the partners themselves. This section focuses on the need to develop a more professional edge as a Business Partner, a challenge which is even more evident if you have worked in an operational HR role previously and need to re-invent yourself in some way to signal the change to managers in the business.

This part of the book is split into three sub sections:

- Creating and Leading Change
- Delivering a Business-Focused Service
- Relationship Skills

Each of these sections provides tools and techniques to develop what we see as some of the critical skills related to the role. The chapters within each section also pick out elements from the behavioural framework for Business Partners outlined in the introductory chapter and reproduced as an Appendix to this book.

# 2a

# Creating and Leading Change

An assumption might be made that skills in creating and leading change are mostly relevant to those working at a senior level in the Business Partner function. However, we see that the skills included in this section are relevant to anyone working in the Business Partner role. Those operating at a more junior level will still need to influence people in the business to take into account the wider business and HR agenda and help them focus on the priorities during times of change.

This section focuses specifically on:

- Influencing and leading change *and*
- Developing your thinking style.

Those of you still working in a more operational role but wanting to develop business partner competencies will, from reading this chapter, be able to identify the difference between thinking from a strategic perspective and applying a more predictable approach. With many organisations going through fundamental change, the ability to think and act from a wider perspective will create the business edge needed for surviving in the present tough economic climate.

This section incorporates the skills under "creating and leading change" in Chapter 1 and written as a self-assessment questionnaire in the Appendix. These skills include: being both proactive and preventive, applying innovation and entrepreneurship and path-finding, which includes the ability to cope with ambiguity and complexity.

Chapter 5 covers in some depth the topic of influencing and leading change – crucial to the success of the Business Partner role. The skills of course overlap with relationship skills more generally but to have the ability to be clear about what you can and need to influence, identify a range of strategies for meeting goals and to work with others to bring about successful change for the greater good of the organisation is a highly valued competence area for Business Partners. This chapter will outline some of the theory and practice around change, offer models and frameworks to add to your toolkit and highlight issues to consider when working with change in the organisation.

Chapter 6 is a new addition to this book, included particularly as we extend our own thinking on the principles of business partner practice rather than solely considering a standard role under the title of Business Partner. The assumption in this chapter is that everyone has a brain of course but that we may tend to rely on a particular way of thinking, based on cultural expectations (both personal and organisational), and what feels more natural and comfortable to us. By practising the art of flexible thinking and extending the way we look at issues facing the business we are more likely to be able to meet the demanding needs of our customers and partners. This chapter looks at three different types of thinking under the headings of rational, creative and strategic thinking. We recognise that these terms will be used differently by individuals and throughout different texts, so ask that you approach the topic with an open mind to our interpretations.

# 5

# Influencing and Leading Change

This chapter pays particular attention to the role of the Business Partner in influencing change and dealing with some of the reactions to change within the organisation. If you already have a seat at the strategic table and are considered one of a number of influential people who can support change within the business, then your job will be much easier. Some of you reading this book will be aspiring to the role of strategic Business Partner and so we hope you will find some useful pointers in this chapter on how to influence change in the organisation from a less strategic position too. Wherever you are in the organisation, and at whatever level you are providing services, part of your role as an HR professional will be to influence others so that the HR agenda stays on track.

When we consider change in this chapter we are paying attention to interventions aimed at improving the business or performance of the business. As with previous chapters, we will draw on research and practice to illustrate both the challenges in implementing change and the methods and practices that have been successful.

## What kinds of change are you likely to be involved in?

First we need to consider the type of changes we are touching on here. You may be required to respond to changes outside of your control as with (for example) the recent financial downturn. The HR Partners need to respond rapidly to radical changes, such as downsizing and redundancies – providing sound advice to support business and people decisions in chaotic times. This means being able to hold your nerve, stay resilient, work under pressure and stay open to multiple possible ways forward.

Depending on the level at which the Business Partner sits, examples of change interventions might include the following:

- Implementing and facilitating mergers/acquisitions and partnerships;
- Restructuring part or all of the company;
- Introducing company-wide policies or systems;
- Cultural change;
- Reward and remuneration programmes;
- Implementing people development strategies;
- Recruitment and retention strategies;
- Strategy on implementing legislative requirements – e.g. around diversity;
- Business process improvements.

Chapter 3 highlighted the range of possible activities from operational people-focused tasks to future process-focused tasks and all of these (and the list is not exhaustive) have two key things in common. They should all have expected tangible business outcomes and they all have both task and people implications. If you are questioning the tangible business outcomes then that is likely to make your job of influencing change in the business much more difficult. A first step for the Business Partner is therefore clarifying the reasons for the change. One public sector company we are involved with at the moment is making significant changes to their structure and processes as a result of the Modernising Government Agenda. This is resulting in some difficult questions about the purpose of the organisation; who the "customer" really is and where the organisation should focus its energies for the future.

If Business Partners are truly working at a strategic level within their organisations, then an understanding of the nature of change at this level will be key to the success of the role. Questions for Business Partners around the implementation of change are likely to be:

- What are the business imperatives for this change?
- How can I get people alongside this change?
- What can I do if there is resistance?
- How can we achieve what is best for the business and manage the change in the timescale available?
- What methods are going to best fit the change that's required?
- Who needs to be involved? Why? How? And when?
- How will it affect me?

The last question is a fundamental one which is often ignored by people working inside the organisation. As internal consultants, we are often so busy dealing with the emotions of others that we forget to take stock of how changes are impacting on us – particularly at an emotional level. Many people within HR have found their own function being restructured over the last few years and so being able to deal with the likely impact on you will be essential before supporting others to deal with some of the changes. We recently heard of a facilitator running a workshop who was so pre-occupied with the changes going on in the organisation that they were coming back late to the start of sessions. Clearly this is not helpful for anyone. Some options for dealing with your own emotions around the change include: having the conversations you need to before addressing other's concerns; putting it to one side emotionally until you can address it more fully or disclosing how you are feeling to your clients. The third option is likely to be more congruent but runs the risk of taking the focus off your client. We will look more closely at dealing with ambiguity as a part of the skills set for the Business Partner later in this chapter.

In this chapter we therefore consider the following:

- What is the nature of change?
- What are the boundaries of your role in influencing and leading change?
- How can you manage the ambiguity that is inevitably around during change?
- What are the issues and implications of change for people in the organisation?
- What are some of the methods and models you might choose to use?
- What influencing strategies and styles can you use?
- How can you deal with resistance?

## What is the nature of change?

Emergent change and the principles of chaos and complexity (Stacey, 1996) are often quoted to help us understand that change is rarely a linear process and goes beyond predicting what the future might look like and planning a strategy to get there. These theories can be helpful for the internal consultant who may feel that there has to be a defined end point to their interventions. Business Partners and those in internal change agent roles can sometimes end up more as project managers if the boundaries are too tightly confined at the outset. Being clear about your role purpose and values which underpin your role is probably more helpful than a tightly defined job description so that you can flex your skills and experience to suit the needs of your clients.

Change in organisations today is rapid and complex. The recent financial crisis (credit crunch) has hit most organisations and individuals in one way or another. Significantly those in the banking and retail industries face redundancies on a large scale but other organisations have also been impacted by the need to cut costs.

Perhaps one of the most common discussions we find ourselves having with individuals and groups in organisations is about the nature and speed of change. People seem to be in overload with many change initiatives overlaying each other, causing an almost constant level of discombobulation. In larger companies there are often a plethora of consultants working with the organisation to help on differing aspects of the business strategy. If these various interventions are not co-ordinated at a strategic level then confusion and chaos are likely to prevail. One important role for the Business Partner is to maintain sufficient clarity about the overall HR strategy for the business and how this links to the company strategy more widely.

If we return briefly to systems theory and our example of the human body, if one medical consultant is concerned with improving someone's blood pressure, whilst another specialist advises on rheumatism without either talking about possible connections between the two, then the overall health of that individual is likely to be compromised.

Chronic illness is a term used when there is a long-standing and continuing health issue. There may be episodes of acute attacks (for example with asthma) but there is often an underlying chronic illness which also needs to be considered. Work therefore in a human system is often needed at a cellular level. In the same way, in organisational change, if we only treat the acute attacks, which might manifest as customer complaints about response times, the underlying and possible longer term causes will not be addressed. The CONSULT framework in the previous chapter can help here in focusing attention on any underlying causes and systemic issues.

## What are the boundaries of your role in influencing and leading change?

In Chapter 4 we considered perceptual positions as a way of positioning yourself with the client and other stakeholders. This can be a useful way to consider how to influence change in the organisation too. Starting with self: how are you experiencing the change? – what will it mean to you? – and what are some of the beliefs and assumptions you might have about the change and how it should be managed?

## Locus of control

The concept of locus of control is not a new one. Developed by Rotter & Company (1991), it is based on social learning theory which makes the link between expected outcomes and behaviour. Rotter's view was that if we believe that a certain outcome will happen we are more likely to act in a way that makes it so. This idea of self-fulfilling prophecy can work either with positive or negative results. So that if I believe that influencing change in this organisation is difficult and going to involve disproportionate effort to outcomes, then it is likely to be so. If, on the other hand, I believe that I have credibility and that people want and need to engage with the change process, then I am more likely to behave in a way that is congruent with those beliefs.

This brings us back to the theme of our own underlying values and beliefs as an internal consultant and the importance of self-reflection for effective practice.

The locus of control is a useful model to consider, not just from a personal perspective for the Business Partner attempting to influence change, but also from your client's perspective. The more you can encourage people in the organisation to consider their own spheres of influence and control, the more likely they are to feel some sense of ownership for the change.

## Difference between internal and external locus of control

Rotter used the notion of locus of control to describe people who either see control in terms of being responsible for events (those who are internally focused) or outside of their control (externally focused). So that when something happens, which results in a positive outcome, someone with an external locus of control may see this as good luck. If something bad happens it may be viewed as "typical" or "they always do that to me". On the other hand someone who sees himself or herself as in part responsible for the outcome, whether positive or negative is more likely to have an internal locus of control.

Business Partners may want to consider the following to help them prepare for influencing change in the organisation:

- What, in relation to this change, is within my control right now? (this might include making decisions about who gets which posts; how the change should be communicated; providing advice to senior managers on the next steps, etc.).
- What, in relation to this change, can I possibly influence? (this might include how the senior management team should deal with communicating the changes; what the company should decide to do when receiving hostile bids; how to change the policy on recruitment and retention, etc.).
- What, in relation to this change, do I have no control over? (this might include the number of posts that have to be cut; amount of money available; who gets an influential senior management post, etc.).

In our view it is always worth challenging further this third category. So even if it seems on a first take that you cannot influence the number of posts that have to be cut, you may be able to influence where those posts are taken from. The idea of considering locus of control in this way is to really challenge your perception of what you have control over and to help minimise the amount of time and energy you might spend on areas that are beyond your spheres of influence.

Some questions you might usefully ask yourself at this stage:

- What *is my* previous experience of organisational change?
- What do I know is helpful in times of change and what gets in the way?
- What do I think about the changes that I might need to implement and influence here?
- What are some of my beliefs and values about change?
- What is my role and what is the role of my internal clients?
- From a "wise owl" perspective how might the change best be implemented and managed? (see Chapter 9)
- What are the benefits of this change to the organisation as a whole?
- What are the drivers behind it?

## Dealing with ambiguity

All of you reading this book, whether or not you have the title Business Partner, will have experienced change and the ambiguity that often surrounds it. When we find it difficult to find the one truth or one right course of action for making sense of change, then the level of ambiguity will be raised. However, the nature of humans is to make sense and meaning out of our experiences and so even if there is no one obvious way, we might find ourselves making connections and patterns to ease the sense of uncertainty that is around. So often we find ourselves talking to managers, particularly in the middle levels of an organisation who feel there must be an answer somewhere on the direction of the company and what the future holds in store. However, it is also our experience that "the future" is becoming increasingly difficult for senior managers to predict. When no one apparently has the answers, the Business Partners can find themselves in the uncomfortable position of carrying much of the ambiguity that surrounds the change for others in the organisation as well as for themselves.

Managing, or perhaps more appropriately, living with ambiguity, involves being able to let go of what is familiar and certain. Here are some ways of stretching your comfort zones around dealing with ambiguity:

- Delegate a pet project (if you have the resources to do this) and try letting go of the control over something you enjoy.

- Rather than coming up with expert solutions to some of your client's issues, try saying "I don't know" once in a while or "what do you think?" and resist giving the answer for longer than you currently do.
- Use lateral thinking approaches, such as boardstorming or Thinking Hats (De Bono, 1996), to open up the possible ways of approaching issues and problems.
- Consider doing nothing as an intervention option and see what impact this has.
- Use re-framing as a way of looking at things from a different perspective, for example, "what if we imagined everyone in the organisation welcomed this change?"
- Pay attention to what is happening within the organisation in the present moment, rather than placing too much attention on the past or future.

Ambiguity, when it exists in one area of our life is one thing. When we find there is too much ambiguity around both at work and home, then this can cause stress and anxiety. It is worth thinking about your own personal levels of comfort around ambiguity and doing what you can and need to in stabilising those areas that you are able to. For example, if you are dealing with a good deal of complex and challenging change at work, now might not be the best time to move house. Having said this, we accept that it is not always possible to create stability in this way and so coping strategies might more helpfully be adopted. Chapter 9 mentions some tips on supporting self in the challenging role of Business Partner.

## What are the issues and implications for others in times of change?

Continuing with perceptual positions, it would be useful early on in the change process to consider how different stakeholders will be experiencing the change and what their likely reactions to this might be. For the most part, even when people know the changes are needed from an organisational perspective, there is likely to be a focus on how the changes will affect them as individuals. The "what's in it for me?" factor.

### Reactions to change – the human element

When major change takes place within an organisation, the reactions of individuals and groups cannot always be easily determined. Many of our readers will be familiar with the idea of the transition curve, much used when considering the emotional stages of change that individuals might experience from shock/denial, to depression and eventual acceptance and integration. Because of the rate of change in organisations, it is not always easy to read reactions. For example, one individual or group might be stuck in denial or blame (of themselves or others), whereas another might be through to acceptance. Where change has been orchestrated by the senior managers, it is common to find acceptance at that level while others in the organisation might be further back on the curve. If senior managers feel they have to shield employees from sharing in the ambiguity and uncertainty that often go alongside change, this can frustrate even further.

The Business Partner working at a more strategic level may find in their close alignment with the senior managers in the organisation that they too have moved more quickly through to acceptance and integration. There is a danger here that you may lose sight of how the changes are being received at a grass roots level. A careful balance needs to be maintained between staying closely aligned to the main needs of your direct partners in the business and being attuned to the needs of other stakeholders.

Agyris and Schon (1978) developed the notion of the learning organisation and how organisations adapt to change internally and externally through single- and double-loop learning. Single-loop learning is fixed and non-adaptive. In organisations it tends towards procedures and adapting procedures to maintain stability. Managers here may make adjustments and change but because underlying principles are not challenged, it is more likely that the status quo will prevail. Trial and error is an example of single-loop learning. In this type of learning, the focus is on using feedback to decide what to do better next time. Generative or double-loop learning is where the individuals or organisations allow their mental models to be influenced and changed by the feedback. This is about questioning assumptions and learning to learn – seeing situations in differing ways. Double-loop learning in times of change means seeking information on which to make choices and involving others through discussion. The learning here is through challenging long-standing beliefs and inviting approaches which might be uncomfortable. This approach is more likely to find the underlying causes and needs for change and how individuals and the organisation overall can learn from the process.

## Change interventions which generate learning

The title "large scale interventions for change" is often given to a range of activities or interventions in organisations aimed at facilitating rapid change. Examples used here include Open Space Technology; Real Time Strategic Change; Future Search; and Appreciative Inquiry. One of the key principles is that of engaging as many people in the "system" as in the change itself. So that rather than a select group of people deciding what the changes should be and how they should be progressed, a critical mass of employees would have a say in both the what and the how of change. These interventions are then based around a Conference, usually lasting from one to three or four days.

People are invited to participate in the process of change so that they:

■ Understand the need for change;
■ Participate in making sense of the current reality and decisions about what needs to change;
■ Generate ideas about how to change existing processes;
■ Engage with the implementation phase(s) and make things happen in reality.

The beauty of these large-scale interventions is that they challenge some of the traditional assumptions about change – i.e. that it has to be slow and painful. Assumptions which underpin a range of interventions in this category include:

■ Change happens most successfully when people have a say in the changes which will affect them;
■ The people who are closest to the issues often have critical information which is vital to share for the overall benefit of the organisation;
■ By engaging a critical mass of people at the same time, the information and change strategy will be enriched;
■ Synergy can lead to innovation and creativity;
■ Diversity of people and ideas is more likely to lead to good solutions;
■ Change can happen quickly.

There are some important underlying principles and values which underpin large-scale change interventions when applied purely:

■ Engagement
■ Selecting the right issue
■ Selecting the right people
■ Structuring the intervention
■ Paying attention to the process.

Adapted from Bunker and Alban (1997).

**Engagement**
Underpinning all the interventions that normally come into the category "large-scale intervention" is one of valuing engagement. It is key that if a critical mass of people within the organisational system is to be invited to take part in the change strategy and process, then a real belief in the value of engagement needs to be

present. There are many examples of people being invited to take part in discussions around the future of the organisation only to find that their views are either ignored or given a token airing.

For engagement to really work and become meaningful for individuals and groups there needs to be a commitment to hearing and taking on board the views of people at the Conference and a willingness to learn from what is being said. This means an attitude of openness and curiosity, on behalf of everyone present. Particularly important for the Business Partner if this is an intervention, which you consider using.

### Selecting the right issue

The main consideration here is that the issue should be systemic. In other words, it needs to be something which affects the system overall. It should also be important enough for people to want to air their views on it. For example, the values of the organisation; reward and recognition strategies; improving customer service; improving quality of products, etc. would be examples of what might be systemic issues. The subject needs to be sufficiently focused so that it is clear what the theme for the Conference will be. The planning group (mentioned below) will normally help to shape how the issue is presented to make that clearer for the conversations. It needs to be meaningful for all those attending including any external stakeholders who are invited to take part. Having a positive and future-focused spin on the issue will help to steer clear of a problem-solving approach and free up lateral thinking. Examples might include:

- Creating excellent customer service;
- Rewarding people to reflect their value and contribution;
- Creating a community of best practice;
- Reflecting positively the communities we serve;
- Getting the right products in place at the right time;
- Developing leading edge practice in research;
- Creating a "fit for purpose" structure which meets business needs.

### Selecting the right people

A planning group will normally be set-up of people who represent a microcosm of the organisation and its stakeholders. One of the main tasks for this planning group is to decide who should be at the event. The focus for deciding is the primary question that needs to be addressed as outlined in the above section. Stakeholder mapping as described in Chapter 4 can be used to determine who needs to be present. Alban and Bunker (1997) give a nice example of a school system holding a meeting about an education issue and inviting a taxpayer organisation. It might be worth thinking about who would be your organisational critics and the potential value of inviting them along as outside stakeholders.

The Conference will also provide a good opportunity for the senior managers in the organisation to have a visible presence, although they will need to be seen to be encouraging engagement by everyone in the organisation, rather than imposing their own view of change.

**Structuring the intervention**

A key part of these interventions is to enable people at all levels in the organisation and sometimes outside stakeholders to have a voice. Change can feel incredibly disempowering if people do not feel like they have had an opportunity to participate in the process. The design and structure of the intervention therefore needs to create opportunities for people to talk and listen to each other. One important reason why these conferences are usually over more than one day is to have the opportunity for reflection time. Real Time Strategic Change for example (Dannemiller and Jacobs in Alban & Bunker, 1997) is based on the Beckhard and Harris (1987) model of change:

$$C = D \times V \times F > R$$

The model states that change will happen when there is sufficient dissatisfaction ($D$) with the present status quo; when there is a clear vision of the future ($V$) and some tangible first steps ($F$). All three elements have to be greater than any resistance to the change or perceived cost.

If any element is not present then the change process can get stuck.

In an intervention which helps people move through these stages, dissatisfaction is sometimes heightened during the first day of the Conference, by holding up the proverbial mirror, sometimes by speeches from external stakeholders or clients so that there is impetus to move from the present unsatisfactory position. The first night therefore of a conference structured with this in mind allows people to face the reality of what is, before moving on to the vision for the future.

The right level of structure for these events is important. If it is too structured people become anxious and if it is not structured enough people can become anxious, so boundary management is important. Generally speaking the structure needs to be designed around the process rather than the content of the discussions.

Organisations that have attempted to speed up the process and deal with all these aspects within a day may have found that although energy is present and people are full of good intentions, there has been insufficient time and attention paid to really bottoming out all of the issues. Sustained change is less likely in these scenarios.

**Paying attention to the process**

As these events usually involve large numbers (anywhere from between 35 to over a 1000) the structure and process issues are crucially important. Tables are normally set up in carousel style with groups of approximately six people sitting at each in a max-mix style (people from different stakeholder groups at each table). The timing and logistics for these large-scale events is crucial. People need to move through the process smoothly, often looking back in some way at the history of either the issue or the organisation; looking forward to the vision for the future and focusing on actions to get there. Creating the right dynamic for people to discuss things in an open environment and feel committed to taking things forward takes light-handed but skilled facilitation and many internal consultants who want to try these methods work with externals skilled in using the frameworks and in facilitating the process.

As examples of the methods you may use to take people through the various stages: storytelling and an environmental scan could be used to bring out the past; boardstorming in groups for considering the present and future around such questions as: what should we stop doing? what should we continue doing? and what should we create? to look at how you want to get to where you want to be. Another method commonly used is that of a "market place" with stalls for various stakeholder groups or topics. In Open Space technology, people decide which topic they want to discuss within a broad conference theme. The "law of 2 feet" gives them permission to stay or leave the discussion when they decide.

With all these methods, the responsibility and ownership for the outcomes remains firmly with the people attending the conference. It is crucial that sufficient time is built in for action planning and follow-up if the change is to be followed through.

## Who uses large-scale interventions?

From Roffey Park's Management Agenda (2006), we find that 26% of those responding reported that they used large-scale interventions as an Organisational Development (OD) tool.

In 2003, we also sent a Web survey to 647 Roffey Park contacts by e-mail. Forty-three people completed the survey and several others responded by e-mail that the survey was not relevant to their organisation due to its size or because they had not taken part in large-scale interventions. Respondents were mostly from the private services sector (47.5%) but other sectors were also represented (15% from production and manufacturing, 27.5% public sector, 10% Charity/Not for profit). They came from organisations of all sizes.

Of the 43 respondents, just over half (53.5%) reported that their organisation had undergone a large-scale intervention to support change. Six (14%) had used

Open Space Technology, seven (16.3%) had used Real-Time Strategic Change, five (11.6%) had used Appreciative Inquiry and six (14%) had used Future Search. Other methods were reported including Action Labs, motivational communication events, organisational transformation framework and employee engagement surveys.

Organisations who had engaged in large-scale interventions most commonly used external facilitators (60.9%). Almost half used HR to facilitate and the same proportion used senior managers. Other facilitators included OD specialists.

## Other aspects of change

The model below (Figure 5.1) highlights aspects of change that might need to be considered if the change is to be managed effectively.

The highlighted areas show the likely impact if any of these elements are missing. So, where there is a lack of vision, but all the other aspects of the equation are in place, you may find there is a high level of confusion in the organisation, or part of the organisation affected by the change.

As we can see, any of the missing elements can trigger either an emotional response or a lack of effective transition to the desired future. Even if the vision of

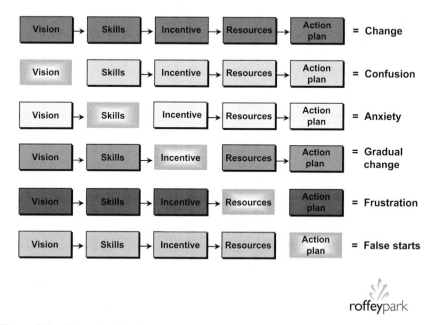

**Figure 5.1** Managing the change process.

the desired future is not entirely clear, people will need to have a sense of where they are headed to feel that their day-to-day efforts are not entirely in vain.

You might find it useful to reflect on the following in relation to changes you are trying to influence in your organisation:

- How clear is the vision or desired future goal for this change?
- What skills do people need to effect the changes? Who needs which skills? And how can they best be developed?
- What incentives are already in place or could be put in place? These do not necessarily need to be financial, but what might be the benefit of the changes that are needed to individuals and teams?
- What resources are needed? This might include equipment, access to people, access to information, etc. and how can you make sure that people have access to the resources that they will need?
- What steps are needed to make the change happen? If there is no formal project plan for this piece of work, calculating the milestones will still be helpful.

You might also find it useful to reflect on Kotter's (1995) steps to organisational transformation shown below. This (as with all other models and strategies mentioned in this chapter) can be applied both in relation to HR transformation from operational role to Business Partner practice, and in relation to other organisational changes which you want to influence in your role as Business Partner.

- *Establish a sense of urgency* – this includes examining the market and competitive realities and identifying and discussing crises, potential crises or major opportunities.
- *Forming a* powerful *guiding coalition* – assembling a group with enough power to lead the change effort and encouraging the group to work together as a team.
- *Creating a vision* – creating a vision to help direct the change effort and developing strategies for achieving that vision.
- Communicating *the vision* – using every vehicle possible to communicate the new vision and strategies and teaching new behaviours by the example of guiding coalition.
- Empowering *others to act on the vision* – minimising resistance to change, encouraging risk taking and changing systems or structures which might get in the way.
- *Planning for and creating short-term wins* – planning for and creating improvements in performance, and recognising and rewarding employees involved in these improvements.

- Consolidating *improvements and producing still more change* – this might include hiring and promoting people who can implement the vision and re-invigorating the process with new projects and themes.
- Institutionalising *new approaches* – articulating the connections between the new behaviours and corporate success and ensuring leadership succession planning.

When considering methods for implementing change it will be important to focus on the outcome you are seeking to achieve. Success, in our view, is more likely if an iterative approach is taken. This means more than one intervention is aimed at achieving the end result with opportunities to reflect on the impact of the interventions at each stage.

## Influencing skills and strategies

The Business Partner will need to draw on a range of influencing strategies, skills and styles to be effective at implementing change at all levels in the organisation. We look at political skills later in the book (Chapter 9) whilst recognising that influencing and political skills are inextricably linked. Both skill sets can be used either ethically or not, for personal gain or for the greater good of the organisation and with an understanding of the culture of the organisation and dynamics or not. Having said that, these aspects of influencing are not mutually exclusive and the effective Business Partner will be able to balance personal, HR and organisational agendas with a good understanding of the organisational culture and dynamics.

### Core skills of influencing

In our view, if you want to be more influential, there are some underpinning assumptions about influencing that might be helpful to consider:

- We all have the ability to influence – it is happening all the time. Just try smiling at someone and see what happens. Even if they don't smile back you will probably get a reaction. By doing something either unconsciously or consciously we will have an impact on someone else. For example, not turning up at a meeting.
- Much influencing behaviour is outside the conscious awareness of the people involved.
- We cannot change other people's behaviour, only change/adapt our own behaviour and through that, increase the possibility of change in others.
- Influencing is more about the process (or how we do things) than content (what we do).

If you have ever been influenced to buy something you were not then particularly interested in when you returned home, you will understand this last point.

We refer to many of the skills of influencing throughout this book, but by way of summary we would see these as being:

- Self-awareness – understanding how you typically react to difficult situations and being able to increase the choices you make in terms of how you react and behave.
- Self-confidence – based on self-acceptance. Having confidence in your internal and external resources in the face of resistance.
- Observation skills – and the ability to pick up on content and process messages (i.e. the non-verbal behaviour).
- Interpretation – making sense of what is going in the moment, based on both self-awareness and wider awareness.
- Listening – actively and attentively to what others are really saying.
- Questioning – knowing when to ask open and closed questions, and asking them at the appropriate level – for example, facts or feelings.
- Having an outcome focus – being clear about what you want from the interaction.
- The ability to see things from different perspectives.
- Flexible communication skills – the ability to put your message across in a variety of ways to suit the style of the other person/group.
- Timing.

## Push and pull strategies for influencing

We cover here push and pull strategies for influencing which can be used in a one-to-one, group or organisational context.

Both push and pull strategies are really about how we use our energy. Energy used to push someone or something in a particular direction or to draw them towards our way of thinking.

**Force-field analysis as a diagnostic tool**
We touched on Force-field analysis in Chapter 4 as a way of considering the driving and resisting forces for the HR move into strategic Business Partnership. Here we re-visit the model in more detail and link it to interventions for influencing change.

**Push and pull strategies as a way of influencing change**
As a Business Partner you can increase your range of options for influencing a change by considering push and pull strategies. For example, in the case of

a recent restructure where jobs are being re-advertised and redundancies may follow.

Examples of push strategies might include:

- Top-down communication, which sets out clearly what is happening and why;
- Statements about what is not negotiable and decisions that have already been made;
- Telling people what the jobs will be and when they will be invited to apply.

*Advantages* of this approach are that it tends to be quicker, people know where they stand and in times of uncertainty a sense of direction from the top can be re-assuring.

*Disadvantages* as you can imagine, people can feel uninvolved and under-valued, as if their views don't count. The organisation might miss out on some good ideas about the way forward. People affected by the change may be the very people who have the best ideas for improving the ways things are.

Examples of pull strategies might include:

- Providing opportunities for discussions – for example through meetings and focus groups or open space;
- Q & A sessions;
- Getting people involved in what the restructure would look like and writing the job descriptions.

*Advantages* of this approach are that people are more likely to be committed to the outcome if they have been involved from the outset. Any ambiguity and fear around the change is shared, rather than protecting people unnecessarily. People get the full picture earlier and can make their own choices about what to do, which may include looking for other jobs.

*Disadvantages* Time is the biggest one. It takes longer to be consultative. People's expectations might be raised and you need to be sure that the consultation is a genuine one, otherwise there could be many disgruntled employees who feel that have been asked for views, which are not going to be taken on board.

For long-term change strategies, a combination of both will be necessary. Some examples of combined strategies to deal with the restructuring example above are shown below:

- Communicating clearly what's negotiable and what's not – message from the top;
- Regular bulletins and updates via a variety of methods, e.g. e-mail, newsletters and intranet;

- Providing forums for discussion and answering questions;
- Workshops on change management;
- Training for those applying for new/existing jobs;
- Project groups across the organisation to look specifically at aspects of the work that need to change;
- Outplacement counselling where necessary.

Both can be very effective and it is important to have enough flexibility of style to be able to draw on the appropriate skills at the right time.

In our view, push and pull behaviours are still responsive to the situation and the individuals, therefore they are all assertive in nature, rather than tipping into aggressive or passive behaviour, which tends to be reactive rather than responsive.

For short-term outcomes, for example to consider influencing someone in a discussion on a one-to-one basis or at a meeting, you might want to consider which set of behaviours would be more influential – push or pull.

**Push behaviour**
Push behaviour includes:

- Being directive (i.e. telling rather than asking);
- Being prepared with information and giving this to others;
- Using facts and logic;
- Enforcing the rules such as policies and laid down procedures;
- Applying sanctions and pressures.

**Pull behaviour**
Pull behaviour includes:

- Drawing others out through the use of open questions;
- Actively listening – paraphrasing and reflecting back what others are saying;
- Offering incentives and rewards;
- Finding the common threads between differing views;
- Inspiring others towards a shared goal.

It is important to consider *how* the behaviour is presented as well as *what* is being said to get a proper indication of push and pull. For example a question, even if openly ended, can be said in a tone of voice which seems to demand an answer. The total message needs to be considered for a true reflection of whether the strategy is push or pull.

It is worth considering if you tend to use the full range of influencing skills or whether you are more likely to rely on either push or pull to achieve your desired outcome. Training in influencing skills can help to develop a wider range of skills and strategies.

## Dealing with resistance to change

Sometimes when attempting to influence organisational change, even if you have used a wide range of strategies and involved people in the organisation, you will be met by resistance and conflict. We believe that you are more likely to experience it if you expect it, but you may also get it if you do not.

Resistance to change can be observed in a number of ways:

- Overt conflict and arguments either between individuals or teams;
- Withdrawal or apathy about the issue, detachment and disengagement;
- Increased political behaviour;
- Drop in performance or productivity;
- Lack of teamwork, more individualistic behaviour;
- Increased grapevine and gossip.

Conflict is often perceived to be negative and as an obstruction to progress. However, conflict can also be a positive energy and a catalyst for movement. Two roles for the Business Partner in helping to support others through the change process are those of mediator and coach. Whilst it would be unrealistic to expect all Business Partners to be trained and experienced in both these skills to the level of full-time mediators and coaches, having an understanding of the skills and being able to apply a sufficient level at the appropriate time will prove very useful, particularly in managing change.

A recent example which comes to mind includes again a restructure within an organisation where individuals in previously secure employment were required to be interviewed for their present jobs, sometimes in competition with close colleagues. There was a great deal of unrest and anger at the "management" in the organisation for seemingly putting them in this difficult position. Whilst the changes were accepted on an intellectual level as being necessary for the business, there was a good deal of dissatisfaction around how the process had been managed. The Business Partner was called in to help facilitate the change process.

Clearly coaching the senior managers to handle this change would be a useful part of the change strategy. Preferably the Business Partner would be asked to help on this before decisions had been made and action taken. However, in this situation the Business Partner was called in after the event – to help mop up the pieces. Where the closest client is the senior manager, mediation in the true sense can be difficult. One of the important principles behind mediation is that of neutrality. If the various parties involved in the conflict do not see you as neutral then mediation will be difficult and you may need to call on outside help. The key skills in both coaching and mediation include:

- Active listening;
- Asking open and probing questions, reflecting back at a content and process level;
- Offering insights on how you see the situation and the behaviours;
- Helping people to re-frame the situation;
- Gaining clarity about what people want and need to move forward and agreeing actions.

Coaching from the Business Partner can happen on both an informal and a formal level. One of the more successful interventions towards change is that of informal coaching of senior managers. Coaching also happens at the early stage of "gaining entry" referred to in Chapter 4 and throughout developing the consultant/client relationship. Knowing when to use a directive or non-directive style in coaching is important. Non-directive coaching where you allow the managers to make their own choices for how to move forward is more likely to help in strategies aimed at long-term change.

Styles of intervention from acceptant to prescriptive can usefully be considered when coaching your internal clients (Cockman, Evans, & Reynolds, 1992).

## Acceptant style

This includes listening in a neutral, non-judgemental way to help relax clients and allow them to confront any blocks at an emotional level in moving forward. It is likened to the early stages of counselling. Here positive regard and empathy will help the client to talk freely.

**When is it appropriate?**
This can be particularly useful at the early stages of a consultant–client relationship or when the client is experiencing pain around something that is impacting them on a personal or an organisational level. It can also be a useful style to adopt with teams or groups who are experiencing problems with change and expressing anger or anxiety.

## Catalytic style

The skills here include asking questions and gathering data with the purpose of helping the client to generate ideas to solve issues themselves. Questions usefully asked here start with: who, what, why, how, where, when and how. The CONSULT framework in Chapter 4 gives some examples of this approach.

**When is it appropriate?**
When the client or group is in a resourceful state and needs help in generating thinking more clearly about the issues. The ways of generating information can include a number of differing methodologies, not just face-to-face questioning. It is a helpful part of the data gathering and diagnostic stage for both the consultant and client.

## Confrontational style

This style is epitomised by "holding up the mirror" so that the client can gain insight into what is really going on. The consultant calls attention to differences between values and behaviours or the espoused theories and theories in use. The skills here would include feedback and presenting information in a way which confronts the issues about what you notice going on.

**When is it appropriate?**
When you have built up sufficient trust with the client or when there is no other option. In other words if you think your client will not move on without a level of confrontation on the issues then this may be the best way forward. When the interests of other clients or stakeholders in the change need to be reflected back so that your client is fully aware of the big picture.

## Prescriptive style

This links most closely to the Expert or Doctor–patient model in our earlier chapter. It involves giving advice and expertise, providing data on the issue presented to you by the client.

**When is it appropriate?**
Sometimes this is a good way to build trust with your clients, particularly those who are looking for an expert view. It is worth being wary here of staying in the role too long in case the client becomes dependent on you providing this service, when they may have the capacity to move things forward themselves.

By developing and extending your style and skills in coaching you will be adding to your already wide skills set and heightening your ability to influence change in the organisation.

## Summary

The ability to influence and lead change is perhaps the key area that sets apart the truly strategic Business Partner from the more operational HR role. As someone working inside the organisation, there will be challenges that present themselves over and above the challenges that are present for external consultants. By understanding the nature of change and how change impacts on people at all levels of the organisation, you are more likely to approach your projects with an appropriate balance of attention to task and process issues. Supporting managers, particularly at the senior levels of the organisation, will be important and is a useful way of influencing how change is dealt with for the longer term. If the senior managers in the organisation are equipped to lead change well, the implementation process is likely to be eased. The ability to coach in both formal and informal situations and influence the way the changes are handled requires high levels of skill and understanding. Supporting yourself through the change and managing the personal impact on you are also important so that you are more able to support others through this process. Influencing, coaching and mediation skills may all come into play in your role in supporting strategic change.

In this section we have covered some skills, which we consider key to the role of successful Business Partnership. In particular, contracting, self-awareness and critical reflection, building and maintaining effective relationships and influencing and leading change. We appreciate that there could be a number of other chapters included skills such as project management, strategic thinking and strategy implementation. However, we have decided to focus on those areas which we think are at the core of the role.

## Checklist

- Are you clear on how the various initiatives and external consultant activities tie in with the strategic business plan?
- Have you got a support strategy for helping you deal with your own reactions to the changes going on in the organisation?
- Have you established those areas that you either have direct control over or can influence?
- Have you let go of the areas that you cannot influence?
- Are you creating some stability in your life, to help support the areas that are more ambiguous and uncertain?
- Are you checking out how people in the organisation are responding to change?

- Have you considered engaging more people in the change process? – either by using large-scale interventions or by applying the principles?
- Do people at all levels in the organisation feel like they have a "voice" to explore the change strategy and their views on it? How do you know?
- Is there a clear vision to support the changes?
- Are you increasing your range of influencing skills and strategies to good effect?
- Are you identifying and dealing with any resistance to change?
- Are you using your skills to coach managers, either formally or informally, to help them deal with the change process in the most appropriate way?

## References

Agyris, C., & Schon, D. (1978). *Organisational Learning: A Theory of Action Perspectives*. Reading, Mass: Addison-Wesley.

Beckhard, R., & Harris, R. (1987). *Organisational transformations: Managing complex change*. Reading, MA: Addison-Wesley.

Bunker, B. B., & Alban, B. T. (1997). *Large group interventions – Engaging the whole system for rapid change*. San Francisco: Jossy-Bass.

Cockman, P., Evans, B., & Reynolds, P. (1992). *Client-centred consulting, a practical guide for internal advisers and trainers*. Maidenhead: McGraw-Hill.

De Bono, E. (1996). *Serious creativity: Using the ower of lateral thinking to create new ideas*. London: HarperCollins Business.

Kotter, J. (1995). *Leading Change: Why transformation efforts fail*. March-April. Harvard Business Review.

Pfeiffer & Company. (1991). *Theories and models in applied behavioural science, Vol. 4*. Organisational San Diego, CA: Pfeiffer & Company. 1991.

Stacey, R. D. (1996). *Complexity and creativity in organisations*. San Francisco: Berrett-Koehler Publishers Inc.

# 6

# Developing Your Thinking Style

This chapter stands back a little from the assumption that you are working as a strategic Business Partner and considers the importance of how we think as a process for Business Partnering practice at whatever level of operation. We find people often talk about the biggest challenge for HR as a "mindset" shift from thinking operationally to thinking more strategically with an emphasis on adding and creating value as well as providing value for money. This perception rather assumes that there is something wrong with current thinking within HR and we prefer to encourage different ways of seeing things rather than changing mindsets which can, (unsurprisingly) be an uphill struggle. The ability to think differently when we have been working in an organisation for a considerable period of time can be challenging. Embedded patterns of thinking and behaviour often go without question both within ourselves and others, so here we encourage an openness and exploration of looking at things through different lenses with the objective of encouraging others in the organisation to do the same.

We will look at the value of thinking under three specific headings and pay attention to how they might add value to those working in a Business Partnering role:

■ Rational thinking
■ Creative thinking
■ Strategic thinking

The diagram shown on the next page shows that the Business Partner, particularly those working at a more strategic level in the organisation, with the remit of advising on approaches to leading and managing complex change must be able to not only apply a rational level of thinking, but also use creative and strategic thinking to enable a range of ways forward for the organisation.

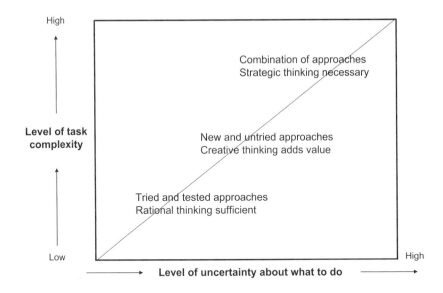

Further exploration of these different thinking approaches is outlined in the next paragraphs with links made to the role of the Business Partner.

## Rational thinking – the detective's approach

This is the typical way of thinking encouraged and valued in many organisations. In Briggs Myers (1980) terms, a preference for "T" in terms of making decisions from an objective, logical and impersonal perspective. Rational thinking will usually involve critical reflection, standing back from the situation to weigh up the pros and cons of any course of action, resisting the temptation to go with gut instinct, challenging assumptions in self and others and basing decisions on facts. A rational perspective suggests a "sensible" or more scientific approach to thinking, avoiding speculation, intuition and assumptions. For a Business Partner supporting managers in the organisation this could involve a range of strategies including:

- Gathering data: usually in the form of quantative information through questionnaires, statistics, existing documentation, structured interviews and surveys.
- Compiling reports, demonstrating differing perspectives on a problem or situation – probably with reference to data and logical analysis.

- Pre-planned strategies for implementing change using a range of tools including: force-field analysis, PEST and SWOT, process mapping, etc. (see Chapter 8 on Project Management).
- Working within the formal organisation; for example, by appropriate reference to hierarchical structures, systems in place and the overt norms and ways of working. Playing to the rules and expected ways of doing things in the organisation.

An example of a rational approach in practice is highlighted in the example below:

A senior Business Partner in a large public sector organisation was asked for advice on a recruitment and retention strategy for front line staff. Previous experience had shown that retaining staff at the lower grades of the organisation had been challenging to say the least with a high turnover of staff – in particular those on the front desk and staffing the customer enquiry telephone lines.

A rational approach might include the following interventions:

- Analysis of exit survey questionnaires over the previous six months;
- Structured focus groups with a sample (statistically valid) of line managers to find out the challenges of staff retention and actions taken to recruit people when vacancies arose;
- Analysis of the current recruitment strategies, job descriptions and person specifications;
- Gap analysis of manager's skills in recruiting the best people for the job;
- Benchmarking retention statistics of different departments to see if the problem occurred in a particular area of the organisation;
- Overall analysis of all information and completion of a written report with recommendations to the "client" or senior manager who has asked for the data.

This can be a useful approach, particularly where the problem is not hugely complex and will be illuminated by straightforward analysis. It will be common practice in many organisations to take this rational, logical approach and will often be both expected and required, meeting the extraverted requirements of the client and the assumptions around within the existing culture of the organisation. However, the limitations of a purely rational approach are probably apparent. How many millions of reports have been written only to be left in someone's in-tray or bottom draw with limited, if any real impact on the ways of working in the organisation? Also, it is worth questioning if the rational approach misses anything out in its very assumption that "thinking outside the box" is inappropriate in this particular situation.

The downsides of applying purely rational thinking to challenges facing the Business Partner include:

■ Transformational change is unlikely – as working within the current constraints and guidelines of the organisation is likely to allow both good and bad practice to flourish.
■ Current mindsets of managers within the organisation remain unchallenged and there may be little opportunity for learning or development of more creative ways of looking at problems.
■ The "tried and tested" approaches are seen to be the best or only way of tackling complex issues.
■ The Business Partner can be placed in a "pair of hands" or "expert" role without consciously being aware of the implications of this.
■ Real problems may have only temporary solutions suggested, so a more short-term or quick-fix approach rather than looking at things from a more strategic or complex angle.

## Creative thinking – the magician's approach

"It has been said that, metaphorically, we live in times of "permanent white-water" (Vaill, 1989), where the way ahead is full of the unpredictable, rather than the calm rivers we were used to in the past. The methods we use to navigate need to adapt. White-water rafts are at their best when there is a team of rafters, each able to take the initiative and quickly respond to whatever they are faced with. Each person needs to have a sense of direction and a view out of the boat, whilst communicating with their fellow rafters. It feels sometimes that we are still trying to navigate unpredictable waters on a rowing boat, with a cox shouting instructions in the belief that they can see the way ahead. Worse still, some organisations seem to have reverted to a slave galley, where most people are in the dark and a few important people crack whips and keep trying to look good on the top deck." (Penn in Kenton & Penn, 2008).

The notion here is that by having an ability to go beyond the expected and traditional ways of working, the Business Partner will have greater influence, credibility and impact; really challenging the status quo, both in terms of the current culture of the organisation and perhaps the expectations of the client or manager. In this process, the creative thinking ability of the manager can be encouraged and developed and the potential for the organisation to really make headway with change rather than struggle against the tide.

According to Van Oech (1983) creative thinking: "requires an attitude that allows you to search for ideas and manipulate your knowledge and experience... using crazy, foolish and unpredictable ideas as stepping stones to practical new ideas... in short, by adopting a creative outlook you open yourself up to both new possibilities and to change".

More than ever in organisations, there is a necessity to be open to these "new possibilities". The credit crunch being experienced in 2008/2009 and beyond means that unforeseen (some would argue predictable) change needs to be navigated and worked with rather than managed in any controlled and systematic way.

In our roles as Business Partners, managers, employees at any level of the organisation or just as human beings in our day-to-day lives, we can limit our ability to think creatively in a number of ways. The following are some examples of limiting assumption that might stop us thinking more creatively about organisational problems:

- *One right way*: If we start from a premise of believing there is one right answer it can limit the opportunities for looking for alternative ways of doing things. Included in ways around this are getting lots of ideas through, for example, brainstorming and reframing the problem to come at it from a different perspective.
- *Rational is best*: Rational thinking has its place but as shown in the diagram earlier, in unpredictable times, a logical or rational approach may limit the possibilities for an even more effective outcome.
- *It won't work here: or "It's been tried before":* It may have been tried before, but the likelihood is that the context, people and other surrounding factors have all changed. As the saying goes: "you cannot jump twice into the same place in the river". So re-visiting an approach that has been tried before may result in a very different outcome.
- *I'll be judged as incompetent:* There may be a risk for a new Business Partner who comes up with ideas completely outside of the box that she/he will be judged negatively and this could impact on credibility and influence. However, part of the Business Partner's role is to hold the proverbial mirror up to clients and the organisation overall and help them see different ways of doing things. Provided the assumptions you are making are transparent and you have built sufficient trust within the client system, this should not be a problem.

■ *Creativity cannot be learned:* This statement could be applied to a number of behaviours that we might feel less confident about including leadership and management and Business Partnering itself perhaps. There are a whole host of assumptions underlying this statement which in themselves need to be challenged including what creativity is and means. People often associate "creativity" with thinking about new and whacky ideas, but there is also an element of creativity which is about seeing things differently and this plus many other aspects of creativity can be learnt. The creative process starts with a belief in the ability to be creative and encourage creativity in others.

For Business Partners in the organisation, creative thinking could manifest through your interventions in a number of ways including the following:

■ Working counter-culturally: encouraging, for example, meetings to be held in different ways, brown bag lunches, standing up meetings, meetings facilitated by the most junior person present, etc. Whatever currently happens as the norm might be challenged to free up different ways of thinking about things and highlights current cultural practice, which might be inhibiting better ways of doing things. Three questions might be useful here:
   – How are things normally done around here?
   – What might be a positive outcome from doing things differently?
   – What's the risk of trying? And what's the risk of not?

A word of warning about doing this: if you analyse it too much you are probably going to fall back into a rational mindset and may talk yourself out of doing anything different, so a suggestion would be: consider it, but not for too long!

■ Applying a range of lateral thinking tools, e.g. brainstorming, mind-mapping, creative visualization, storytelling, use of metaphors, etc. Encouraging right brain as well as left brain thinking.
■ Ask more questions than giving answers: for example, what if? Questions can be particularly useful in freeing up some of the assumptions that might be around in the organisation. For example: "what if you had a free reign to tackle this problem yourself?"
■ Thinking and going "outside the box" by looking at how different sectors and organisations are handling issues. For example, how are the problems of queuing in the supermarket dealt with? and how might the approach be applied to any backlogs of work in your own organization/Department?

An example of a creative approach in practice is highlighted using the same example as before:

A senior Business Partner in a large public sector organisation was asked for advice on a recruitment and retention strategy for front line staff. Previous experience had shown that retaining staff at the lower grades of the organisation had been challenging to say the least with a high turnover of staff – in particular those on the front desk and staffing the customer enquiry telephone lines.

A creative approach might include the following interventions:

- Working counter-culturally – inviting the senior manager or client to spend a day on the front desk and/or manning the telephone lines. In this back to the floor exercise the manager might find out directly the challenges leading to high turnover of staff.
- Getting staff currently on the front desk to visit other organisations and see how things are managed there to learn and apply to their own area of work.
- Having an "ideas" room or box for staff to say how things could be improved.
- Conduct a "mystery shopper" exercise to see first-hand the customer experience in the section. The mystery shopper could be a front line member of staff from a different area of the organisation which is functioning well.
- Invite a local college to conduct a research exercise into the issues and ask them to present back to the front line staff.

In working with the client and these interventions, sufficient trust and credibility need to be built up, so that there is support on the way forward. Keeping an open mind, asking good quality questions and using the rapport building skills highlighted elsewhere in this book will help.

## Strategic thinking – the leader's approach

We have aligned this kind of thinking to leadership because the qualities of strategic thinking are necessary to make a real difference in the role and include both rational and creative elements. Leadership here is distinct from management and important for those in a Business Partner role so that you can remain influential and credible. It is not just about implementing HR strategies, which puts the role back at the operational, reactive end of the HR spectrum. Rather it's about crafting strategies aligned to the needs of the business, and in order to do this all the skills mentioned in the other chapters are necessary, e.g. relationship skills, influencing skills, consultancy skills and political savvy.

It might be useful to be clear about the difference between strategic and operational thinkings as those of you in less strategic roles can still develop your strategic thinking capability to good effect.

The table below highlights some differences:

| Strategic thinking | Operational thinking |
|---|---|
| ■ Seeing things from a global (helicopter) perspective | ■ Thinking of the practical/day to day implications |
| ■ Concepts and generalities | ■ Concrete and evident |
| ■ Double loop learning (taking a step back to consider "what are we learning from the process of what we are doing?") | ■ Single loop learning – action to fix immediate problems |
| ■ Looking for new opportunities and breaking new ground | ■ Sticking to what's been tried and tested |
| ■ Doing the right things | ■ Doing things right |
| ■ Systemic, whole systems perspective | ■ Application to present system |
| ■ Standing back | ■ Getting stuck in |

It is also important for Business Partners to develop their strategic thinking capability, so that they in turn can generate better strategic thinking in the organisation. Better business decisions will tend to come from managers in the organisations if they have thought about things deeply and widely rather than superficially. Part of the role of the Business Partner is to support and challenge managers to help them develop that capacity. A typical challenge around this is that of available time. Both managers and those working in HR will often say the ability to think strategically is hampered by lack of time and pressures of work. Yes, the demands of the job can mean little time for thinking about things more strategically and yes, the ability to think strategically needs quality time given to it. It's a catch-22 position, so unless you commit to thinking and working in a more strategic way, it is unlikely that you will really fulfill the challenges of Business Partnering practice.

If we incorporate the elements of strategic thinking highlighted above into our example shown earlier and combine both rational and creative options that might look something like this:

---

A senior Business Partner in a large public sector organisation was asked for advice on a recruitment and retention strategy for front line staff. Previous experience had shown that retaining staff at the lower grades of the organisation had been challenging to say the least with a high turnover of staff – in particular those on the front desk and staffing the customer enquiry telephone lines.

- The initial conversation with the client or manager includes an assessment of his/her ability to think widely or strategically about the problem that has occurred. The use of questioning at this stage and good listening skills are combined to build rapport and challenge current thinking.
- Using the process or collaborative consultancy role (see Chapter 4), the Business Partner works *with* the manager to decide a range of interventions most likely to effectively diagnose what's going on and solve the problem.
- Together, they map out the stakeholders who have a vested interest in the recruitment and retention of staff and decide how best they can be influenced to take ownership of the issues and contribute to a successful way forward.
- A range of interventions including their possible pros and cons are discussed. In particular the short, medium and long-term aspects are considered. For example: strategies for covering current short-term sick absence by seconding staff from other sections; further analysing the trends in this area and why they have arisen (which might include the manager in a back to the floor exercise or the mystery shopper) and/or stakeholder focus groups to look at the wider issues of recruitment and retention in the organisation and the factors impacting on this.
- A range of "reporting back" methodologies might be used, tailored to the differing needs of individual stakeholder groups, both in terms of content and process.

---

The different thinking approaches can be applied of course in either doctor-patient, purchase supply or process ways of working with the client, so we do not intend to imply here that strategic thinking will always align itself solely with the process model. What we are suggesting is that to be successful in the Business Partner role, the ability to think both creatively and rationally is helpful and may make the difference between maintaining the status quo and really making a significant difference to the business.

An important model applied to Business Partnering is that of the value triangle The notion here is that value needs to be determined in the eye of the client, rather than assumptions made about what would constitute value by the Business Partner or the consultant.

Using the idea of the value triangle (Fig. 6.1) (Ingham, 2006), links are made to the different areas of thinking as highlighted below:

**Figure 6.1** Value Triangle.

For the most part, HR is expected at the very least to provide value for money. This means providing what the customer or client expects; delivering services on time; dealing with customers professionally; people getting paid on time; recruitment to posts carried out with due consideration to employment law; disciplinary procedures carried out in accordance with legislation and organisational requirements and so on.

Creative thinking is necessary when we think about adding value to our customers and clients. Here, the Business Partner needs to go beyond the expected, anticipate customer or client business needs and provide services and products which break the mould. Examples include: delivering things more quickly than expected; providing one-to-one personalized support when there has previously been little if any choice and tailoring an approach to a specific client rather than giving them off the shelf tools which might not be appropriate.

Strategic thinking aligned to created value is about asking some fundamental questions to start with such as:

■ What does the client want and expect and what is needed in this situation to support both the client and the business?
■ What have they not said but I know is a challenge in their area of the business?

- What do I know will help both the client and the business in the future if it's given some attention now?
- How can I surprise and delight them in the service they get?
- What does the business not yet know it needs but the external and internal environment is flagging up?

For example, how might strategic thinking have helped in the current financial crisis? Both of us have been working with clients through this difficult period of change and noticed that quick decisions have been taken to deal with immediate shortfalls in finance. In our own line of business, many of our colleagues in the freelance world have either taken up full time jobs (rational perhaps?) or diversified into other areas (creative thinking definitely needed) or taken stock on what's happening in the current climate and weighed this up against the long-term prospects of being able to survive as a freelance consultant. Rational thinking might say: many businesses are in a downturn and there are limited funds around for training and development, so this is likely to be the first thing to go. Thinking more creatively we might consider not just offering the same services, at the same price and in the same way as we have before but asking what current needs are particularly highlighted through this difficult period? – Change? Conflict? Team-building? Coaching? Career counselling? etc. And how can you be best placed to offer these interventions?

Strategic thinking takes all of these into account and helps us to make both rational and creative decisions based on all the information available. This means intrapersonally: – what do we know in our bones about the present situation and how are we experiencing it directly? Interpersonally: – what do we pick up in the day-to-day conversations that we have with others in the organisation that tell us what's important to people in the organisation right now? And (in the words of our colleague and Barbara's co-author Suzanne Penn, 2009) extrapersonally: – what else is going on around here, in the environment at large, that is impacting on the present situation?

## So how can you develop your strategic thinking ability?

There are a number of ways the ability to think more strategically can be developed including a range of training programmes on the topic that might suit individual needs. Other ways in which you might develop your skills in this area include:

- *Research* – particularly about the business and the sector you are in but also more widely about the world of business. Allocating time to reading and digesting newsletters, articles, newspapers, briefings, etc. In some orga-nisations, summaries of the latest news report are sent to employees to help them keep up to date.

- *Work on projects with others* who can contribute in this area (see also Chapter 8). For example, do you have researchers or people with the specific role of strategy implementation in the organisation? What do they do to keep their strategic thinking skills honed?
- *Take time* – If you are feeling stuck about a way forward on a particular issue, try doing something different – take a break, go for a walk, try a mind mapping of ideas, draw an interpretation of what seems to be happening to illuminate different aspects of the issue.
- *Ask questions* – Chunk up the issue by asking questions such as – what else is contributing to this? And how does this impact on the business more generally? Who else has a view? All these questions and more will help reveal the bigger picture perspective.
- *Stay interested* – particularly stay curious about what other businesses are doing, where and how they are successful and what contributes to good and bad services.
- *Step into others shoes* – either literally or metaphorically. Do your own back to the floor exercise or spend some time shadowing others to find out what is going on from their perspective. The broader perspective you have on things, the more likely you are to come up with effective ways around organisational problems.
- *Network* – inside and outside the organisation to keep up to date and get different perspectives.

See also Chapter 9: Understanding self and organisational awareness.

## Summary

In this chapter we have looked at the importance of thinking in different ways to really add and create value for the business and for our clients from the Business Partner role. Rational thinking will help us to be seen as sound practitioners who have well thought out solutions and can work within the more formalized structures and systems of the organisation. We are likely to be seen as "sensible" people who will be trusted with our judgements because they are based on logic and well-reasoned approaches. Creative thinking will be necessary when we are presented with problems which may not have been surfaced before and/or when a rational approach just will not help move the client and or the business further forward. Some clients will actively expect you to be able to help them think differently about the complex challenges which they are now facing in the business. If we are to create real value in the Business Partner role, it is more likely that we will require both rational and creative thinking, combined in our description here of strategic thinking. By showing an ability to think more deeply about the issues you are challenged by and by taking a more long-term and holistic approach, you will be modeling vastly needed skills for managers in the organisation. Strategic thinking ability can be learnt through critical reflection, widening your network and keeping up to date with current trends both within and outside your own field of expertise.

## Checklist

- What current thinking do I typically adopt in my role? Rational? Creative? Strategic? And how do I know?
- Given the nature of the business I am in and the current culture, which form of thinking is most prevalent amongst managers here?
- What are the implications with the current ways of thinking in the organisation?
- If more attention was paid to thinking in different ways, what might be the beneficial effects?
- What could I do more of to increase my capacity to think differently about the challenges facing the business and my clients?
- How can I encourage different ways of thinking within the management community?
- What opportunities are already in the system to take advantage of? For example: Training programmes? Workshops? Coaching and mentoring? Project groups?

## References

Briggs Myers, I. (1980). *Gifts differing: Understanding personality type.* Davies-Black Publishing. (Reprint edition (May 1, 1995)).

Ingham, J. (2006). *Strategic human capital management – Creating value through people.* Oxford: Butterworth Heinemann.

Kenton, B., & Penn, S. (2009). *Change conflict and community.* Oxford: Butterworth-Heinemann.

Vaill, P. (1989). *Managing as a performing art.* San Francisco: Jossey-Bass.

Von Oeck, R. (1983). *A Whack on the side of the head.* New York: Warner Books.

# 2b

# Delivering a Business Focused Service

In this edition of the book we have added in a new section on project management, which in our experience of working with Business Partners is becoming a more valued skill. Working as a Business Partner requires a disciplined approach to both managing projects and managing relationships. As a result, this section focuses on two of the fundamental skills in this respect:

– Consultancy Skills and
– Managing Projects and Reviewing Performance.

Developing skills in these areas will not only build your credibility as a Business Partner, but will also ensure that your day-to-day actions are clearly focused on the service you provide to the business.

This section incorporates two of the categories from the skills and behaviours highlighted in Chapter 1 and written as a self-assessment questionnaire in the Appendix. These are firstly, "Delivering to the business" – which encompasses the need to have a holistic overview; adapting your role and keeping a long-term perspective and secondly, "Maintaining a business focus" – which encompasses prioritising effectively; utilising feedback and demonstrating effectiveness.

Chapter 7 explores the use of a consultancy framework to provide the ability for Business Partners to engage effectively in all their interactions with the business. An awareness of the many different styles of consulting allows Business Partners to make some more strategic choices about the type of consulting role which is most effective at a particular point in time. This chapter focuses initially on the consultancy cycle as a backdrop to working inside organisations and providing a client-centred approach. The remainder of the chapter concentrates on the art and science of contracting and highlights considerations around whom to contract with, issues to cover in the contracting process and how to avoid some of the pitfalls. Contracting is an aspect of internal consulting that is often given insufficient attention and yet is crucial to ensuring understanding of what is needed for the business as well as setting clear expectations about delivery and responsibilities.

Chapter 8 is a new chapter focusing on project management skills, which provide the essential discipline of prioritising and planning change processes effectively for long-term benefit. Project Management disciplines also enable Business Partners to ensure that mechanisms are in place to utilise feedback from the business to adjust and adapt their approach as required. In addition to providing an overview of project management, this chapter also explores the process of reviewing performance and eliciting feedback from the client system. It includes a topic which many internal consultants find difficult, which is to draw a close to projects they are working on and move on from a piece of work without impacting the relationships amongst those remaining. This requires both good project management skills as well as effective influencing to position the client so that you can move on to higher value work.

# 7

# Key Consultancy Skills

The Business Partner role has many similarities to that of an internal consultant and as a consequence, many of the consultancy skills are included in the behavioural framework we have developed. In order to get a better understanding of consultancy skills, this chapter outlines one of the commonly used frameworks for consultancy and focuses on some of the key skills applicable to Business Partners, in particular the need to contract effectively with clients.

**What is consultancy?**
Before exploring consultancy skills, it is worth revisiting some of the definitions outlined in the introduction. There are many differing definitions of consultancy, and depending on the primary purpose of your role, different definitions will have a lesser or greater "fit". However, all consultancy will in some way have the purpose of providing help to a client and for the purposes of this chapter, a simple definition provides us with a focus:

> *"A 2-way interaction – a process of seeking, giving and receiving help"*
> (Lippett & Lippett, 1986)

or

> *"A person in a position to have some influence over an individual, group or organisation, but who has no direct power to make changes"*
> (Block, 2000)

As we explore the skills in more depth, you will see that the role can be complex and so you may like to develop your own definition and understanding of consultancy in the context in which you work. Having this understanding of what consultancy means can help us to be clear with our clients about the service we aim to provide.

## The consultancy cycle

Consultancy skills are often described with reference to the life cycle of a project. Figure 7.1 shows how the consultancy cycle typically appears.

Each of the stages shown in Figure 7.1 highlights skills needed by the practitioner:

### Phase 1 – gaining entry

This phase involves being able to build a good rapport with your clients and establish credibility and visibility within the wider client system. It includes a whole range of sub-skills including: being sensitive to client needs, effective communication and influencing skills and the ability to attend to both the content and process of communication.

Whilst internal consultants may have their projects given to them rather than having to sell themselves to gain a piece of work, the initial discussions about the project are still critical in terms of setting expectations and establishing relationships. Creating early impressions and "Getting in" with your client were discussed in the earlier chapter on positioning yourself with your client, as was the need to market yourself even if you have a monopoly position.

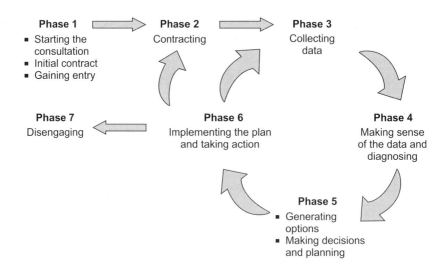

**Figure 7.1** The consultancy cycle.

## Phase 2 – making and maintaining effective contracts with your clients

This phase is critically important and will be discussed in more detail later. It refers to setting contracts in terms of what, how, where, when and who. This will include being able to analyse the stakeholders with a vested interest in the work, contracting with them as necessary and engaging them throughout as appropriate.

## Phase 3 – skills and tools to collect information about a presenting issue

This might include the ability to design questionnaires and interview people effectively. Good observation, listening, questioning and analytical skills will also be needed at this stage. Familiarity with diagnostic tools may also be critical if you are gathering data at a more strategic level.

## Phase 4 – diagnostic skills

This phase entails making sense of the information in the context of what else is happening in the organisation or part of the organisation within which you are working. This stage requires a good understanding of organisational development and organisational and group dynamics, plus the ability to stand back and interpret what is really going on in any given situation; so, political awareness is useful here.

## Phase 5 – generating and selecting options

In this phase, you need to be able to work with your clients to decide the most appropriate course of action. This could include a training intervention; recommendations about systems, structures or processes that need to be changed; recruitment and retention strategies or other interventions aimed at improving the business and/or people's experience in the workplace. This stage will require good presentation and influencing skills, plus political skill and sensitivity.

## Phase 6 – implementing the recommendations

The skills needed in this phase depend very much on the intervention. Facilitation and change management skills are likely to be needed as well as some expert knowledge.

## Phase 7 – the ability to disengage effectively

This phase refers to knowing when you are helping and when you need to hand over the process to your client. The ability to disengage effectively is a skill in itself and is explored in more detail in Chapter 9.

Many of the underpinning skills in this phase model will be familiar to HR professionals – such as the ability to question, listen, develop rapport, facilitate discussions and present information. Whilst not straightforward, developing these skills is covered comprehensively in other publications, and it is not the intention to go over these here. Some of the other skills mentioned, such as positioning yourself with your client, influencing change, political aptitude and disengaging, are covered in other chapters of this book. Consequently, this chapter focuses primarily on the importance of Phase 2 of this model, which is the ability to contract effectively with clients.

However, projects are rarely as neatly presented as a consultancy cycle. As a Business Partner, you may get brought into a project at the implementation stage in the role of a pair of hands. If you have concerns about what you are being asked to do, then the ability to challenge and backtrack through the cycle will be a critical skill for maintaining your credibility. One Business Partner commented that *"being presented with the solution which someone thinks is right to implement, rather than being allowed to research the issue/problem and complete a full consultancy process"* was one of the most challenging aspects of her role.

## Benefits of internal consulting

Whilst this model applies equally to internal and external consultants, Lacey (1995) points out that there are advantages and disadvantages that come from having an internal perspective, some of those are outlined in Table 7.1.

The diagnostic phase of the consultancy cycle, for example, can provide challenges for both the internal and external consultants. On the face of it, the internal consultant should more easily be able to access information in the organisation either through primary or secondary methods. However, sometimes the role of someone working internally can be viewed with suspicion and so access to certain individuals or information may prove difficult if full trust has not been established. A positive advantage for the internal consultant can be an ability to identify with the culture and values of the organisation and how they impact on behaviour. Skilled consultants will be able to identify how they are impacted by what is happening in the organisation as a member of that system and use themselves as a live part of the diagnosis. For example, if communication of change is leading to confusion and anxiety in the organisation, the internal consultants are also likely to experience this. If they are able to stand back and assess what they are experiencing, this can be another valuable source of data contributing to the overall picture of what is happening.

Those working internally will have to deal with their own feelings of discomfort and anxiety about the changes before they can effectively support

**Table 7.1**  Advantages and Disadvantages of Being an Internal Consultant

| Advantages | Disadvantages |
|---|---|
| *Phase 1: Gaining entry* | |
| Familiar relationships | Must work with everyone |
| Little marketing required | Cannot drop a project |
| Steady pay | Less prestige than externals |
| Less conflict of interest | Work may be boring/routine |
| Familiarity with jargon | |
| *Phase 2: Contracting* | |
| Ease of verbal contracts | Informality may lead to lack of clarity |
| Knows the systems and players | Juggling demands of changing confidentiality and openness |
| *Phases 3 and 4: Collecting data and diagnosing* | |
| Knows where to look for dysfunction | Can be part of the problem |
| Moves freely in the organisation | May not have the latest techniques |
| Can involve the right people | Client retaliation or dependency |
| Understands the culture | Prestige determined by job level |
| | Change anxiety in consultant |
| *Phases 5 and 6: Selecting options and implementation* | |
| Knows the "fit" of options proposed | May have limited vision |
| Identifies the key power sources | Free and informed choice is unlikely |
| Ensures proper follow-through on ideas | Project failure may humiliate |
| *Phase 7: Disengaging and evaluating* | |
| Success may be linked to status | Failure may lead to loss of status |
| Success broadens opportunities | May experience alienation/isolation from client system |
| Get to see long-term impact | May get little recognition for themselves |

others – working to uncover dissonance in their own value systems before working with others. The internal consultants can easily find that clients become overly dependent on them as experts. Managing client anxieties as someone working internally with their own fears and concerns about change and how this might impact on them can also result in unhelpfully co-dependent relationships.

It will be really important for the internal consultants to demonstrate the behaviours they are trying to influence on others when selecting methods for data gathering and diagnosis. In this way they will be able to build credibility and respect by "walking the talk". Issues of confidentiality are also important during this process. External consultants are more likely to be trusted to respect confidences and act impartially, so the internal consultant needs sometimes to work harder at demonstrating a commitment to keeping confidences.

As internal consultants, Business Partners would benefit from reviewing this list and thinking through how they can counter some of the potential disadvantages. Some Business Partners for example will bring in external consultants to work with them if they feel they are too close and immersed in the problem they are working on.

## The importance of contracting

> *"Consultants naively imagine that contracting is a short, straightforward business deal and not the complex social-political interaction that it is"*
> (Neumann, Kellner, & Dawson-Shepherd, 1997)

At first glance contracting with your client appears to be a straightforward task. There are a number of different elements that need to be discussed, debated and agreed at the start of any project, and once this has happened, the end outcome is usually documented in some way to provide evidence of the discussion and clarity about how you will work together. However, as you dig deeper into what makes a successful Business Partnership between HR and the line managers, it becomes increasingly clear that the effectiveness of each stage of the process, from initial data gathering through to implementation, is dependent on the quality of the contracting meetings with the client and that if these discussions are not thorough enough, many misunderstandings or unrealistic expectations can occur as a project develops.

According to Roffey Park Research (Kenton & Moody, 2003), only 6.9% of companies include contracting in their top three competencies for internal consultants. Yet having a clear contract with the key decision makers is critically important when working as an internal consultant, perhaps more so if working internally where the boundaries of the relationship can be less clear. It seems that those working internally are often faced with competing priorities and this, combined with a lack of perceived power and influence, can mean that it is a challenge to define the boundaries and priorities for work presented by clients.

Contracting on an internal basis tends to take place in an informal way and with little attention to defining the time and other resources, which might be needed for the work (including access to people). Whilst there are constraints to having a too tightly defined contract, which leaves little flexibility, some defined parameters can be extremely useful for helping to establish roles and responsibilities for both the consultant and client.

As well as a focus on the "what" of contracting, i.e exploring the different elements of a project, Business Partners also need to examine the "how" in terms of establishing how the relationship with the client will operate. Whilst it is easy to get drawn into a discussion on the issues presented by the client, it is equally important to discuss early on how consultant and client will work together in order to lead into an exploration of the consultant role.

## Do I even need to contract?

Business Partners who work predominantly for one client, or for whom the role is less tangible than project delivery, may feel that there is less of a need to contract with their client. Whilst specific projects may require scoping and clear terms of reference, on-going process interventions may be harder to tie down, or the way of working with the client may be very established. Many organisations, such as *Severn Trent Water*, used their Business Plan as terms of reference for the work of the Business Partners, as this provides clear goals, timescales and deliverables. However, as one Business Partner described it, *"my work is like a bottomless pit and I need to prioritise and manage expectations constantly. Holding contracting discussions is a way of achieving this"*. We would echo these words and suggest that contracting on the less tangible aspects of the role is often *more* critical than on the key deliverables.

Contracting with your client and setting terms of reference for a particular project, or elements of your role, has a whole range of benefits:

- It can help the clients to develop their thinking about an issue and work out what they really need from you, rather than what they first think they need;
- It leads to a mutual understanding of the "what" and the "how" behind the contract;
- Jointly exploring a problem will help you to establish a better understanding of the business issues and background to the issues;

- It provides an opportunity for you to redefine your role from one of a support function to that of an equal partner; and
- Clear terms of reference provide a benchmark for assessing the effectiveness of your performance.

However, even when the benefits are evident, it can still be hard to tie down a client as an internal provider. *Airbus* aim agree a charter with their clients to prevent constant change to the project brief, but admitted that there was resistance to being tied down by the client system.

## Whom should you contract with?

The consultants in the Roffey Park Research (Kenton & Moody, 2003) identified a difficulty in establishing exactly *who* the client is and some even cited "the whole organisation". In a sense it is often true that the client is the organisation and this makes it even more important to identify key members of the client group in order to gain access to the more senior levels and decision makers in the organisation, which can often be difficult. One internal consultant from *The Body Shop* stated that they "*spent time getting clear client relationships – recognising that in every piece of work there is likely to be more than one client – users, deciders, influencers etc*" (Inside Outreach, 2002).

This issue of who is the real client becomes even more difficult to establish when the Business Partner has dual reporting lines. Determining whether a project is being driven by the HR business or the operational business may not be that easy to assess and as a consequence loyalties may well come into play. One way to help with this is to establish success measures which are agreed with both reporting lines as a way of clarifying which client agenda you are following.

Even when the Business Partner is clear about who the client is, it can sometimes become apparent during contracting meetings that the client does not really own the problem and that the true owner is elsewhere in the organisation. If this occurs, it is important to question whether the issue should be re-contracted closer to the source of the issue if at all possible, as this will help to provide the level of commitment required to make any recommendations effective.

## The sponsorship role

It is also important to consider the other stakeholders in the client system, such as any suppliers, consumers or sponsors. Section 1 examined the role of sponsors and other stakeholders in the organisation. A sponsor for the piece of work may or may not be identified by the client, but where the Business Partner is involved in helping with an aspect of change, it will be important that they are not seen as the "champion" for the work. If this occurs, the Business Partners may become the scapegoat if the change does not go to plan, or feel an increasing need to justify their position. Rather, it might be more appropriate if sponsorship comes at the most senior level of the organisation.

In discussions with consultants it seems that there is little exploration in the contracting stage about the role and responsibilities of the sponsor. This may mean that the role becomes more of a token gesture than a committed and valued contribution. Contracting needs to include consultant expectations of the sponsor. This is a potentially difficult conversation for those working internally. Useful questions to ask might be:

■ What would effective sponsorship look like?
■ How would this be demonstrated so that people throughout the organisation know that the work has commitment and backing at the most senior levels?
■ Would multiple sponsors be appropriate for this project?

*Nortel* ensure that they appoint "sustaining sponsors" as part of their steering committee for new projects (Morris, 1996). The role they have defined for these sponsors is to:

■ Remove political and organisational impediments;
■ Seize opportunities to champion the project;
■ Help market and sell it to other leaders;
■ Give advice on politics to the team;
■ Keep the team motivated to achieve; and
■ Hold the team accountable for meeting milestones

The role is clearly defined as a leading and active position, rather than just that of a spokesperson.

The Hyde Group also renamed their sponsors "saviours" to reflect their championing role.

## What to do at the initial client meetings

When you first meet the client or hold an initial meeting with them by phone, the client will be making almost instantaneous impressions about you. Having gained entry, the next step is to hold a more in-depth discussion with the client on a particular issue or project. Whilst there is usually a need to negotiate a formal agreement for any piece of work, equally important in these initial client meetings are the aspects that focus on the psychological or unspoken contract which is being established between the Business Partner and the client.

Before we go on to discuss the practicalities of contracting skills for Business Partners, it may help to include a short paragraph about content, procedure and process and how we are defining these terms here.

## Content, procedure and process in an organisational context

*Content:* In an organisational system, this will include the overt policies, structures, business plans and strategies. It also includes the task focused elements that are in place and make explicit what we are here to do. It can also be the explicit agenda at a meeting.

*Procedure:* This will be the "how" we go about doing the business. It will include processes and systems in place, the methods by which we get things done. The meeting in itself is an example of procedure – it is the method we choose to get something agreed or discussed. Other methods might include training, telephone conferencing, workshops, interviews, etc.

*Process:* These are the things below the surface in the classic iceberg model – the beliefs and assumptions that people carry, the pre-conceived ideas, the gossip and grapevine, the shadow system that can either help the organisation achieve its goal or get in the way. In our meeting example, some of the process will be visible around non-verbal body language, the asides, doodling, tone of voice, etc.

The Business Partner needs to be able to determine at which level interventions are needed and what else needs to happen to support change. For example, in an organisational context, if an appraisal system is changed at a content level, how will this impact on the way appraisals are carried out? What needs to happen to pay attention to the procedure? And what might the underlying feelings of the appraisers and those being appraised be? (process).

## Content and process between individuals and groups

Here, content is about the words people use. The language chosen can give you an important indication of what else is going on at an individual level. For example is your client saying "we" and meaning "I"? This may mean that the client wants to disagree with what you are saying, but does not want a confrontation; so, pulling others into the conversation can be a way of feeling safe. Are they putting their "but" in your face? – I remember hearing Marshall Rosenberg, founder of Nonviolent communication (NVC), speaking at a recent conference about the aggressive use of the word "but". Usually, the use of this word will mean that someone is feeling defensive or not listening to what you want to say (Rosenberg, 2003). By paying attention to your own words and those used by the client you may be able to make the communication clearer.

The tone of voice and non-verbal behaviour is the "process" of the conversation, otherwise known as the music and the dance behind the words. The tone of voice someone uses can give invaluable clues as to how they feel about a suggestion or a piece of feedback, for example. Mixed messages tend to arise when someone says one thing, but their voice or facial expression gives you a contradictory message. You might choose to reflect this back to your client by saying "you don't seem too sure" or "you're looking a little puzzled about what I've just said". The aim again would be to clarify the communication between you.

Noting content and process at an organisational and individual level can help to extend our choice of interventions. It will not always be appropriate to pick up on process explicitly, but it can help to aid our understanding of what is really happening.

## Formal contracting issues

The more formal part of the contracting process is content based and entails discussing and debating on a number of issues and drawing up a contract, or initial terms of reference, based on what is agreed. A good contract is likely to:

1. Agree on objectives and the overall scope of the work
   - What type of outcome is expected – a change, a solution or recommendations?
   - What does success look like?
   - What is the purpose of the project?
   - Who are the people involved?
   - What are the boundaries of the work?

2. Set timescales and plan the phases of work
   - Is it fixed or open ended?
   - Whose time will be needed at each stage?
   - What are the key deliverables?
   - When will they be delivered?
   - What are the key milestones?

3. Agree who has responsibility for each aspect of work
   - Who is the sponsor and what is his/her role?
   - Who is in a steering role for the diagnosis and design?
   - Who has decision-making capability?

4. Agree on data gathering methods and access issues
   - What methods are appropriate for the project?
   - What methods suit the context?
   - Whom can you talk to?
   - Whom and what must you avoid?

5. Agree how the work will be communicated
   - Frequency of contact
   - Method of communication
   - Confidentiality agreements

6. Outline the finances and any financial implications
   - Which budget is it coming from?
   - Who can authorise payments?
   - Are there penalties for late delivery?

7. Detail other resource allocations
   - Staffing
   - Materials/equipment

8. Outline any dependencies and risks that may affect the intended outcomes
   - What assumptions are being made?

9. Establish a review process and a process for re-negotiation
   - How will the project end?
   - Will any on-going support be required after completion?
   - How will the project be reviewed?
   - What methods of evaluation are appropriate?
   - Who will instigate re-negotiation of the contract if there are changes?

Each of these elements is essential in the contracting process as problems can easily arise if they are omitted. Attempting to spend two or three days carrying out a thorough evaluation of a project at the end of the process, for example, is almost impossible if this was not discussed and agreed up front.

Many of the items on the list also require a skilled conversation to get to the root of what is required and how the contract will be carried out. Confidentiality for example is an important issue, which is often raised, but seldom explored, in sufficient depth. Cockman, Evans, and Reynolds (1992) suggest that an effective discussion on confidentiality will cover the following:

- What confidentiality means with respect to the issue;
- Whether data gathering will be collected and reported openly;
- How the findings will be distributed;

- Whether access to the data will be given for other purposes; and
- What levels of involvement are appropriate.

This list alone however is fairly formidable as an agenda for a meeting; so, it is important not only to prioritise the key elements so that they are discussed and clarified as soon as possible, but also to flag up any items which don't get covered and ensure you gain agreement to come back to them at a future meeting. Often the initial contracting process can take several meetings, depending on the complexity of the project. For highly complex projects, Gantt charts are often used as a project planning tool.

## How formal do you need to be?

In some organisations there is a need within the existing process to formalise and sign off an agreement for every project. This may seem overly formal in small companies and the contract does not necessarily need to be the type of document that requires joint signatories. A detailed e-mail may be sufficient if this suits the culture and management style of the organisation. However, even in companies where it is not common practice to formalise verbal agreements, it can still be very useful for the Business Partner to summarize the contents of a contracting meeting and send this to the client to check that there is a common understanding of the points raised.

## The informal contract

Much of the discussion at the initial meetings with the clients is likely to focus on the issue they are seeking to address. The Business Partners will be using their skills to probe the client about the nature of the problem in order to help gain clarity on the task at hand and establish the formal contract. Mixed in with this, discussions may also take place on various aspects of the informal contract, such as the role expectations (expert, pair of hands, collaborative, etc.) and how the client and partner would ideally like to work together.

As if that wasn't enough, there will also be a whole host of non-verbalised perceptions taking place at a process level, such as:

- Do I really want to work with this person?
- Do I trust them?
- Do I like them?
- How competent do I think they are?
- Do I agree with what they are saying?
- How knowledgeable are they?

- Do I feel a sense of rapport?
- Do their questions make me think?

From a Business Partner perspective there a number of mini-agendas which are worth holding in the back of your mind during the initial set of meetings with a client.

## What is the bigger picture?

Useful information to get at this stage is a sense of the department, its objectives and customers as well as how the issue fits and what has already been tried and with what outcome. Background information, such as why the client has chosen you (if they had an option), may also be useful.

It is important for the Business Partner to check out any assumptions about how the problem is defined and any possible solutions that are raised. Often a client will have made some preliminary diagnosis about their particular situation and may be resistant to suggestions that more data need to be gathered before devising a solution. The Business Partner needs to try to retain an open mind on the likely reasons for the problem occurring and continually encourage the client to question their assumptions and take a wider view of the possible options.

## Where does the power lie?

It is important to get an understanding of who has the power to make which decisions in relation to the assignment. Getting an understanding of the key stakeholders and who needs to be involved in the process of decision-making can be essential if you are to avoid treading on people's toes and wasting a lot of time tailoring the project to the wrong people.

Exploring what you are prevented from doing with the client can be a useful way of finding out some of the power politics occurring. Are there certain things that you can only talk about to certain people for example. Getting a good understanding of the organisational relationships and how these help or hinder the situation is vital information and is often one of the key advantages that Business Partners have over external consultants.

## What are the potential underlying problems?

The "presenting problem" which the internal consultant is asked to tackle is often complicated by the overlaying culture of the organisation. For example, a request for a team-building event may, on further diagnosis, show that a controlling leadership style or unfair reward strategies are the main contributors towards dysfunctional team behaviour. Internal consultants can find it difficult to get permission to go behind the presenting issue and get to the root cause of problems – often due to the issues of role, status and power highlighted above. Effective contracting plays an important part here in clarifying the expectations of both the consultant and the client.

## What are my needs and expectations from them?

It may be important for you to convey certain information about yourself or the way you like to work to your client and gain commitment to this. For example, you may have particular biases which you would like them to acknowledge. Block (2000) recommends making a list of essential and desirable needs which you can then hold in your head when entering into a client discussion. Possible needs include:

| | |
|---|---|
| Essential needs | Client support for a particular approach |
| | Establishing co-operation for data gathering |
| | Commitment to the project by the client |
| Desirable needs | Open and honest feedback |
| | Tolerance of mistakes |
| | A share of the credit if all goes to plan |

If your essential needs are not met, or there is a mismatch between your values and those of your client, you need to consider whether it is possible to turn down the work. In the Roffey Park Research, internal consultants identified difficulties in saying "no" to work even when it did not seem to be high priority. The culture of the organisation will have a significant impact on the consultants' ability to set priorities and manage the boundaries of their work as well as the expectations of their role.

## What are their needs and expectations of me?

As well as overtly discussing what a client needs from you as a partner and how they expect you to work with them, a Business Partner also needs to be constantly on the lookout during the initial meetings for subconscious cues stemming from the client. Often consultants will say that they have discussed their role with their clients and that the clients have agreed that they would like to work collaboratively with the Business Partner. This is not surprising as this can often sound like the right thing to say. However, if a Business Partner is able to pick up on the nuances of the client's body language, they will be aware of any confusions or insincerities and explore these further. It can be more fruitful to start from a point of asking what expertise the client is looking for, which will bring out collaborative skills if these are required.

Responding appropriately to the client's emotions can often be a challenge. Business Partners often try to rescue the client rather than remaining neutral in the situation. Table 7.2 illustrates some of the possible emotions that might be exhibited by a client during an initial meeting. For each emotion there is likely to be an emotional reaction which is triggered, but the skill of the Business Partner lies in being able to respond in a neutral way.

Clients will also have needs and expectations about how they want you to behave towards them and how much commitment they expect from you. Once again, the more you can draw these thoughts into an open discussion, the more clarity you will have.

## Will I have the level of access to people and resources I need to be effective?

During the contracting discussions Business Partners are often faced with a dilemma as to whether to work within the constraints on offer, or to negotiate for what they ideally need. For example, your client would like you to find out about a particular aspect of work, but is not prepared for you to question some of the key stakeholders or ask particular questions. This is a difficult judgement to make, as the partner is often balancing the need to appear helpful and flexible towards the client against a need to work in the most effective way. However, effective partners will challenge and explore the resources on offer before deciding how far to push. Ultimately, if partners take on an assignment without the permission they need to access adequate resources or people their credibility is likely to suffer more than if they advise the client up front that a particular course of action won't work in the way proposed.

## Gauging success

At the end of the discussion, if it has gone well, there will be a greater sense of commitment between the client and the Business Partner, and the trust and respect between the parties will have grown. A quick test of the success of a contracting meeting is whether the Business Partner has managed to bring out all the anxieties of both parties and gained a clear commitment of how to proceed.

**Table 7.2**  Partner Responses to Client Emotions

| Emotion | Neutral reaction | Emotional reaction |
|---|---|---|
| Confusion | Clarify issues<br>Clarify roles<br>Provide a structure<br>Restrain action<br>Assess the impact<br>Provide models/maps | Get sucked into the confusion<br>Oversimplify<br>Fight<br>Take sides<br>Accept one frame of reference |
| Conflict | Learn its history<br>Welcome it and understand it<br>Value the differences<br>Provide an arena<br>Model conflict handling | Fear it<br>Minimise it<br>Ignore it<br>Take sides |
| Worry/fear | Listen<br>Acknowledge feelings<br>Explore sources and nature | Teach<br>Falsely reassure<br>Contract unrealistically |
| Stuck | Establish what they have<br>Find out what worked before<br>Find out what hasn't worked<br>Start where they are<br>Establish needs and wants<br>Provide relevant input | Do it for them<br>Work with solved problems<br>Solve symptoms<br>Suggest your favourite solution |

Adapted from Clarkson and Kellner (1995).

## Avoiding some of the pitfalls of contracting

### Perceiving contracting to be an up-front activity

Whilst the majority of the issues for any assignment will need to be clarified and agreed early on in a project, it would be wrong for Business Partners to assume that once they have a written agreement there is no more contracting to be done. Each review period, project milestone or emerging issue is an opportunity to revisit some of the initial assumptions that were made with the client and re-negotiate the contract if appropriate. The client contract should be a live agreement that is continually challenged and amended as appropriate.

Having said that contracting should be an on-going activity, there is also a danger in this, in that the client may use it as an opportunity for continued re-negotiation of the contract and the ground rules. Steps also need to be taken therefore to set expectations up front about the nature of any re-contracting that might take place. In addition, the Business Partners need to be prepared to challenge their clients if they feel they are being taken advantage of.

## Straying too far into data gathering

In trying to establish the underlying problem being presented by the client, it is easy for a Business Partner to risk straying into an unplanned phase of data gathering. Whilst this might not be a problem, it can lead to difficulties if it either gets in the way of other aspects of the contracting which should be taking place, or leads to assumptions being made on how to progress the project without a more accurate diagnostic study. One of the key skills of the Business Partner is the ability to gather enough data on the issue to be able to draw up an initial contract, without getting too drawn into the work to be able to take a step back.

## Starting to carry out work before a contract is agreed

It may seem obvious that work should not begin on a particular project until the contracting issues have been discussed and agreed, but often there is a pressure to begin the work beforehand. It may be, for example, that a key stakeholder is only available for interview the next day or that a particular department needs a key deliverable on a set date. Whilst this is not quite as critical if there are no cost or fee issues involved in the partnership, it is still equally important that the contract is fully discussed before work commences. Without this happening, mis-understandings are likely to occur, expectations will not be met and it will become increasingly difficult to revisit some of the initial conversations, which still need to take place.

## Acting unprofessionally

It is particularly critical in the early stages of a project that you make every attempt to convey a respectful, open and honest manner towards your client. Over-familiarity with a client or a sense of inferiority compared to the client can lead to the Business Partner acting unprofessionally. Key guidelines for dealing professionally are:

- Arrive on time;
- Be clear and open about your objectives;
- Acknowledge your clients' opinions and respect their values;
- Be honest about the limitations of your work;

- Challenge your client if you do not understand anything they are saying;
- Actively listen and appreciate your client's position;
- Be prepared to admit any misunderstandings on your part;
- Avoid giving personal opinions on people in the organisation; and
- Provide your client with choice as to how to proceed.

Things to avoid are:

- Talking more than listening;
- Not managing the time during the meeting;
- Voicing recommendations too soon;
- Appearing inflexible in your approach; and
- Leaving the meeting without a clear agreement on next steps.

It can be useful, particularly if you are working as part of a larger partnership group, to document client meetings. If someone needs to pick up on your work or follow up in your absence then the partnership can then be seen to act far more professionally. Figure 7.2 is an example of a meeting report form.

## Ignoring a lack of commitment from the client

Sometimes a Business Partner will come away from a meeting with a feeling that the real issues or anxieties were not openly discussed. This can occur when the Business Partner is enthusiastic and confident about a piece of work and the client is not totally committed to what is being discussed, or it may just be that the client is very trusting of the partner and abdicates some or all of the responsibility for the issue without the necessary willingness to participate in the discussions.

One of the key skills of effective Business Partners is that they will raise concerns they may have and even when they are not clear where the concerns originate, and will be prepared to say so and explore this with the client. Whilst Business Partners can potentially be effective at instigating organisational change without a strong client commitment, their effectiveness and perceived success will be greatly enhanced by ensuring that they gain commitment up front.

Sometimes a client may just have a low motivation for either the project in hand, or for a full contracting discussion of the type described. One reason for this may be that they don't see the value in the process and need to be helped to do this. Another possibility may be that they do see a value, but their priorities are not in your favour! In these cases, taking small steps and contracting on each stage at a time may be a better way forward, or alternatively, negotiating with your client

---

**Meeting Report Form**

**Date:** 24<sup>th</sup> January 2005

**Location:** Glasgow Office

**People present:** PG, AW, ST

**Objective of meeting:** To get an understanding of the client issues concerning turnover.

**Background/Structural information:**
Turnover currently at 35% in the call centre. Previous year was 26%. Currently 6 call centre teams of 10, each with a team leader.

**Issues arising:**
Newer recruits are turning over faster – possibly due to less opportunities for promotion to team leader – possibly due to graduates working before getting a "proper" job.
   Induction training is good, but existing staff feeling a bit neglected.

**Suggestions made:**
Talked about exit interviews for staff leaving; morale of current staff; change to IT processes; Team Leader skills; competition in the area.
   Discussed need to do more analysis of the possible underlying causes before making recommendations.

**Actions:**
AW to come back in 2 weeks to propose a way of gathering more data to diagnose the cause.

---

**Figure 7.2** An example of a meeting record.

to work with another person from the client system on the contracting issues may be a way forward.

## Reaching an impasse

It is easy to reach an impasse in your initial discussions with a client, as it will be the first time they have thoroughly explained their needs and expectations and you have raised yours. If these needs and expectations do not match, which typically occurs in areas such as required timescales for delivery, then you may hear yourself repeating your points over and over again, or your clients may continue to state their position and be unable to move on. You are likely to feel a sense of irritation at this point, but the blocks may not always be evident, as the language used is often coded. For example:

The client says:          "Why don't you think it over and get back to me?"
The client means:      I want you to do it the way I'm suggesting.

The client says:          "Lets gather some more evidence"
The client means:      I don't agree so you can prove it if you like.

The client says:          "Right" or nothing at all
The client means:      I'm confused and don't really understand what you're saying.

It is important to recognise that you have reached a blocking point before you can move on from it. Ways forward include:

- Revisiting your own needs and expectations to see if they are realistic;
- Pointing out the impasse to the client and getting agreement to put it to one side and move on; and
- Thinking creatively with your client about how to get around the different needs.

## Closing the contracting meeting

It is useful to allow some time at the end of your initial client meetings to summarize all that have been agreed and take time to review the process. Asking how the client felt about the meeting, the project and you as a Business Partner may be difficult questions to pose, but will be invaluable in launching you into an open and honest relationship.

## Summary

Consultancy Skills are an essential part of a Business Partner's toolkit. The abilities to establish yourself with your client and contract effectively are critical building blocks to your success. In addition to the key skills that underpin the consultancy model, such as questioning, listening and building rapport, there are higher level skills involving political influence, awareness of process issues and ability to diagnose.

This chapter focused predominantly on contracting, which is a key component of the consultancy cycle and is not just about establishing the parameters of a piece of work. Done well, it is about having some difficult conversations with people in the organisation about roles, responsibilities and expectations. It takes guts for more junior Business Partners to have an honest conversation with senior sponsors about what they need them to contribute rather than just accepting them as a figurehead for a project.

Due to the vast number of issues which require clarity at the start of any project, contracting is not something that can be tied up in one meeting with the client. The formal elements of the contract alone can take some time, and it is also important to raise and deal with the intangible process elements. Effective contracting provides a thorough basis for a continued relationship with your client and provides greater assurance that your work will be focused appropriately and valued by the client and organisation.

## Checklist

- Have you got a good understanding of the consultancy cycle?
- Are you taking steps to minimise the disadvantages of consulting internally?
- Are you clear you are contracting with the right client?
- Have all the tangible elements of the contract been agreed upon?
  - Objectives and scope of work
  - Timescales and milestones
  - Responsibilities
  - Data gathering issues (including access)
  - Communication
  - Resources – finance, staffing, facilities, etc.
  - Dependencies and risks
  - Review and evaluation procedure
  - Process for re-negotiation
- Have you developed a sense of the potential underlying problems to what is being presented?
- Do you have a clear sense of the surrounding issues?
- Have you gained sufficient data to be able to progress?
- Have you left the way open to revisit the contract?
- Have you clarified roles and expectations for both yourself and the client?
- Have you challenged and explored any emotional responses stemming from the client?
- Have you acted professionally throughout the process?
- Have you raised any reservations you have about the contract?

# References

Block, P. (2000). *Flawless consulting* (2nd ed.). San Francisco: Jossey Bass/ Pfeiffer.

Clarkson, P., & Kellner, K. (1995). Danger, confusion, conflict and deficit: a framework for prioritising organisational interventions. *Organisations and People, 2*(4), 6–13.

Cockman, P., Evans, B., & Reynolds, P. (1992). *Client-centred consulting: A practical guide for internal advisers and trainers.* Maidenhead: McGraw Hill.

Inside Outreach. (2002). See www.inside-outreach.co.uk.

Kenton, B., & Moody, D. (2003). *The role of the internal consultant.* Horsham: Roffey Park Institute.

Lacey, M. Y. (1995). Internal consulting: perspectives on the process of planned change. *Journal of Organisational Change Management, 8*(3), 75–84.

Lippett, G., & Lippett, R. (1986). *The consultancy process in action* (2nd ed.). San Francisco: Jossey Bass/Pfeiffer.

Morris, D. (1996). Using competency development tools as a strategy for change in Human Resource function: a case study. *Human Resource Management, 35*(1), 35–51.

Neumann, J. E., Kellner, K., & Dawson-Shepherd, A. (1997). *Developing organisational consultancy.* London: Routledge.

Rosenberg, M. B. (2003). *Nonviolent Communication – A language of life.* Encinitas, CA: Puddledancer Press.

# 8

# Managing Projects and Reviewing Performance

As Business Partners operate more strategically, their role increasingly involves shaping and managing projects that add value to the business. Whilst HR has historically often had a co-ordinating role and implemented new initiatives (such as new appraisal schemes, for example), it is rare for those to have been approached with rigorous project management disciplines. Larger scale, more complex projects, however, require a more structured approach to managing projects and it is becoming essential that Business Partners have an awareness and ability to deploy these skills.

Project Management is a profession in its own right and there are many software tools that can help with the complexities. The aim of this chapter is not to provide the details of these tools, but to outline the different stages of managing projects and to highlight some of the more frequently used tools.

Reviewing performance and eliciting feedback from the client system can take place at any time throughout a project and continual feedback should be encouraged. Formal reviews tend to take place at key milestones and at the end of projects. As a consequence, one of the first steps in ensuring high-quality feedback is to establish an end point in the work you are undertaking.

At first glance, it may seem strange to include a section within this chapter on bringing projects to a close, as surely it should be obvious when a project reaches its conclusion. However, this is one of the areas where external consultants have the advantage over internal consultants. For them, the end of a project is signalled by either delivering a final piece of work or being paid for the final time. For internal consultants and Business Partners, however, their continued presence in the business can mean that the end point is less clearly defined. A key part of their role is therefore to signal completion on a particular piece of work to their clients, in order that it can be thoroughly reviewed and so that they can move on to something new and of more value.

## So what is project management?

In essence, project management is about having a clear and structured process for utilising the resources of the organisation, in order to achieve a defined objective within a set of constraints. Typically, projects will aim for achievable outputs and are unlikely to involve behaviour change. This is interesting, in that often the very thing Business Partners are seeking to achieve as a result of implementing a new process or approach is a change in behaviour. Programmes, on the other hand, do aim to achieve longer term outcomes that often encompass behaviour change.

The type of change projects that HR Business Partners are involved in are likely to be steps along the way to achieve a longer term outcome and may sit under an umbrella of a wider programme of change. It is important to keep this broader perspective in mind as each project is undertaken.

Project management can seem a rather formal approach and is quite disciplined in the way that it progresses through certain phases. The six key phases are illustrated in Figure 8.1.

At each of these phases there is a requirement to manage stakeholders effectively and to manage the issues and risks that emerge. Projects are quite formal in their approach and each phase needs to be signed off before the next one can begin.

### Project conception – developing the business case

When a new project is first conceived there is usually a need to gain approval in principle for the idea before the more detailed project planning begins. At this stage HR Business Partners are increasingly likely to get asked to develop

**Figure 8.1** Project phases.

a business case for a particular course of action, which highlights the key issues, a recommended course of action and the potential impact on the company. Reddington, Williamson, and Withers (2005) suggest that a business case has three key purposes:

- To get other people to understand the vision;
- To get approval for funding; and
- To act as a reference point for decisions during implementation.

For Business Partners, developing a business case is an excellent opportunity to both build your credibility in the business and actively influence and build relationships with the key stakeholders. A good business case will answer questions that people might pose, such as:

- Why is this important?
- Why is it a priority?
- How can this help us achieve our goals?
- What are the business benefits?
- What resources do you need?
- How will we measure our success?
- When can I expect results?
- Why are you the right person to lead on this?
- What period of time are we looking?
- How does this proposal fit with the strategic objectives of the company?
- What are the options and the pros and cons of each?
- What changes will this mean?
- What is the financial cost/benefit of the proposal?
- What are the risks involved?
- What are the critical success factors?
- What skills and competence are required to deliver it?

Just thinking through your answers to these questions can be a useful practice prior to any project you undertake, whether a business case is required or not.

Often, in the course of their work, Business Partners may start off by making an initial proposal for change, which, if it is accepted, is then developed into a more comprehensive business case in order to seek more formal approval for the idea. More formal business cases are typically quite lengthy documents and typically companies will have a set format which needs to be followed. The key elements of the document would normally include an Executive summary; a description of the current situation and the issues faced; the proposed strategy and risks associated with it; cost and benefit data; and a high-level implementation plan.

## Tools to support the business case

A number of tools can be used to draw together your business case. Some of the more commonly used tools are:

- Situation Analysis
- SWOT (Strengths, Weaknesses, Opportunities, Threats)
- PESTLE (Political, Economic, Social, Technological, Legal and Environmental factors)
- Benchmarking
- Stakeholder analysis
- Competency Analysis
- Competitor Analysis
- Market Analysis
- Customer profiling
- Cost Benefit Analysis
- Resource Planning
- Scenario Planning
- Risk Analysis

We touch on some of these tools throughout this book and focus particularly in this chapter on Risk Analysis, due to its relevance to project management.

## Gaining support for your business case

Developing a business case provides an ideal opportunity for Business Partners to consult with a wide range of people and build strong relationships across the business. It is imperative that a broad spectrum of stakeholders are involved early in the review process so that assumptions can be discussed and key people have time to be influenced about the benefits of your approach. The wider you consult, the greater the ownership of your case.

Mapping your stakeholders' interest, commitment and influence is a useful technique for ensuring that you have thought through your approach from different people's perspectives and this tool is discussed in Chapter 4 of this book. Identifying potential sources of resistance and listening and acting on stakeholder concerns are critical in ensuring a business case that meets with their approval. Before you even present your business case you will need to be influencing and managing your stakeholders in order to establish your credibility and identity and demonstrate your ability to manage the project.

Gaining business buy-in is a critical step in making the business case and cannot be over emphasised. Selling the vision is often about showing how it is going to have a positive impact on the bottom line. Talking to your stakeholders in their language, making links to customers and the competitive position, as well as using techniques such as the balanced scorecard, will be critical.

Understanding the barriers you might come up against is a critical part of putting your case forward. Cannon (2006) recommends considering the following questions:

- Do you know what you want to achieve?
- Do you really believe in it yourself?
- Have you got all the facts that support your case?
- What are your strongest arguments?
- What are the benefits to your audience?
- What else is affected by your proposal?
- What are the key arguments against your proposal?
- Is the timing right?
- How will you sum up?
- What would a critic pick up on?

## Project definition – scoping the project

Once the business case has been approved, the more detailed project planning can begin. Initially this will involve scoping the project and producing a number of key documents (see Figure 8.2). This set of documents will normally need to be approved by a steering group before the next phase – project planning – can begin.

Whilst this may seem like an administrative and rather bureaucratic stage, in reality producing each of these documents requires quite complex negotiation, influencing and extensive communication. Without strong interpersonal skills,

> Project Brief with clear project objective

> Stakeholder lists

> Statement of requirements

> Scope of Work

> Risk Assessment

> List of Project Team contact details and roles

> List of Project Steering Group details and roles

**Figure 8.2** List of key documents.

Business Partners are unlikely to get the right people in the project team and steering group and have a fully supported project brief.

Experienced project managers will be the first to tell you about the importance of the project brief. They find that when difficulties emerge on the project and resistance to change is starting to happen, referring back to the original brief and re-stating that with the steering group can be invaluable in moving the project forward.

## Project planning

Project planning is the phase that typically involves the use of software. Before any data can be input the Project Manager needs to:

- Identify all the project activities and who will carry them out;
- Get time estimates for each activity;
- Determine activity dependencies to assess which can run in parallel and which need to follow in sequence; and
- Note any constraints on timings.

Projects can then be depicted on Gantt charts (see the IT change programme example in Figure 8.3) and a Critical Path Analysis (CPA) can be carried out to show the earliest possible completion time and project critical activities.

It is not the intention to go into more detail on this here; however, one more term which may prove useful to be aware of is a PERT estimate. This stands for

**Change Programme - Overview**

**Figure 8.3** Change programme – overview.

a Programme Evaluation and Review Technique and is a way of calculating the time for each project stage. A PERT estimate:

$$\text{PERT} = \frac{\text{optimistic estimate} + (4 \times \text{most likely estimate}) + \text{pessimistic estimate}}{6}$$

This can be particularly useful with more unpredictable activities as a legitimate way of guessing the timing!

All projects are a balance between delivering on time, to cost and with quality. This cost, quality, time balance is quite critical and can often require quite open and honest conversations about the priorities for the task and is often at the heart of concerns as the project progresses.

Consider for example the move to service centres for transactional HR activities. Whilst the cost argument may be clear, sticking rigidly to a project timetable may well mean that people are not given sufficient time to buy-in to the concept, or understand how the new system will operate. Equally, over-focusing on quality, by trying to plan in every eventuality, will inevitably lead to unnecessary delays. Understanding whether concerns raised about a project stem from quality, cost or time drivers can help you as the project manager to influence the process and achieve the best possible outcome.

## Project execution – managing risks and monitoring progress

The on-going management of a project can be a challenging role. Not only are you potentially juggling the needs of different stakeholders, but you are also needing to respond to changes and issues that arise, perhaps due to timescales, costs, quality or predicted benefits of the project. In project management terms these are termed "issues" and "risks".

Most large-scale projects have on-going risk analyses, which will not eliminate potential risks, but will identify the likely impact of an event and strategies for minimising the risk. Risks are defined in a number of ways:

Unacceptable risk – the project cannot be processed without immediate action to reduce the risk;
High risk – it will have a major impact on the schedule and costs;
Medium risk – it will have a significant impact on the project and possible knock-on effects; and
Low risk – it is not expected to have a serious impact.

Risks are typically reported regularly to the steering group in the form of a table depicting likelihood of the risk occurring and anticipated level of impact (see Figure 8.4).

## Managing Risk

|  | Low impact | Medium impact | High impact |
|---|---|---|---|
| High (7-9) Likelihood | Medium Risk | High Risk | Unacceptable Risk |
| Medium (4-6) Likelihood | Low Risk | High Risk | Unacceptable Risk |
| Low (1-3) Likelihood | Low Risk | Medium Risk | High Risk |

**Figure 8.4** Managing risk.

High-risk items will need actions specified within the business plan. Any medium-risk items may need preventative measures. For example, if the only supplier is not of the quality expected, then piloting a project, or delaying more risky aspects of a project may be useful.

For lower risk items, there may also be a need to put in place monitoring mechanisms.

Similarly, issues are usually put to the steering group in the form of an issues register, which specifies questions that have been raised, when and who raised them and what priority they have in terms of action. Project progress is often monitored using an RAG report (Red, Amber, Green), which shows progress on each of the project activities and draws the attention towards the problem (Red) issues. Figure 8.5 is an example of an RAG project report.

## Monitoring: RAG Report

| Project Activity | Red, Amber, Green Status | Comments |
|---|---|---|
| Briefing Managers | Green | Invites issued |
| Workshop for unions | Amber | Room still to be booked |
| Briefing packs | Red | No resource in publishing |
| Announcement | Amber | Draft for approval |

**Figure 8.5** Monitoring RAG report.

## Changes to the project

At the start of projects only certain elements are predictable and can be planned for. Consider for example a project to implement a new mentoring scheme. Whilst some elements may be decided in the initial scoping phase – such as how many mentors are needed, how they will be trained and who the recipients will be – it is inevitable that as the training takes place more questions will emerge. If for example concerns were raised about keeping the line managers updated, this would need to be highlighted as an issue to the project board. It may even be necessary to raise a change request to the project, to allow extra days and costs to produce a briefing pack for line managers.

These change control protocols are established at the start of the project and are needed when the inevitable changes that occur have an impact on the cost, quality or timing of the project.

## Project closure and post-project evaluation

Most larger projects require a formal project sign-off and once this has taken place, it is good practice to review the project and evaluate the success.

This aspect is explored in more detail in the next section. However, the main points to explore are the degree to which the project achieved its intended outcomes; an exploration of how the project group worked together so that improvements can be made for the future and feedback can be given; a celebration of success and a review of the processes used.

## Reviewing performance

Reviewing performance can take a number of different forms including:

- Self-reviews;
- Client–partner relationship reviews;
- Feedback from the client system;
- Project process reviews; and
- Business Partner function reviews.

Each of these provides vital data for enhancing the performance of both the Business Partner and the business as a whole. Within this chapter we will be exploring the first four of these and the function as a whole is explored in Chapter 11.

### Recognising the need for closure

One of the hardest parts for internal consultants is to recognise the end point and the need for closure on a particular project for themselves. If Business

Partners are working effectively then at the end of their project the ownership should lie with the client and it should be straightforward to draw a line under the project and move on. However, for internal Business Partners this is fraught with difficulties as the partner is keen to ensure that the relationship is sustained and one way to do this is to help out with extra little tasks that need doing, or by providing expertise when requested at key meetings or events. The client may be equally keen for the relationship to continue in this way, as it may provide an extra free resource!

If the project has been carefully monitored and progress has been tracked against a plan, it will be apparent when the tasks have been completed. However, there may still be some lingering activities that require your attention, or it may be "easier" for the client or people in the client system to ask you to assist them in something rather than doing it themselves or through newly established processes. It is essential that the Business Partner continually asks himself/herself "am I still adding value?" or "am I just carrying on to meet my own needs?". If you truly do feel your presence is still necessary in the project, then there is a need to re-negotiate an extended contract with your client, or set some new terms of reference to cover a transitional period. If not, then you need to be assertive with your client to clarify your current priorities with them. The ability to say no to your client when necessary has already been discussed in earlier chapters and is equally critical in the later stages of a project if you are to maintain your credibility.

**Moving on from a project without impacting the relationship**
Business Partners are human beings, and it is human nature to feel wanted. Ending a project, particularly a significant one, can leave you with a sense of loss and concern that important relationships may come to an end. Where the Business Partner model is based on the individuals gaining their own work, there will also be added concerns that losing contact with your client may lead to a loss of further work. It is essential therefore that the Business Partner ends each project professionally and takes steps to continue to build on the relationships that have been established. Just because a project comes to an end, it should not mean that key contacts are lost, although it will mean that the nature of the relationship will need to change. The networking skills outlined in Section 2 will come into play as a means of maintaining relationships, as relationships are an area that need to be actively managed to ensure success in the role.

## Guidelines for moving on

There are a number of steps a Business Partner can take to ease the transition at the end of a piece of work. Each of these will help to transfer the ownership of the project back to the client system and should ensure that the clients are fully equipped to take on the different aspects of their role. This process is often referred to in consultancy terms as disengaging.

## Establish the process at the start of the contract

It is essential that Business Partners establish a plan for disengaging early in the project. At the initial contracting phase, the partner needs to be working with the client to establish:

■ When each aspect of the project will be completed;
■ Who will be responsible for what at completion;
■ Any on-going support that may be required after completion; and
■ How the project will be reviewed.

Many of the companies we spoke to, formally disengage from a major project by signing off agreement that the initial terms of reference have been met. They then set up a maintenance contract, if required, to cover any on-going support that is needed.

## Incorporate symbols of completion

Holding certain events or providing awards can be a useful signal to the client that the project is coming to an end. Celebrating the success of a project is a helpful acknowledgement of completion and is useful for both the client and Business Partner in terms of cementing their relationship and demonstrating their value. This does not need to be overly formal, and as one Business Partner we spoke to put it "*I drag them (the client) down the pub whenever I've done anything I want to show off about!*".

Carrying out a thorough review of the project and the partnership is also a useful symbol of completion. This will allow for the partner to formalise any on-going support which may be needed, and depending on the original terms of reference it may also be necessary to produce a written report that needs to be signed off by the client.

More subtle signals can also be appropriate, such as a gradual spacing out of meetings or contact, or where cross-payment is made, a reduction in the per-centage charged towards the end of a project.

## Identify the right time

It can be useful for a Business Partner to ask himself/herself "am I still adding value?". Although it is often nice to be working with a good client and feeling valued by them, partners may have an increased sense that they are not doing anything the client groups can't do for themselves. At this time, done properly, partners will enhance their credibility by stepping out of the project.

## Ensure you follow-up

It is critical that partners maintain the relationship they have built with the client group, so whilst they need to be clear that their role in the project is ending, they should also find ways to keep the contact going to continue the relationship. Follow-up dates are very useful, not only in reviewing the project, but also as a way of legitimising continued personal contact with the client and key stakeholders.

## Reviewing the effectiveness of the client–partner relationship

The end of a project is a good time to review your effectiveness as a Business Partner. In addition to evaluating the success of a particular project, which is discussed in more detail in Chapter 11, it can also be an ideal time to review the effectiveness of your relationship with the client. Where you have a constant client within the business, the appraisal process may also provide an established review point, as is the case within *Barclays* and the *Inland Revenue*. In the *Inland Revenue* the customer account managers establish a customer agreement at the start of each project and when the project is completed they evaluate the performance of the consulting partner as part of their performance appraisal.

The review is likely to cover a number of different aspects, depending on the length and complexity of the partnership project. In many organisations, such as the *BBC*, the process starts with a self-assessment, sometimes using the aid of a tick-box questionnaire. The questionnaire is also given to the client to complete and is used as a framework for the discussion, which follows. Generally, reviews take place in a number of different ways, which include:

■ Self-reviews – assessing your own performance;
■ Client feedback;
■ Feedback from the client system;
■ Project process reviews;
■ Business Partner function reviews; and
■ Project outcome reviews.

### Assessing your own performance

The Business Partner behaviours, outlined in Section 2, provide a useful frame for assessing performance, both from your own and from the client's perspective. The behavioural framework has been adapted into an assessment questionnaire outlined in Appendix A. Many organisations we spoke to had established competency frameworks that were used for self-assessment in a similar way.

Thomas and Elbeik (1996) also provide some useful checklists for carrying out a review of your own performance as an internal consultant. Some of the key questions which they suggest are useful to reflect on include:

- To what extent were the original goals met?
- Did the project stay within budget?
- Was the project delivered on time?
- What did I do well on this project?
- What would I do differently if I were to do it again?
- How effective was my relationship with the client?
- Was I always open and honest in my dealings?
- Have I left a positive impression with my client?
- What elements of this project can I use as an example of best practice?

## Assessment from the client system

The client system includes not just the clients themselves, but also other members of the project team, customers, sponsors, other stakeholders and key contacts throughout the project. There are advantages in gaining feedback on the relationship as well as the project. It can often help the partners' credibility by admitting that their approach was not perfect and establish a firmer foundation for future to work together.

Many organisations, such as *Royal and Sun Alliance*, use 360-degree feedback to provide data from a wider source within the client system. However, often more valuable than a questionnaire is the opportunity to hold structured interviews with the client system. Particular questions that could form the basis of a structured interview are:

- What do they see as my main contribution to the project?
- What specific actions helped in meeting the project goals?
- What specific actions hindered or delayed meeting the project goals?
- What could I have done differently to be more effective?
  - How proactive was I?
  - How prompt was I in dealing with queries?
  - How professional was I?
  - Were there any aspects I needed to understand better?
- How effective was the communication between us?
  - Did we have good rapport?
  - Did we have a high level of trust?
  - Was I listening as well as I could?
- Was the level of involvement appropriate?
- Did my service provide value for money?

**Table 8.1**   Client Rating Scale

| Business partner is... | | Business partner is... |
|---|---|---|
| Challenging | ⊢┼┼┼┼┼┼┼┼┤ | Accepting |
| Clear | ⊢┼┼┼┼┼┼┼┼┤ | Unclear |
| Practical | ⊢┼┼┼┼┼┼┼┼┤ | Theoretical |
| Provides value for money | ⊢┼┼┼┼┼┼┼┼┤ | Over priced |
| Open and friendly | ⊢┼┼┼┼┼┼┼┼┤ | Distant and defensive |
| Trustworthy and honest | ⊢┼┼┼┼┼┼┼┼┤ | Not to be trusted |
| Efficient with time | ⊢┼┼┼┼┼┼┼┼┤ | Wastes time |
| Develops joint solutions | ⊢┼┼┼┼┼┼┼┼┤ | Imposes solutions |
| Credible | ⊢┼┼┼┼┼┼┼┼┤ | Lacking in confidence |
| Willing to adapt and change | ⊢┼┼┼┼┼┼┼┼┤ | Inflexible/resistant |
| A true partner | ⊢┼┼┼┼┼┼┼┼┤ | Unequal partner |

- Would they recommend you for other projects?
- How could I do a better job if we were to work together again?

A visual continuum is another good way for Business Partners to understand whether they are achieving the right balance in their approach to the client relationship. An example of the types of scales that might be appropriate is shown in Table 8.1.

## Reviewing the effectiveness of the project

In addition to reviewing the effectiveness of the relationship between the Business Partner and the client, there is also benefit to be gained from reviewing the way the project was managed. Often these discussions can get mixed together. Whilst this is sometimes inevitable, it can be hugely advantageous to separate the two, to prevent the discussion taking a bias towards either the relationship or project issues. Particular interventions or projects will benefit from having their own review process, in terms of the quality and approach used. This is different again from evaluating the outcomes of a particular project, which is discussed later in this book.

It is good practice to produce either a written or verbal report at the end of each project, as this then provides a structured method for conducting a review, as well as symbolising the end of your involvement in the project to the client. The review can cover a number of different aspects, depending on the length and complexity of the partnership project. Completing a "learning log" as you progress through the project may help with the review.

The review of the project may contain:

- A review of project effectiveness, i.e. did it meet the outcomes intended?
  - Has it delivered the intended benefits?
  - Has the original problem been addressed?
- A review of the process effectiveness
  - What helped the project go smoothly?
  - Were the right people involved?
  - How effective was the communication?
  - How effective was the planning?
  - What got in the way of progress?
  - What should we do differently next time?
- A review of project and process efficiency
- Customer satisfaction
  - What do you like about the outcome?
  - What are you not so sure about?
  - Have you experienced any further problems?
  - What further changes or additions would you recommend?
- Client/others reporting on the project

Sometimes the client may need help to recognise different stakeholders' perspectives on the project and it may be appropriate to gather data from a range of sources.

This review process is not intended to evaluate the business impact, but will provide useful data to enhance the service provided.

## Utilising feedback

If you follow the guidelines set out in this chapter then you will gain a lot of information about yourself, your client and stakeholder perceptions of you and the effectiveness of the processes that were used. However, this is not the final step, as it is essential that this information does not disappear into a vacuum, never to be referred to again. Some of the Business Partners we spoke to said "*I wish I could find more time for proper reviews*", but unless you prioritise your time to incorporate reviews then it is unlikely you will be enhancing your performance at an optimum rate.

The data need to be utilised in some way to enhance the service provided and your own performance. Carrying out a mini diagnostic study on your own feedback will provide you with the insights needed to decide what actions to take forward into the future.

Members of CIPD can use the data to review their Continued Professional Development (CPD) and establish new learning targets. More importantly, credibility with clients and key stakeholders can be hugely increased by demonstrating learning from the feedback, and by working in different ways with people as a result of the learning.

## Summary

Business Partners engaging in strategic change are likely to find themselves increasingly in need of strong project management skills. Even if they are not required to do the detailed planning, an awareness of the disciplines of project management will be essential in their partnering role. Some of the more formal elements, such as risk analysis, change control protocols and critical paths may seem to some not only an alien language, but a little like obstacles to be overcome in achieving progress. However, used effectively, these tools can be immensely useful to Business Partners in engaging stakeholders and influencing people in the business.

Project management can be a huge lever for HR. Business Partners can build credibility through developing more robust business cases and ensuring that the people elements of business change projects are fundamental and built into the project planning process as opposed to being something which sits alongside.

Reviewing your performance as a Business Partner is an essential and often neglected part of the role. The information you can glean from taking time out to reflect on your performance and gather data from those around you can be invaluable in terms of providing new insights and learning to enable you to enhance your performance. Not only that, but the process of gathering the data can also help to build more solid relationships with those around you, particularly if you ensure that you act on the information you receive.

Often the difficulty in reviewing progress comes from Business Partners having difficulty in detaching themselves from particular pieces of work and clearly signalling to their clients that their involvement has ended. Contracting effectively, setting time aside in the project plan and incorporating symbols to indicate completion can help with this process.

Questioning is a vital skill of any Business Partner and this chapter contained many suggested questions to assess projects and performance both by yourself and others. More important than the questions themselves, however, is the way in which the information gleaned is used and the useful dialogues that asking such searching questions can lead you into.

## Checklist

- Does the business case engage all the stakeholders?
- Have I thought through the possible barriers to successful project completion?
- Am I using the project management disciplines to the best advantage?
- Am I continually reviewing whether I am adding value on this project?
- Do I feel as if I am still holding the client's or consumer's hand for my own benefit or for their benefit?
- Have I taken steps to signal the end of a particular project to the client?
- How do I review my own performance as a Business Partner?
- Is there a clear and effective process for reviewing the effectiveness of my relationship with the client?
- Is there a clear and effective process for reviewing each project?
- Are the customers and other stakeholders involved in any review?
- Do I make time to make sense of the feedback and analyse the data?
- Am I demonstrating learning and applying new ways of working as a result of the review process?

## References

Cannon, J. A. (2006). *Making the business case*. London: CIPD.

Reddington, M., Williamson, M., & Withers, M. (2005). *Transforming HR, creating value through people*. Oxford: Elsevier.

Thomas, M., & Elbeik, S. (1996). *Supercharge your management role: making the transition to internal consultant*. Oxford: Butterworth Heinemann.

# 2c

# Relationship Skills

Successful relationships are at the heart of the Business Partner role and to be effective you need a strong understanding of your own biases and style as well as the ability to tune into others and their links to the business. This is not an easy process and as a result, this section focuses on two of the fundamental skills in this respect:

- Developing yourself and organisational awareness
- Interpersonal skills and challenges

Developing skills in these areas will not only build your credibility as a Business Partner, but will also ensure that your day-to-day actions are clearly focused on the people to which you provide a service in the business.

This section incorporates two of the categories from the skills and behaviours highlighted in Chapter 1 and written as a self-assessment questionnaire in the Appendix. These are firstly, "Working alongside managers in the business" – which encompasses the need to operate collaboratively, empower others and maintain a people perspective; and secondly, "Self awareness and impact" – which encompasses self-expression, dynamism and continual learning.

Chapter 9 explores the use of reflective practice to develop a greater self-awareness and understanding of others in the organisation. The ability to question oneself and continually strive for self-improvement have been found to be critical to the development of effective Business Partners. This chapter also focuses on the use of power in organisations, and the need for Business Partners to take a more political stance and improve their networking capability in order to achieve greater influence. This recognises the need for Business Partners to develop their own resilience in the face of change and act as a role model for others in the organisation.

Chapter 10 focuses on developing more advanced interpersonal skills, which go beyond effective listening and questioning, which are not covered here.

Instead, this chapter explores how to develop rapport and trust with clients, particularly when the client is resisting change. The steps in building personal credibility and credibility for the HR department are discussed, along with strategies to deal with some of the pressures and challenges that are often posed.

# 9

# Developing Self and Organisational Awareness

For organisations to survive and thrive when change and uncertainty are prevalent there is an increasing need for Business Partners to go beyond the fundamentals and build their capacity to really understand themselves in the context of the organisation.

As we have explored in previous chapters, consultancy skills are key to really working alongside managers and helping them to understand and work with the organisational issues that challenge them.

If we look at the consultancy cycle, at one level it seems a straightforward process; however, in reality things are often more complex. If we take contracting, for example, we may think we have agreed a contract with our clients which is about providing a management development programme for all middle to senior managers to help them improve their ability to motivate and develop their staff. We have agreed the expected outcomes with our client and we may expect to have access to the senior management population as a way of ensuring that the changes that are needed are made effectively. However, unless this has been made explicit in the contracting stage, we may find our attempts to engage and work with the senior managers thwarted. Contracting is just one stage of the cycle that needs a more in-depth understanding and awareness to be able to really carry it out effectively.

## So what are the more advanced skills of consultancy?

To be really effective in the consultancy role, however, that is defined; we need the ability to think in different ways (as discussed in Chapter 6) and be critically reflective in our practice. More recent organisational change models highlight the importance of continual environmental scanning, so that the organisation is adaptable and ready for change (Stacey, 1996). In the same way, consultants need to be continually able to tune into their own practice; reflect and evaluate what they are doing in the moment and match that to what is happening outside in the group, organisation or other system in which they are working. It is also about the ability to draw together underpinning theory and knowledge and apply this, together with a heightened self-awareness, in day-to-day practice.

At the top of the model below "reflective practice" is shown as the end result of a number of other key aspects of advanced consulting (Figure 9.1).

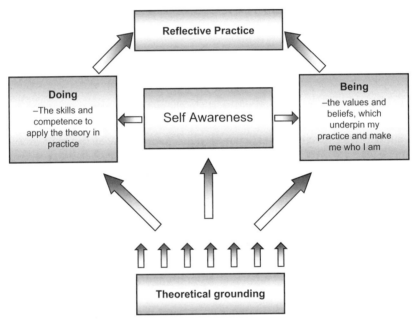

**Figure 9.1** Kenton and Moody (2004).

Let's take each of these in turn:

## Theoretical underpinning

As most, if not all people, applying consultancy skills within an organisational context will be facilitating change at some level, certain underpinning theory will be helpful to understand.

Below are some examples of theoretical underpinning that might be helpful for Business Partners:

- Organisational development and culture – models of culture, systems theory and thinking, models of OD

- Organisational design – models of organisational design, business process mapping, designing organisational structures, aligning strategy and structure
- Organisational and group dynamics – stages of group development, team roles and preferences, theories of conflict and behaviour, psychodynamic theory
- Change theory – transition curve, linear and complex change, emergent and chaotic models, large scale interventions for rapid change
- Business strategy – links to HR strategy, business process management, business performance measurement
- Quality systems
- Research methods – including quantitative and qualitative research, grounded theory, action research, project management
- Learning and development methods – what they are and how they can be applied – in what contexts – coaching, mentoring, shadowing, action learning and projects (for example).

At a more advanced level of consulting, the practitioners will need to go beyond understanding the theories and be able to judge what they mean in the context in which they are working; drawing on relevant theory in the moment and, where appropriate, bringing this awareness into conversations with the client. We do not intend to go into all these theories in more depth in this book. However, the reader is referred to our recommended reading section at the end.

## Awareness of self, others and the system as a whole

We all have a level of self-awareness, which helps us to exist in the world. I am aware that I am hungry and I eat (although even some of these basic levels of awareness are becoming under developed). For those of us in roles that involve helping other people and organisations, our level of self-awareness needs to be more acute. "Getting our own house in order" is an expression which is often used in relation to the helping professions and while most of us might not be professional counsellors, there will still be a requirement to deal with some of the "messiness" that goes with organisational and personal change in-terventions. It is important for those of us working as consultants and/or using consultancy skills to be aware of the interventions that we make and the likely impact on others. This includes how we behave from moment to moment and our personal process as well as the more content-driven processes and

171

interventions that we might make. A fictitious example here might help to elaborate on this point:

> *Debbie is a Business Partner at Performican. She has been called in at short notice to a meeting with Mr Jones, one of the senior managers and is feeling a bit flustered about what he may want. Shortly after arriving in his office it is clear that he expects her to come up with some expert suggestions about how to increase low morale in his team, which has escalated to the point of someone walking out that morning. Debbie knows the individual and is concerned and anxious about how he may feel and the impact on the other team members but feels unable to say this. Instead, under the pressure of time and Mr Jones's insistence that she "sorts something out quickly", Debbie finds herself promising to facilitate a meeting with the team that afternoon.*

This example raises a couple of important points about self-awareness as a key part of the advanced consultancy skill set:

- Knowing and paying attention to any ingrained patterns of behaviour that we might have. For example, drivers such as "please me" or "try hard" (Berne, 1969);
- Paying attention to our ability to keep grounded in challenging situations;
- Paying attention to our needs and emotions from moment to moment;
- Recognising what is happening in the here and now and how we are reacting on both an emotional and a behavioural level;
- Being able to self-evaluate the effectiveness of our reactions and responses;
- Knowing what our strengths are and hooks, triggers and limitations; and
- Knowing when our own overall health and well-being needs attention.

If we are self-aware, then even if our behaviour is in some way inappropriate given the situation, it can be rectified. So Debbie, in the example above, may have been aware of how she was feeling about the situation in Mr Jones's team and consciously decided not to disclose these. Facilitation of the team meeting might be a useful intervention, if Debbie is consciously choosing to do this from a basis of self-awareness, rather than as a reaction to Mr Jones's insistence that some-thing is done quickly.

Self-awareness can be thought of as part of our "*Being*" and "*Doing*". Doing is about our competencies to fulfil our role; having the skills set to carry this out and the tools and techniques to be effective. The toolkit, if you will of the Business Partner including the technical aspects of consultancy.

Debbie in the example above has a CIPD qualification and good facilitation skills, she is accredited to use psychometric instruments and has built up good knowledge and skills in facilitating change over a period of 10 years. She has the skills to coach individuals and experience in facilitating numerous events for managers and teams in challenging change situations. This knowledge and skills set make up the "doing" part of what makes Debbie effective. Her self-awareness will let her know where her strengths are on the doing side and where she might need further development.

"Being" is more about the energy we bring, our personality, our integrity and ability to relate to the client at some human level. So this is about who Debbie fundamentally is as a person; her values, beliefs and sense of self. This side can be strongly developed as in a healthy plant; like an early shoot that needs some attention, or even an unfertilised seed. Being clear about our values and beliefs can strengthen our capacity to work congruently with our clients. Debbie may want to re-check some of her beliefs in working with managers in the organisation and consider the implications of these. For example if she believes:

■ The more senior the manager the more respect he/she needs to be given;
■ Her role is to provide the service as specified by the manager;
■ That she must have all the answers all of the time;
■ That doing something is better than doing nothing;
■ That the manager's needs are more important than the members of his team; and
■ That she should never say no.

The list is not definitive! You can see how these beliefs may lead to ineffective behaviour in this situation. However, Debbie may have a healthy, strong and supportive set of beliefs, which are then not played out in her behaviour. This mismatch can lead to incongruence. Therefore, Business Partners applying consultancy skills well will be able to identify when their behaviour is congruent with their beliefs and the values of the organisation and when they are not.

## Reflective practice

*So what then is reflective practice and how does it link to the advanced consultancy skills set?*

Schon (1983, 1987) challenges the conventional view of professional practice in that practitioners need to draw, not only on their technical knowledge and specialist skills, but also to draw on tacit knowledge and understanding, which he calls "knowing-in-action", learning how to re-frame difficult problems into situations which can be helped. This is more about the art of consultancy than the science. This capacity to reflect, both in day-to-day practice and as part of our continuous development is, according to Schon the key to professional practice.

If Debbie in our earlier example had the ability to reflect well, a number of things might have happened. Her reflection in the moment may have highlighted how she was feeling about the situation, and she may have decided to disclose her own reactions to the news of the recently departed team member. By role modelling congruence in this way, Debbie may allow the manager to get in touch with his own feelings about what has happened.

By reflecting after the event, Debbie may have pondered on how Mr Jones was acting and made links to both her experience of him in other situations and her knowledge and understanding of people and how they react in change situations. For example Mr Jones may have been quite shocked at the sudden departure of one of his team members and projected blame onto Debbie. Her understanding of group dynamics may have given her some insights into how the team was responding to a relatively new boss and other changes that had taken place recently. By being able to reflect both in the moment and afterwards, Debbie's choices of interventions are immediately increased.

Part of the advanced skills set is the ability to bring our reflections on what is really going on into conversations appropriately.

## The use of power in organisations

To understand the organisation, its culture and ways of working, we also need to consider the question of power – what it is, whose got it, how they use it and how to draw on power to help us achieve our objectives. Power does not have to mean domination, rather it can be thought of as energy, or drive, to achieve goals.

### Power bases

Power in an organisation can be used constructively or destructively. The uncontrolled use of power in an organisation can mean that people achieve their goals at the expense of others or the organisation overall. We all need enough power to enable us to get things done, and a first step is recognising what power we have.

There are many sources of power that people have in organisations – often without realising it. It is important not to overlook the power of the stationary clerk for example or the finance manager. One reason to consider power bases is that you have an idea about what power the people you want to influence have. Another is to consider for yourselves which of the following you already have and which you could usefully increase towards greater organisational influence. Examples of power bases are the following:

- Resources – to give out or to take away resources such as people, money and equipment;
- Information – access to information which might be useful to other's in the organisation;
- Specialist knowledge – this could be on a range of topics, for example reward strategies, quality management tools, etc.;
- Status/authority – this might link to position but could also be job title or role;
- Position – in an hierarchical organisation, the higher up in the organisation, the more power someone will tend to have;
- Reward – to be able to reward people by for example giving them a good appraisal, or a pay rise, or the ability to take these away;
- Reputation – being able to command respect based on previous deeds
- Interpersonal – using good interpersonal skills to create impact and respect;
- Personal – a sense of self-worth which creates personal presence in the company of others; and
- Political – a good understanding of the informal networks, how these work and how to use them to influence others.

Which of the above do you have now? And which could you build on? Which are valued most highly in your organisation?

In our experience the sources of power, which have either remained constant or are on the increase are interpersonal, personal and political. In the knowledge age, specialist knowledge and information will often have credit too. Status/authority and positional power tend to be on the decrease in organisations that are flatter for a quicker response to change.

## Understanding the politics

As well as thinking about the sources of power that you and your internal clients will be operating from, an understanding of the organisational politics will be key to influencing successfully.

Politics with a small "p" within an organisation can still have negative connotations. We often come across individuals who are working in an internal consultancy role who would prefer not to engage with the organisational politics. However, it may depend on whether you view political activity as neutral, negative or positive. Linda Holbeche's research on political activity in organisations draws on data from 120 professionals across Directors/senior managers and middle managers (one focus group consisted of HR professionals) (Holbeche, 2002).

In the research, respondents rated political behaviour in the following ways:

- Using strategies to achieve personal goals at the expense of others/the organisation (27%)
- Using strategies to achieve personal goals irrespective of the impact on others/ the organisation (33%)
- Using strategies to achieve personal goals which also benefit others and/or the organisation (40%).

Interestingly, in the last category women respondents outnumbered men (25% to 16%).

Some of the other findings from the research are shown below:

- 65% of respondents agreed that political behaviour is part of natural human behaviour
- Men were slightly more inclined to see politics as natural human behaviour (38%, with women at 27%)
- 63% of survey respondents agreed with the statement "people engage in political behaviour as a defence mechanism"
- 87% of respondents felt that political behaviour was most likely to occur in large organisations
- 49% thought organisational politics was on the increase, 44% said they thought it was about the same over the last three years and 7% felt there was less politics.

## What does it mean to be political and to have political skills?

This links closely for us to questions of ethics for Business Partners, which are discussed in more detail in the next chapter. However, it will certainly include having an understanding of the informal networks and the culture of the organisation and using that knowledge and understanding in a way that best serves the business and the individuals within it.

James and Baddeley (1987) developed a four-part model to highlight different aspects of political understanding and behaviour. These include the ability to "read" and understand the political environment and "carry" certain political behaviours into situations. The levels of awareness are shown from "politically unaware" to "politically aware" and the behaviours and skills from "psychological game playing" to "acting with integrity". The skills shown on the left-hand side of the model tend to be more focused on achieving personal goals at the expense of others and on the right-hand side behaviour which has the organisational needs in mind.

## Model

Business Partners will need to be skilled at both understanding the political environment and acting in a way which best serves the organisation and individuals within it. The model can also help in developing our awareness of other's behaviour and how best to respond, particularly with individuals you want or need to influence.

### What it means to be an innocent sheep

When individuals come into an organisation they may be unwittingly acting as "innocent sheep" in that there is a sense of naivety about how things really work in the organisation. So if the policy says all annual leave needs to be agreed by the senior manager, the assumption may be that that is the reality. The innocent sheep may find in practice leave is taken on a first come first served basis and they miss out on taking leave at their preferred time. By sticking to the rules and acting on principles, the innocent sheep is at risk of being attacked or gobbled up by the fox!

### Possible actions for supporting innocent sheep

It does not necessarily pay for the organisation to have too many people in this category, partly because it is more about maintaining the status quo than engaging with the change process. Some ideas on developing innocent sheep include:

- Having a good induction scheme which talks about the values and culture of the organisation as well as the overt rules and policies
- Having a buddy system, so that individuals can draw on the experience of others to find their way around the informal systems
- Training programmes which cover political skills and influencing
- Offering a mentor – using some of the wise owls in the organisation.

### What it means to be an inept donkey

The inept donkey according to the James and Baddeley model describes someone who is still politically unaware, but through their own self-interest engage in psychological game playing. This term comes from Transactional Analysis (Berne, 1969) and demonstrates how people get their needs met at a psychological level, through their interactions with others. The donkey then is someone who is emotionally illiterate and uses unprincipled and unethical interventions to get noticed and increase their influence.

However, because this is done in a somewhat clumsy way, you may notice a lack of tact and diplomacy here. Examples would include disclosing unhelpful gossip in an inappropriate environment, the proverbial "putting one's foot in it".

## Possible actions for supporting inept donkeys

You may feel that donkey behaviour needs to be ignored or put down, as it certainly seems to be an unhelpful and possibly destructive set of behaviours. However, it is difficult to really be clear about the intention of using this behaviour, without knowing the individual concerned. If, for example, we believe that everyone's behaviour has a positive intention for that person, i.e. they have a basic need, which gets met by their behaviour at some level, we might approach it differently. Certainly left to their own devices, people behaving in this way can cause an annoyance at best and provoke conflict and tension amongst others at worst. Here are some options for dealing with donkey behaviour:

- Pick up on any underlying message – for example: "are you really saying that all the support staff performing under the standards expected?"
- Pick up on any underlying feelings – for example: "You sound angry about being left out of that decision"
- Give direct feedback – for example "I feel uncomfortable about you talking about George when he isn't here and would prefer you talk to him directly"
- Ask questions to find out what their needs are, for example, to be more directly involved in things or for greater social contact.
- Involve them more – it may be that showing some trust is just what they need.

## What it means to be a clever fox

When we include a session around organisational politics in any of our programmes for Business Partners or managers, the behaviour that most people recognise readily is that of clever fox. This set of behaviours includes the ability to read the organisational politics and use it to one's own advantage. It differs from the inept donkey in that it is a much more subtle set of behaviours and skills. It could include someone who is in a post for a short period of time and gets their objectives met, but at the expense of others around them. The fall-out from this behaviour is not always seen until after the event, if at all. There is a charming veneer, which disguises the intention in a way, which makes it difficult to spot. This individual can recognise the power bases and use them well, exploiting weaknesses to meet their end goal. Sometimes in organisations this behaviour is seen as valid and is actively encouraged and valued. It often will mean that short-term goals are met, as with other aggressive behaviour strategies. However, the long-term implications are usually serious. It can create an environment where people are "watching their backs" and levels of trust and openness are low.

Possible actions for dealing with the clever fox:

Here, more than with the other behaviours, you may well be questioning the need to support the clever fox, although the same question applies to the fox as to the donkey: "what needs are not being met, which results in expressing behaviour in this way?" As a first step you might try some of the strategies mentioned for the inept donkey. However, you could spend a lot of time and energy trying to understand the behaviour, when what you may need to do is limit the damage done by the clever fox. As a first question it will be important to be clear about the behaviour and whether it really is clever fox or wise owl. Your reading of the situation will be key to this. Is the behaviour fundamentally serving the purpose of meeting the individual's needs at the expense of others and/or the organisation? If you are not sure, you may want to check out some of your assumptions before jumping to conclusions. Some suggested actions for dealing with clever fox behaviour are shown below:

- Use your observation and listening skills to really hear and understand the behaviour.
- Check out any assumptions, by asking questions of those who might be impacted by the behaviour – for example: "how did Jo's decision affect you/your team?" Try to remain neutral.
- Find out where their allies and enemies are and get to know them – what is their experience of this person.
- Use some of the skills referred to for dealing with donkey behaviour – pick up on the process as well as content of what is being said but be careful about how you do this and in what company!
- Support others who might need help in dealing with the behaviour. Use your coaching skills.
- Chunk up important decisions, which will impact on other teams or the organisation more widely. At meetings, bring these wider issues to the attention of the group. For example – "how will this affect the finance people? And our longer term strategy?"
- Choose methods for your projects which include a wider range of diverse people, so that it is not just the clever foxes who get to say how things should move forward.

## What it means to be a wise owl

We should say at this stage that rather than seeming to label everyone else's behaviour around these descriptions, in our view, we can all be behaving in some of these ways at any time. This is more about being attuned to the behaviours that are displayed by individuals in organisations including ourselves and giving consideration to some of the choices we may have about how we deal with them. Wise owl behaviour in the model is about understanding the political terrain and acting with integrity. The wise owl has not only the interests of others at heart, but also the interests of the organisation. They are interpersonally skilled and politically sensitive. In our view, this does not mean being totally open all the time. Rather, it is about paying attention to what is going on between different people and groups in the organisation; understanding the nature of the business and what needs to happen to get the business needs met and using their sources of power in a way which supports others rather than subjugates them.

Using wise owls in the organisation and developing more wise owl behaviour

Fortunately, many people we have worked with also recognise the wise owl behaviour in their organisations. These tend to be the people who have earned respect and credibility and are both approachable and diplomatic. It should be stressed here that these are not necessarily people who are at the most senior level of the organisation. They do though recognise their own sources of power and use these to help others and the organisation overall.

- Use wise owls to mentor others in the organisation;
- Get them involved in championing specific projects and influencing others in the organisation;
- Use them as a role model – notice what they do and how they do it, if you want to develop more of these skills for yourself;
- Ask for their views at important meetings if they are not being expressed and get the organisational take from them to widen other's perspectives;
- Is there anyone amongst the wise owls who would be a good mentor or coach for you?
- Develop your own political awareness. Talk to people in the organisation about its history and listen to stories about how things are done around here;
- Keep in mind the first, second, third and fourth perceptual positions, to make sure you are paying attention to the wider needs; and
- Get feedback on how you are perceived in terms of your political skills and sensitivity. This could be either by way of 360-degree feedback or more informally from people you trust and know will be honest.

## Networking

Ask anyone who works as an external consultant about the importance of networking and they will be quick to confirm, that their success will be in part as a result of the networks they have built. A lot of time and effort will often be put effective. This might include spending some time talking with colleagues in your immediate work environment; having an internal or external coach or mentor; being able to discuss work issues with a supportive partner or family member (although beware here that you're not offloading too much on to one individual); belonging to appropriate professional networks; and regular and planned meetings with colleagues in a similar role. The use of learning sets or support and challenge groups can also be extremely helpful to maintain effective practice.

## Commit to continuous professional development

In our view, no one should be in a supportive profession without making a commitment to continuous professional development. How you do this, will be very much up to you – it might include training programmes, coaching, mentoring, reading, writing articles, attending network meetings and so on. The list of possibilities here is quite long. Make sure that some of the development focuses on you getting to know you better.

## Summary

Key skills for Business Partners and internal consultants will include: organisational and business awareness; influencing and political skills; excellent interpersonal skills; specialists HR skills, consultancy and change management skills. Above all, though, the ability to understand the organisation as a system and develop the skills of a reflective practitioner will be key to success in the role. Developing your understanding of how organisations and systems work, together with an ability to reflect on your practice both in the moment and between actions will help you to make more informed choices about how you work with your clients and within the organisation.

In certain professions such as law and medicine, practitioners are required to commit to a number of days per year for their continuous professional development. While this is not the case at the moment for Business Partners, we recommend that you build in time to develop your own practice each year. Working with others in a supportive capacity means you are offering them expertise and advice which need to be kept up to date. Having some clarity about what is happening in the wider business world, your own particular niche and your organisation in particular will help inform your work and the advice you offer to others. Knowing the self and developing your self-awareness and resilience will also help you to be more grounded practitioner.

## Checklist

- What are you doing right now to develop your self-awareness and awareness of others?
- Have you established regular links with other Business Partners/internal consultants in the organisation to discuss how your work links with theirs?
- Have you established a personal development plan for yourself towards continual professional development?
- What reading/research are you doing to update your knowledge and skills on how organisations and systems work?
- Have you targeted specific individuals who can help you understand the organisation or parts of it better?
- Have you established a good support network?
- Are you taking time for reflection each day?
- Have you got at least one project which stretches you at the moment?
- Have you got too many and if so, what are you doing to limit the number of these?
- Are your feedback systems in place and working?
- Have you clarified your job purpose?
- Are you clear about the boundaries of your role?
- What strategies have you got in place for influencing change? And how do you know if they are working?
- Which sources of power are you actively engaged in building?

## References

Belbin, M. (1993). *Team roles and work*. Oxford: Butterworth-Heinemann.

Berne, E. (1969). *The games people play*. London: Penguin.

Holbeche, L. (2002). *Politics in organisations in conjunction with Director Magazine*. Horsham: Roffey Park Institute.

James, K., & Baddeley, S. (1987). "Owl, Fox, Donkey or Sheep: Political Skills for Managers". *Management Education and Development, 18*(Pt1), 3–19.

Kenton, B., & Moody, D. (2003). The Role of the Internal Consultant. Horsham: Roffey Park Institute.

Schon, D. (1983). *The reflective practitioner: How professionals think in action*. London: Maraca Temple Smith.

Schon, D. (1987). *The reflective practitioner: How professionals think in action*. London: Maraca Temple Smith.

Stacey, R. D. (1996). *Complexity and creativity in organisations*. San Francisco: Berret-Koehler Publishers Inc.

# 10

# Interpersonal Skills and Challenges

*"For us it comes down to 3 things – Relationships, Relationships, Relationships and through these enabling our clients to do so much more for themselves"*

Jean Floodgate, The Body Shop International

It is almost impossible to describe the numerous immeasurable factors that go into creating an effective relationship between Business Partners and their clients. However, it is clear that before you can even begin to build a sound relationship with a new client, you need to develop good rapport and empathy with them. Once you have a good rapport, you need to start to build your own credibility as a Business Partner and operate within a set of values that show integrity and professionalism. As if that isn't enough, effective Business Partners also need to be able to deal with the pressures and conflicts that are likely to emerge during the course of a project. Business pressures as well as political pressures from within organisations are part of everyday life, and the ability of Business Partners to deal effectively with these pressures is critical in sustaining an effective role.

## Developing rapport and empathy with your client

### Understand the client's perspective

Clients like to feel comfortable with the person they are dealing with, and one way to build and sustain rapport with your client is to identify common interests or values. If rapport does not come easily to the relationship, then showing a genuine interest in and understanding of the issues and constraints facing the client can go a long way. The Business Partner needs to put himself/herself in the client's shoes and gain a real understanding of the client's personal and business goals from his/her partner's perspective.

## Be genuine

There is a strong temptation when faced with a client to adapt your style and suggestions to suit what the client is explicitly asking for and the way they operate. This is particularly the case when there is a perception that the Business Partners' credibility stems from demonstrating their expertise and that their added value comes from providing lots of ideas and answers to questions. Ineffective Business Partners who follow this approach will soon find that they are putting forward suggestions and ideas that they themselves are unsure of. Whilst it is true that Business Partners do need to draw on some expertise, partners who have a mindset that it is the client who adds the value (as they hold the real key to the problem or the situation) find it much easier to show a genuine interest in the client's issues and work with their agenda to help move the project forward. The evidence suggests that the people whom clients continue to use are those who think about and are genuinely interested in what the clients' needs are and how to address them, rather than continually suggesting their own preferred approach. Business Partners should still use their own expertise, knowledge and ideas, but need to tailor them to the context of the client.

## Go beyond the expressed needs

Developing rapport requires the Business Partner to empathise with the clients and understand not just the words being said but their thoughts, emotions and interests as well. A truly collaborative approach is rarely reached by working only on the expressed needs of the client. Valued relationships between clients and Business Partners operate at a deeper level, where both have professional as well as personal trust in each other.

There is a need to listen to what is *meant* rather than what is *said* by the client. This entails picking up on clues in the client's body language and emotions and reflecting back your interpretation. For example, when a client says "That might work" this could either mean the client really does believe it will work, or that there is a small possibility, or that it is unlikely to work for them. Partners need to sense any lack of conviction in the client and ask questions to draw out the true meaning behind the words. In this case, the Business Partner might say, "I am getting the feeling that you are not really sure it will work – tell me why that is". Given that only about 7–10% of the impact of communication comes from the words that are used, tuning into the non-verbal cues and the tone of voice is essential. It is not possible to overstate the importance of active listening, paraphrasing and checking understanding as key skills for an effective Business Partner. Effective partners are likely to do twice as much listening as talking.

## Understand the whole person

To gain empathy Business Partners need a real understanding of their clients on a number of different levels.

- Character: How do they operate? What are their preferred ways of working?
- Perspectives: How do they see the future? What do they see as the company's position?
- Motivation: What is their interest in the project? How important is it to them? What really motivates them in their role?
- Values: What principles drive the way they operate?
- Understanding of the pressures on the client at that moment:
  - The political situation
  - Their relationship with their peers
  - Their relationship with their seniors
  - The marketplace
  - Their satisfaction with work
  - Factors affecting them in their home life
  - Their hot-spots

## Understand your own biases

In order to be sure of your own biases, it is useful to have a clear understanding of your own personality type as a Business Partner. People tend to ask questions within their own frame of reference and when we hear something we attempt to evaluate it, rationalise it and make an interpretation in a way that makes sense to our own models of behaviour. The more you have an understanding of what your own filters are, the easier it is to suspend judgement for a longer period and seek to expand your own frame of reference to allow an increased number of possibilities. As an example, a Business Partner may have a bias towards team-building activities as a way of improving relationships within teams. It may be that they have had a lot of success with this method in the past. However, it may be that the situation presented has an underlying problem that would make team building less effective on this occasion, and jumping too early into discussing possible solutions will limit the partner's ability to understand the complexity of the situation and reach a more effective resolution. The less quick you are to judge as a Business Partner, the more likely it is that you will reach an optimal solution.

## Establishing and maintaining trust

Developing rapport and empathy with your clients is the first stepping-stone in building their trust. How you choose to operate and act beyond this will determine whether you can sustain your position and build trust and credibility (as shown in Figure 10.1).

### Manage expectations

People buy from people and a client will only continue to use you if you establish trust.

However, trust can easily be destroyed and is particularly impacted by taking risks, which may backfire. Without encouraging some risk-taking, however, it is unlikely that the Business Partner will be adding significant value to the business. So, what is important is that the partner manages the client's expectations when faced with a risky situation. Face-to-face time with the client is essential, not only in providing an opportunity to set and manage expectations, but also in helping to increase the level of rapport and empathy. Pfau and Cundiff (2002) argue that one of the key factors in establishing trust is for the Business Partner to help stakeholders understand the strategic human-capital issues facing their organisation and to explain the rationale behind change-related decisions. Only in this way will the client group understand what the Business Partner is trying to achieve.

**Figure 10.1** The building blocks to trusting relationships.

## Show loyalty

Loyalty is an important part of trust. If your client always comes second or third on your list of priorities, they are likely to sense this and will feel that you can't be trusted. Partners can demonstrate loyalty by putting the client's agenda first.

## Deliver on what you say you are going to deliver on

Trust is usually broken by not following through on actions, or letting your client down in some way. This may sound straightforward, but the quickest way to lose both trust and credibility is to not todo what you have committed to up front. Even if there are perfectly valid reasons why something is not happening as planned, it is important that this is communicated effectively to *all* involved, or you risk damaging your reputation. Trust is broken very quickly and clients may not explicitly tell you that they are unhappy. The first indication that trust is broken is likely to be a slight change in behaviour towards you and a sense that there is a vague dissatisfaction, which is not being aired. Regaining trust is hard work, and it is much better to admit mistakes or inability to follow through on promises before the client finds out.

## Respect confidentiality

With an effective partnership, confidentiality issues are addressed up front and it is clear who has access to what and which conversations are open and which are not. This is not always easy to sustain as an internal Business Partner. Often you will be asked for other people's views or for your own perceptions of individuals or situations and it is not always clear how open you should be. It is important to avoid criticising others or being indiscreet if you want to maintain a sense of trustworthiness. Coupled with this is a need for Business Partners to have a strong sense of what their own principles are, so that when they are faced with difficult situations it is immediately clear which path to follow.

## Building credibility

Credibility is critical both for the partnership function as a whole, in terms of its marketing and perceived value, as well as at an individual level. Table 10.1 illustrates the key factors in establishing credibility for both aspects.

**Table 10.1**  Key Determinants of Credibility

| Individual credibility | Functional credibility |
|---|---|
| ■ Work on the client's agenda | ■ Increase visibility |
| ■ Go for quick wins | ■ Understand the business |
| ■ Be proactive in providing information | ■ Use appropriate procedures |
| ■ Use your expertise appropriately | ■ Gain relevant qualifications |
| ■ Have conviction in what you say and do | ■ Pull in expertise from outside when it is needed |
| ■ Work only in areas that add value | ■ Stay in touch with the market |
| ■ Be responsive | |
| ■ Don't get emotionally drawn in | |
| ■ Always get buy-in to the solution | |
| ■ Present messages carefully | |

## Individual credibility

### Work with the clients on their agenda

Credibility comes from working with the clients on their agenda rather than your own. To be truly credible you need to get a real understanding of where the client is in relation to the project and use listening, empathising and questioning techniques to great effect in order to draw the links between what is being said and the bigger picture.

### Establish some quick wins

Individual credibility is built primarily from positive feedback from significant players in the organisation. When first starting out "quick wins" are useful for establishing a reputation for delivering change. "Clients for Life" (Sheth & Sobel, 2000), and "The trusted advisor" (Maister, Green, & Galford, 2002) describe how Business Partners always need to start from the position of being a hired expert and that the first step in building a longer term relationship is to move to become a steady supplier. This move comes from showing reliability in what you do and doing what is expected. Once you are a steady supplier for a particular client, then you can strive to the position of "trusted advisor", where the Business partner can add real value by working collaboratively with the client to help provide real insights. They argue that you cannot expect to start a relationship in a truly collaborative way (as shown in Figure 10.2).

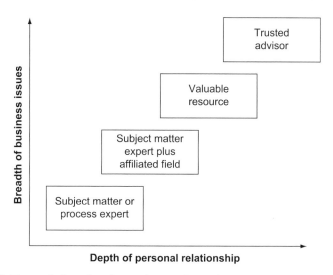

**Figure 10.2** The evolution of a client–advisor relationship.
Source: Drawn from Maister et al. (2002).

However, despite this being a natural development of the role, there are dangers if the quick wins are not utilising the whole range of partnership skills. An internal consultant from *HBOS* described to us how during the restructuring of the Royal Bank of Scotland, they had been primarily used in a purchase–sale role and were attempting to re-position their Business Partnership as more of a process role. However, they found that you soon get a reputation for delivering in a certain role and that it is then difficult to break the mould. They managed to find a way round this by getting in on the early stages of strategy discussions, before the diagnosis began. This does serve as a word of warning, however, that if your quick wins are based on effective implementation and delivery of projects it may not be as easy to develop into a partnership role and that quick wins carrying out effective diagnosis or design may be a more useful starting place.

## Be proactive in providing information

Anticipating information which may be useful to your client can provide a real opportunity to gain unexpected praise or positive feedback. Clients are often too busy to keep on top of all the management information which may be useful to them and unexpectedly being presented with something pertinent to their issues can be very powerful in leveraging your credibility. Having the client's agenda in mind when going about other things may lead to you picking up on thoughts, ideas or written documentation which is of use to their project. Surprising your client with information they haven't asked for can be very useful in building your relationship as well as benefiting the business.

## Use your expertise appropriately

If you are positioning yourself as an expert in a particular aspect of the project, it is important that you do have this expertise. You need to be honest about what you know and what you don't or the client group will see through you.

There is a difficult balance between credibility and expertise. If you ask clients what they value in a Business Partner it is not often that they state expert knowledge at the top of the list. More often the ability to trigger thoughts and ideas in the client is the skill that is most valued. If Business Partners continue to provide sound expertise without building a strong relationship then it is likely that eventually the client will go elsewhere to buy the same expertise at a cheaper price.

## Have conviction in what you say and do

Although Business Partners often have concerns that a decision is not based on sufficient data or that it appears based more on intuition than fact, if you believe in a particular course of action then credibility can come through pursuing it with conviction. The beliefs and passions of Business Partners can help to create an energy which influences the client system and helps to move a project forward when people have doubts.

## Work in areas that add value

In order to be seen as credible, Business Partners may need to turn away work when it is not appropriate. Working as an internal consultant may mean that you get asked to do work that is helpful for your client, but doesn't add value to the business. Often there is a pressure on internals to help out in these situations, but doing this on a long-term basis will damage both your credibility and your perceived value.

There may also be occasions where there is work that will add value, but you do not have the time or resources to take on the task and give it your full attention. Much as you would like to work on a particular project or with a particular client, doing so at this time would leave you overstretched and consequently ineffective as a Business Partner. Effective partners will be assertive with their clients when these issues emerge and will be honest about the situation.

## Don't get emotionally drawn in

If a project or situation is interesting it is likely that there will be conflicting views emerging and this may lead to heightened emotions. It is critical that partners

196

remain calm and level-headed about the situation in order to take a more rational view. Conveying energy and interest is important, but emotional involvement will restrict your ability to see the bigger picture. In order to do this, individuals need to have a clear sense of their own emotions and biases and put these to one side. Having said this, it is also important that Business Partners pay attention to what their own emotions may be telling them and use these feelings to raise any concerns or ideas that they may have.

## Get buy-in to the solution

If you are working effectively as a partnership then the client will have worked with you to develop a solution. However, not all clients have the time or interest to devote to projects and you may find yourself working in a harmonious way with a great deal of delegated authority. Whilst it may be clear to both you and the client that the decision on what will happen is down to you, it is still essential that you deliver what is expected by the client. It is imperative that you take the time to explain your intentions and rationale as early in the process as possible, in order to ensure that the client gains some ownership for the solution. You sometimes need to educate your client in order for them to understand your value.

## Be responsive

A client needs to be able to count on you to do what you say you are going to do. Partners need to be both consistent and reliable, as clients wants to know where they stand and what they can expect from you. Business Partners need to be responsive in a number of aspects:

- Timings: Being flexible with scheduling to suit the client's needs as well as ensuring that all the milestones are met.
- Needs: Ensuring that all their needs are met by the solution.
- Budget: Ensuring that the diagnostic work and recommendations can be achieved with budget
- Other departments: Your main client should be your priority but your reputation will also come from being responsive to others within the client system, so it is also important that you remain responsive to others.
- Accessibility: Make sure that you can be reached or that people can leave messages for you. It can be very frustrating for a client, if they are not able to talk to you when they need to and it is good practice to respond to client's questions and calls as quickly as you can, even if it is just to say you need more time to formulate an informed response.

## Be careful about how messages are presented

Often people will ask for you to "tell it straight", but in reality will be sensitive to feedback they are linked with in any way. Clients can easily get defensive or take things personally and it is not uncommon for the Business Partner to be used as a scapegoat. Effective partners need to be very tactful about how information is presented. A good approach is to invest as much time working on how to communicate and on your engagement strategy as on the activity itself.

## Credibility for the function

### Ensure there is visibility in the organisation

The Business Partnership Function needs to be visible in the organisation and provides a clear sense of the type of work that is being undertaken and the value that the partnership brings to the company. Newsletters, brochures, involvement in organisational events, etc. with success stories and feedback from projects can all add to this. High-level sponsorship for projects can also be vital in drawing attention to the work taking place.

### Establish appropriate procedures

The Institute of Management Consultants (IMC) has a code of conduct which principally covers the following:

- Meeting the client's requirements
- Integrity
- Independence and objectivity.

It may be appropriate for the internal partnership group to use these as a basis for an organisationally tailored code of conduct, which would have the added benefit of raising some of the less talked about issues of confidentiality and ethics to the fore.

Other aspects which may require more consistent approaches are setting clear terms of reference and contracting for each project, communication between Business Partners and feedback processes. Project management disciplines are often used to structure the process throughout an assignment.

### Gain appropriate qualifications

Where Business Partners need specific expertise, they need to ensure that they have appropriate qualifications. For example, it may be that an HR Business Partner needs to be licensed to deliver particular psychometric tools.

## Pulling in expertise

Neumann, Kellner, and Dawson-Shepherd (1997) highlight the relationship with external consultants as key to the success of internal Business Partners. He argues that the more effective partnerships will build good relationships with external consultants and are more prepared to draw in their expertise when it is missing internally. This can also be used as a learning opportunity for the internal partners, if they choose to work alongside the external partners, although it needs to be carefully managed to ensure that perceptions of credibility are not damaged.

## Stay in touch with the market

Keep a strong network of contacts inside the organisation and outside. Good Business Partners need to keep up to date with changes in the company and the section therefore needs a process for collecting relevant company literature and information on the business and market changes.

## Dealing effectively with pressures along the way

Even when Business Partners have a good rapport with their clients and have established a strong sense of credibility and trust, there are still likely to be pressures impacting on the relationship that could limit its effectiveness. Some of these pressures will stem from the business and some may come from the clients or partners themselves (as shown in Figure 10.3).

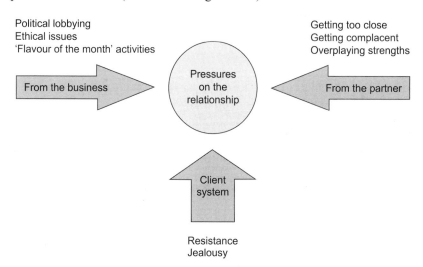

**Figure 10.3** Pressures on the relationship.

## Pressures stemming from the business

### Managing political pressures

Internal Business Partners are much more susceptible to political pressures due to their longer term contract with the organisation, and they can sometimes be asked to bias a report or outcome to suit a particular audience. The more controversial the recommendations for change are, the more likely it is that they will have added value for the organisation. However, it is also more likely that this will lead to greater political objection to the suggestions for change.

This is no different to the pressure an external consultant might be put under and your credibility and business ethics are at stake in this situation. Unlike externals, however, there is a greater need to cover your own back as a Business Partner. Having put up an appropriate level of challenge to a politically led decision, a good approach would be to explicitly re-negotiate the terms of reference or to get agreement from the client, so that you can make it clear to key members of the client system why a particular approach is being taken.

### Dealing with ethical issues

However, hard you plan for all eventualities and contract effectively with your client, it is likely that at some stage you will be put in a position which compromises your ethics to a degree. As a first step, with each project you need to know in advance what you are willing to do and approach the task with a clear view of what is and isn't appropriate. However, you can't plan for all eventualities. Cohen (1991) lists a number of ethical problems consultants face such as:

- Being asked to tailor a report to suit a particular audience and re-word your recommendations in some way to omit key information;
- Being asked to deliver a particular solution to the problem that you know to be wrong or inappropriate;
- Being asked to use information as part of the data gathering that was not gained in an open and honest way; and
- Being asked to set aside a contradictory finding to make the diagnosis easier.

A code of professional conduct, as discussed earlier, may help to address some of these issues. However, a clear sense of your own principles is often more important in helping you to make judgements when faced with ethical dilemmas.

Lynch (in Neumann et al., 1997) suggests that the two key tests for ethical dilemmas are:

■ How transparent is the situation – i.e. how much openness is there?
■ How vulnerable are the stakeholders as a result of the proposed action?

If there is a lack of transparency, or the stakeholders may be vulnerable, then the consultant must weigh up their position and balance this against loyalty to their client. Lynch suggests that it can often be useful to put the dilemmas into context by asking yourself questions such as:

■ Have you defined the circumstance accurately?
■ How did the situation occur?
■ What is your role in it?
■ Are you confident that your position is valid in the long term?
■ Under what conditions would you allow exceptions to your stand?
■ What options do you have?
■ What opportunities are there to discuss the situation with a third party?
■ What are the consequences for each stakeholder as a result of your action or inaction?
■ To whom and to what do you give your loyalty?
■ Could your actions withstand cross-examination in a court by a barrister?
■ Can you discuss the problem with the client before you make a decision?
■ Would you feel comfortable explaining your behaviour to your family, friends and peers?
■ Could you explain your actions to the media?

By answering these questions, the "right" approach can often seem obvious. If this is not the case then, interestingly, the IMC has an ethical helpline which is aimed at providing confidential and non-judgemental feedback on ethical approaches.

## Avoiding being drawn into "flavour of the month"

It's easy to do what will please your client rather than what is right for the business and partners need to ensure that they are continually managing internal customers as professionally as an external consultant would. Focus on activities that make a real impact on the business rather than getting led into flavour of the month activities, which will begin to devalue your impact. Business Partners need to use their judgement about what is right for the business and be prepared to challenge if they are asked to do work outside this scope.

In becoming a Business Partner, you are attempting to move internal relationships onto a more professional basis and provide a real improvement in business results. Establishing who are your prime customers and stakeholders and targeting them is a key part of this process. The initial contracting phase is critical in ensuring that your work is likely to add value.

## Pressures stemming from the business partner

### Getting too close

Business Partners need to maintain independence from their client to avoid getting into a similar mindset where it is difficult to add value. Initially partners can fall into the trap of working too much on the HR agenda rather than respecting the client's agenda, but as the relationship grows there is also a need to maintain an emotional independence to prevent you from over-empathising with the client's position. Effective partners will be prepared to speak their mind, air concerns and views and be open and honest about what they think and feel.

Block (2000) warns against identifying too closely with your clients. He states that we cannot view the clients' triumphs and failures as a reflection of what we do or who we are – particularly if working in process model. Gallwey (1997, p. 36) distinguishes between Making something happen and Letting something happen.

### Getting complacent with good clients

When Business Partners achieve a strong relationship with their clients, it becomes much easier to work with them. The meetings feel comfortable and relaxed and the themes emerging are likely to be familiar. Like any good partnership, there is a danger that the client and partner begin to take each other for granted. Assumptions are made, rightly or wrongly, about what is required and the approach to be taken. Business Partners may even find themselves giving their established clients less of a priority and saying things like: "I know you won't mind if..." or "I'm sure you'll understand if I just...".

It is essential that the Business Partner gives the same level of attention to established clients as new ones. Trust and respect are easily broken in a relationship and not easily regained and often unintentional problems can begin to occur when the client and partner begin to make assumptions without conferring with each other.

### Overplaying your key strengths

Effective relationships stem from an effective balance of your skills and strengths. If you have a particular strength it can be all too easy to over-use it and start to have a negative impact. For example, always acting with strong integrity or conviction can lead a client to view you as inflexible or arrogant. Even gaining too strong an empathy with clients can lead to a weakness stemming from over-identification with their issues at the exclusion of the bigger picture.

Sustaining a positive relationship with your client comes down to establishing an effective balance between a number of key characteristics:

| | | |
|---|---|---|
| Close | vs | Distant |
| Supportive | vs | Challenging |
| Integrity | vs | Inflexibility |
| Conviction | vs | Over-confidence or arrogance |
| Empathy | vs | Over-identification |
| Independence | vs | Aloofness |

## Pressures stemming from the client system

### Viewing resistance as personal

No matter how good your rapport-building skills and credibility are, there is likely to come a time when the client puts up some resistance to progress. This can be a very frustrating time for the partner, particularly as resistance often comes from an irrational behaviour stemming from the client's concerns.

One of the key skills of Business Partners is not to take the resistance personally and to help the clients to verbalise their position. It may be that the client is confused by the amount of information, or is feeling threatened by other people in the organisation. Some clients may just need time to see a particular perspective. The natural tendency when faced with resistance is to either back away or overly justify your position. However, it is at times like these that the relationship needs to become the focus rather than the project.

Often the resistance will not be exhibited in an aggressive way, but will be indicated by passive behaviour, such as limited feedback and lack of conviction through words like "carry on, that's fine". Sometimes the client will be constantly pressing for more information or evidence as a stalling mechanism, or will be more interested in the methodology than the solution. Only by drawing out what lies behind these states will the partner be able to move forward. Block (2000) in his book "Flawless consulting" suggests using phrases such as:

"You seem to be willing to do anything I suggest. I can't tell what your real feelings are." "You are questioning a lot of what I do – you seem angry about something".

The skills needed are excellent observation of the underlying feelings in the client and an ability to ask these more challenging questions about what is driving the behaviour.

## Jealousy

If you are successful in your Business Partner role, build strong relationships with key players and are seen to have a positive impact on the business, it is possible that some of the client system or your peers could become jealous of your success. One Business Partner told us that dealing with jealousy was an unexpected challenge of his/her role, which has meant that they have to be extra conscious of being open and approachable and not "over-precious" about his/her roles.

## Summary

The ability to build strong and effective relationships is a key behaviour for Business Partners. Whilst some people naturally build rapport and empathy, it is a skill which can be developed and enhanced, by being genuine with the clients and trying to get a real understanding of their perspective. Empathetic relationships provide an essential foundation for starting to build credibility.

Credibility comes from both the individual and the more general perceptions of the Business Partnership Function. Individual credibility can be enhanced initially by going for quick wins, being responsive and generally being professional about the way messages are presented and how you use your expertise. To sustain individual credibility, you need to have conviction in what you say and do and be prepared to say no to work that does not add value to the business. Whilst it is important to work from the client's agenda rather than your own, you also need to ensure that you don't get emotionally drawn in and "go native".

Increasing the credibility of the Business Partnership Function comes from effective marketing. In addition to the marketing advice in Chapter 4, this involves gaining a sound understanding of the business; increasing visibility in key areas; using appropriate procedures and drawing on knowledge and expertise from inside or outside the company when it is needed.

Even when Business Partners have strong credibility, there will still be pressures and conflicts which emerge. Political pressures from within the organisation may lead to ethical dilemmas and relationships may become strained if there is resistance to ideas or jealousy stemming from your success. Business Partners need to recognise these pressures and develop strategies to deal with them.

## Checklist for the quality of the relationship

- You show a genuine interest in the client's issues;
- You understand what makes your client tick on a personal and business level;
- You are aware of the pressure faced by your client outside the project;
- You notice and comment when the clients behave in a way which is inconsistent with their body language/meaning;
- Your client responds positively when you summarize what has been talked about;
- You do twice as much listening as talking when you are with your client;
- You have a clear sense of your own preferences and principles;
- You ensure that the client has clear expectations of the project deliverables;
- You are often asked for advice by the client;
- There is mutual trust at a professional level
- There is mutual trust at a personal level;
- You enjoy spending time with your client;
- The client comes to you to talk things over;
- You are consistent in the message you give;
- You have a clear understanding of the boundaries of confidentiality;
- You collaborate extensively on the product or service;
- You approach the client with new ideas or information they have not asked for;
- You constantly deliver value related to the business;
- The client doesn't check up on you;
- You come across with conviction;
- You resist taking sides and getting emotionally drawn into debates;
- The client is understanding if you have pressures that prevent action;
- The client believes you are competent to do the job;
- The client values your integrity;
- You spend time getting buy-in to the solution;
- You are responsive to your client's needs;
- You rarely take your client's needs or views for granted;
- You have consistent and clear procedures to operate by;
- You are prepared to challenge inappropriate recommendations or work; and
- You feel comfortable giving and receiving feedback to and from your client.

## References

Block, P. (2000). *Flawless consulting* (2nd ed.). San Francisco: Jossey Bass/ Pfeiffer.

Cohen, W. A. (1991). *How to make it big as a consultant*. New York: Amacom.

Gallwey, W. T. (1997). *The inner game of tennis*. New York: Random House.

Maister, D., Green, C., & Galford, R. (2002). *The trusted advisor*. London: Simon and Schuster.

Neumann, J. E., Kellner, K., & Dawson-Shepherd, A. (1997). *Developing organisational consultancy*. London: Routledge.

Pfau, B. N., & Cundiff, B. B. (November 2002). 7 Steps before strategy. *Workforce, 81*(12), 40–44.

Sheth, J., & Sobel, A. (2000). *Clients for life*. NewYork: Fireside.

# Part 3

## Benchmarking Your Progress

This section focuses on one of the key sets of behaviours required of any Business Partners, which is to ensure that they are focusing on the key requirements for the business as a whole rather than just delivering to the clients' needs. It is critical that Business Partners obtain and utilise business data and seek to improve their service and gain insights from others as well as the feedback they receive.

Chapter 11 examines the difficult topic of measuring the impact of the Business Partner role to gain some evidence to demonstrate the value of the role and measure progress in terms of the outputs. Evaluation is a difficult topic and one which few companies have got to grips with, so the chapter starts by examining what gets in the way of evaluation and setting out some good practice guidelines to help establish a focus on evaluation. New to this chapter is an explanation of the value triangle, a tool we have found helpful in measuring HR progress. The chapter then moves on to outline some of the models of evaluation stemming from traditional HR and OD that might apply to Business Partnerships and ends by focusing on more recent Business Partner models.

Chapter 12 is a new addition to the book and incorporates case study examples from a range of organisations. Each of the case studies covers a different aspect of the Business Partner role and includes the initial challenges of transition to partnership from an operational HR role; developing the skills and understanding of the Business Partners role; the challenges of outsourcing elements of the HR function and developing the principles of Business Partnering for longer term success.

# 11

# Measuring Your Impact

Many of you, I feel sure, will have turned to this chapter with the hope of finding an easy solution as to how to measure the success of HR when working as Business Partners. Yet interestingly, in all the research which took place for this book, very few of the organisations we spoke to were taking any active steps at all to measure their effectiveness, beyond evaluating the delivery of specific projects. So do you need to bother measuring your impact? And if so, how do you go about doing it?

The immediate value in moving an HR department to a Business Partner model is sometimes hard to envision when the focus is on costs alone, and as such a paradigm shift can be hard to quantify. Yet there is no doubt that working at a strategic level has significant impact. The Corporate Leadership Council (2006) found that successful execution of talent development programmes, for example, contributes to increased organisational effectiveness and profitability, leading to as much as a 15.4% advantage in shareholder returns. Watson Wyatt's Human Capital Index also shows that the five-year returns of shareholders for companies with a high human capital index was 64% compared to 21% for those with a low score and people management practices have been found to lead to 20% productivity and profit improvements.

Interestingly, Ulrich and Brockbank, in their study of HR professionals (outlined in their book "The HR value proposition") revealed that what HR professionals do best, such as doing what they say they'll do and interpersonal skills, have only a moderate influence on business performance. Meanwhile, what HR professionals do only moderately well (strategic contribution) has almost twice the influence on the business where it occurs. They identified HR Business Partner's four main value-adding activities as being culture management, fast change, strategic decision-making and market-driven connectivity. They found that in high-performing organisations, "market connected" HR professionals use their knowledge of the external environment to ensure important signals (for example, customer information) are spread throughout the company so employees respond in unison to market place demands. They also found that these same HR professionals help block relatively unimportant information to help their organisation focus on changing customer and shareholder requirements.

## Evaluating the success of the partnership

Unless the partnership function is still being established, one of the key questions facing Business Partnerships is, "how can I show the Business Partnership Function adds value?". As pressures on businesses increase and there is a continual need to justify costs, there is likely to come a time when Business Partners need to invest some of their time justifying their own existence. If a partnership project goes well then there will be a sense of satisfaction and verbal recognition from the client that the Business Partnership has been of value, but this is rarely enough in today's world of constant justification of costs within the business. Business Partners need to take more active steps to ensure that they are constantly demonstrating value for money.

The shift from operational HR to strategic HR partnerships has meant that traditional measures of efficiency and effectiveness of HR processes are no longer appropriate. To demonstrate business improvement, Business Partners need to collect information which will show the added value the partners are having on the business and their strategic contribution. This, in turn, will help justify the function. The evaluation data can also be used to enhance the credibility of the function, by illustrating the work it undertakes and marketing the Business Partner role, using examples of past successes. If Business Partners are responsible for gaining business internally, this will be an essential marketing lever.

However, evaluation is not easy. Interestingly, in a recent study of HR evaluation practices, whilst the majority of directors (95%) agreed that it was important to measure the strategic impact of HR, only 40% believed it was possible to do so, and this lack of knowledge about *how* to approach evaluation is a key deterrent to any evaluation taking place at all (Cabrera, 2003). It is evident that organisations struggle to evaluate the organisational impact of change processes effectively and with ever increasing pressures on time and resources, success is often seen as stemming from a lack of negative feedback rather than real added value to the business. Yet the pressure on internal service departments to evaluate the impact they have on the business is growing and for HR Business Partners this is no longer about what they do, but whether they deliver business improvement.

One of the possible reasons for the increased pressure on HR to evaluate is the number of companies seeking to obtain accreditation for Investors in People. Achieving IIP status has become a prestigious achievement for many organisations and for HR moving towards a Business Partnership model, achieving IIP is almost essential. The IIP framework is based around four principles, the fourth of which is evaluation of the business benefits. IIP is a total quality framework and works on the premise that evaluation sits in a cycle of planning, doing, evaluating and reviewing. Whilst there is limited guidance on evaluation methodologies, the need to evaluate as part of the IIP standard has been significant and 45% of organisations cite this as a prime reason for carrying out evaluation (Industrial Society, 2000).

Very few of the organisations carrying out evaluation, however, do so in a way which determines the business impact. Traditionally, Training and Development functions have the most expertise within HR for evaluating their success. However, if Business Partnerships follow the trend set by training functions then it makes sorry reading, as the training in Britain survey has estimated that only 19% of organisations try to evaluate the business benefits of training and only 3% of those attempt any sort of cost/benefit analysis.

This chapter will examine how Business Partners can seek to establish better processes for measuring their success and will review some of the more traditional as well as emerging models for evaluation, in order to give an insight into the variety of approaches on offer.

## What gets in the way?

If the pressure to evaluate is getting stronger and the benefits of evaluating are evident, it is worth starting out by looking at what gets in the way of effective evaluations. Even when there is a clear intent on the part of the Business Partner and client to evaluate the project, there are immense pressures within the organisation that run counter to any meaningful evaluation taking place.

### Time

At the end of a project, the pressure is often on to finish quickly and move on to the next job. The client is likely to lose focus and a sense of priority towards a task nearing completion and be motivated to "not waste time" discussing it. This is particularly the case if the project went very well or very badly. In order to overcome this, the Business Partners need to make sure that they have an earlier agreement to evaluate and review that they can refer back to, as well as the courage of their convictions in pressing for the review to take place. Being clear of the benefits in your own mind is imperative if you are to overcome resistance from the client, as is the need to have contracted some time up front to carry out the review.

## Events have changed

During a lengthy partnership project, the chances are that significant organisational changes will be taking place alongside the work being undertaken. More frequently than ever before, companies are re-structuring, downsizing, de-layering, revising working practices and bringing in new technologies. It is all too easy to get to the end of a project and agree with the client that "things have moved on" and that attempting to draw a line between the outcome and the starting point are now inappropriate, despite good intentions at the start. Once again, contracting and re-contracting throughout the project are imperative to prevent this happening.

## Inappropriate measures

What is valued in organisations is often what is already being measured and reported. Linking in with these measures can therefore be highly beneficial for Business Partners, as they will not have to collect new data and will be working with established reports. However, many of the measures existing in organisations focus on "hard" rather than "soft" data and even where hard measures change, it is often difficult to produce evidence about how the partnership intervention impacted the change. Business Partners therefore need to be careful to choose measures that are both relevant and easily attainable in the business.

## The need to focus on "quick wins"

At the start of any Business Partnership there is a pressure to establish your credibility by delivering quickly and effectively in a number of areas. The investment of time is viewed as better placed on meeting the client's current needs rather than following up on the outcomes of previous work. Whilst this is a good model to follow in some ways, it does have the consequence that a pattern is being established whereby it becomes normal practice not to build in a process for review and evaluation. Many Business Partners we spoke to said that they would like to carry out more evaluation, but at the current time the focus needed to be on delivery as a means of establishing themselves in the Partnership role. Having established themselves as Partners who deliver without taking time to review however, it will be difficult to reverse this mould once the partners are more established, as client expectations will already be set.

### Good practice guidelines for establishing a focus on evaluation

So what can Business Partners do to prevent this happening? As a first step, Business Partners need to ensure that they focus their role towards evaluation.

This is not as easy as it sounds, but if partners hold certain principles in mind throughout their role then it should be possible to achieve this. Listed below are a number of good practice guidelines, which are aimed at establishing an appropriate focus on the evaluation process.

Good Practice Guidelines:

- Don't partner for the sake of it;
- Set measures and contract up front;
- Assess the time frames;
- Choose your measures carefully;
- Continually involve your client;
- Let the client take the credit;
- Separate out validation from evaluation; and
- Choose an appropriate level for analysis.

## Don't partner for sake of it

When you first get involved in a Business Partnership project, there needs to be some assessment of the importance of the project and the impact on the organisation. Through careful questioning, the partner should be able to glean whether the proposal is critical to the business, important to the business or more administrative. Kearns (1998) illustration below shows where he perceives an effective Business Partnership Function should be operating.

Even if a Business Partnership appears very attractive (perhaps due to lack of other business or a desire to work with a particular client), in order to sustain credibility and value, Business Partners should not accept work that is not going to add value to the business. If they do, then the evaluation phase will be an unwelcome addition to the process for the Business Partner, as it will more than likely show that they achieved little more than building a new relationship!

When *Coca-Cola* first repositioned their HR function as a Business Partnership, one of their first steps was to identify criteria to evaluate the work they were asked to do (Brocket, 2004). In true partnership style, they involved business managers to help develop criteria which they then used to identify the relative importance of HR projects. The criteria they developed were:

1. Contributes to business performance;
2. Promotes early delivery of business benefits;
3. Maximises employee engagement;
4. Improves or simplifies people management activities; and
5. Supports legal or regulatory compliance.

Each of these criteria was given a weighting and existing projects were ranked against this in order to prioritise the HR project portfolio.

This type of approach provides a clear understanding of why the partnership is taking place and what the areas of impact a particular piece of work is predicted to have. If there is not a strong priority for a particular project, this will be clear from the outset.

## Set measures and contract up front

Although evaluation is often left to the end, it cannot be stressed enough that to be effective measures need to be discussed and agreed at the contracting phase. It is much easier to carry out a thorough review if there is buy-in up front and time has been allocated to it at the start of the project. For example, *Frizzell* go through an explicit process of "contracting" with the line, where programmes are devised and prioritised against the business needs and strategy. This makes it much easier to assess whether those business needs were met at completion.

As discussed in the previous chapters, the purpose of the initial contracting discussions is to ensure that the customer's requirements are accurately translated into actions by the Business Partner, and have measurable outcomes. As with any good project management processes, it is important to get the scope and specification right before committing the necessary resource. It not only conveys a professional image to the internal customer, but also allows misunderstandings to be picked up at an early stage. Some external consultancies, such as *Leaps and Bounds,* are paid on achieving the success measures set up front and this provides a useful focus for their activity. This model could usefully be transferred to internal partnerships.

Although the measures are ideally agreed up front, there also needs to be flexibility and the measures should be continually reviewed. The partner needs to be continually asking, "what does success look like for you?" so that as the project progresses the appropriateness of the original success measures is challenged and re-contracted if necessary.

## Assess the time frames

It is important to evaluate within the time frame that is given for a particular project, rather than an ideal position. If, for example, a project is only given six months to run, when both the partner and client agree that eight months would ensure the quality outcome required, then the measures should be set to reflect the shorter timescales.

However, much strategic HR activity has a longer payback period than the partnership project is likely to last. Work on a new succession planning process, for example, will typically not show its true value until some years after being put in place. In these cases, it is recommended that the risk of not taking any action is built into the cost analysis. In this example, it would mean costing delays in recruitment to key positions, or assessing the predicted impact on turnover. Softer measures may also be more appropriate, such as the level of awareness of the new process amongst key managers.

## Choose your measures carefully

Carrying out evaluation overtly carries a strong message. The questions you choose to ask will give a strong message in themselves about what you are really aiming to achieve. Measuring the quantity of sales calls and not the quality of the calls, for example, will indicate that the intervention is aiming to improve efficiency, possibly at the expense of effectiveness.

Effective partners will discuss with their clients the impact of choosing particular measures and will ask probing questions to ensure that the client has a clear understanding of what they are aiming to achieve with the evaluation.

Typical questions might include:

- "How engaged or active do you want to be?"
- " How much risk are you willing to take?"
- "Who should set the standards and measures?"
- "How are they going to be used?"
- "What message do these measures send?"

## Continually involve your client

Abernathy (1999) makes an important point when he says, "any good manager knows how her work unit is performing and is paid to make some well-informed judgements about what's causing the performance to change". Some organisations have had a lot of success by discarding formal evaluation processes and using line manager perceptions on the impact of change.

Whether you take this approach or not, you will want to get your internal customer involved in the process of establishing measures as early as possible in the project. It can be useful to get their agreement on the benchmarks and measures you are going to use and also establish when and how the results will be tracked. It is also worth discussing any variables which may affect the outcome of the project, so that causal links can be established.

Many Business Partners also choose to seek feedback from other parts of the client system, such as the stakeholders, customers, people involved in the data gathering process, etc. Surveys and focus groups are common methods used for this process. However, the partner needs to be wary of creating a project in itself from the evaluation. The extent of the feedback needs to be appropriate and not overly time consuming and it is therefore important to balance the need for feedback with the cost of gaining it. Evaluators need to work as "real partners" with other managers in the organisation to gain a greater understanding of the relevant performance measures and the causal links.

## Let the client take the credit

If you are good at what you do, it is often said that the client will think that he or she was responsible for it happening. Working as internal partners, the satisfaction comes from client satisfaction and watching change projects become institutionalised into the new culture and organisation. The word-of-mouth recommendations and demand for your services are the credit you receive from a job well done and these allow you access to more interesting projects and areas of the organisation.

## Separate out validation from evaluation

There are many things that can be measured and reviewed within the scope of a Business Partnership and it is important to be clear with your client and yourself on what you are seeking to achieve at any one time. It can be helpful to differentiate between *validation*, which is concerned with whether the intervention or process achieved what it set out to do and *evaluation*, which focuses on the impact of that intervention on individuals and the business. Validation is therefore more about the quality and appropriateness of what went on, and evaluation is more about results. Both of these approaches are likely to have value.

## Choose an appropriate level for analysis

Business Partners need to work with their constraints and opportunities to use evaluation tools to best effect. It is important to clarify why the information is being collected and what use will be made of it. Different types of evaluation can then be used, depending on the nature, scope and purposes of evaluating the intervention. Gathering customised data can be a time consuming business, and the level of the analysis needs to reflect the size of the project and the likely benefits of demonstrating bottom-line results.

Certainly companies with comprehensive evaluation processes such as *IBM, Motorola and Arthur Anderson* evaluate in response to customer needs rather than to justify the activity or maintain a budget. At *Arthur Anderson* bottom-line results are measured less than 10% of the time, but the studies have been very useful to them in increasing customer confidence generally. Business Partners can therefore benefit from choosing where to place their effort in terms of evaluation and not investing unreasonable amounts of time proving business benefits for every piece of work they are involved in.

## Make it worth your while!

Anyone who has tried to do a comprehensive evaluation of an HR project will be aware that it is a time-consuming and frustrating activity. Even when measures are discussed and agreed up front, the changing nature of the business can make it difficult to establish causal links. In my experience, no Business Partners in their right mind are likely to embark on evaluating a piece of work unless there is an incentive for them to do so. If it is something you believe is necessary, however, then establishing evaluation as one of your key performance indicators is one way of encouraging activity in this area. Given that the whole purpose of Business Partners is to have an impact on the business, then financial rewards based on business improvement are also worth considering.

## Reviewing the effectiveness of the business partnership function

As well as assessing the impact of Business Partners on the organisation, it may also be appropriate for the Business Partnership Function to review its own position from time to time and get together as a team to analyse the areas they want and need to improve the most.

A useful exercise that we adopt in working with HR teams is to get them to map their current activities against the value triangle depicted in Figure 11.1.

This model (Ingham, 2006) suggests that HR can provide value to the business in three different ways: At the base of the triangle, HR provides value for money when it increases the efficiency of HR activities. An example would be speeding up the time it takes to issue new appointment letters.

The next level is adding value. This is about helping the business to implement its strategies by translating business objectives into people management activities. An example here might be identifying issues and amending the appraisal process so that it has a more significant impact on performance management.

The highest level is termed creating value and is about HR generating value for the business by taking strategic initiatives which enable the organisation to set different or more stretching business goals. An example might be developing an employer brand to position an organisation as an employer of choice, and by doing so, significantly increasing its potential to grow. Mapping day-to-day activities onto this triangle can give a real insight into the impact Business Partners might be having on the business.

However, the perceptions from the people in the business are also important to gauge. Table 11.1 provides a set of questions which provide a basis for

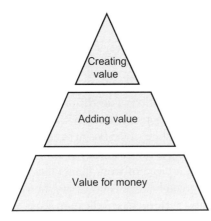

- Creating capacity for the future
- Driving and accelerating business strategy
- Taking advantage of exceptional opportunities
- Producing strategically innovative solutions

- Focussing HR on business strategy
- Creating capacity to perform now
- Ensuring effectiveness and alignment

- Administrating HR operations
- Ensuring efficiency e.g. through outsourcing

**Figure 11.1** The Value Triangle.

a functional review. This can either be completed together as a team, or it can be individually completed and the results compared.

Even without such a formal review, posing questions for discussion at team meetings such as:

- What are the greatest challenges facing the organisation at the moment and are we partnering in those areas?
- How strong is our brand image within the organisation?
- What can we do to improve our network?
- Where do we sit on the value triangle?

can be a useful stimulus for ideas and a focus for developing the function as a whole.

## Establishing clear priorities

Business Partner functions are faced with a myriad of choices about how they spend their time and focus their energy. Key challenges mentioned by Business Partners we spoke to included:

- Culture change
- Re-engineering HR processes
- Communication
- Employee Relations issues
- Skills training
- Redeployment
- Executive coaching
- Cross-functional working

**Table 11.1**   Review of the Business Partnership Function

| Rate each of the following factors according to how you perceive the Business Partner Function meets the criteria given | Score between 1 and 10, 1 = Poor; 5 = OK; 10 = Excellent |
|---|---|

*Business credibility*

1. Understanding of the business needs
2. Credibility with Line Managers
3. Perceived level of customer service
4. Sufficient budget/resource to meet needs
5. Relationships with key stakeholders
6. Brand image
7. Broad network across all areas

*Future focus*

8. Understanding of the challenges facing the company
9. Priorities are towards the longer term company goals
10. Involvement in strategic discussions
11. Linkage of HR activities to Business Challenges

*Business Partner teamwork*

12. Sharing best practice and transferring knowledge
13. Celebrating success
14. Building skills and knowledge

- Technology integration
- Performance Management
- Competency development
- Motivation and morale
- Mentoring
- Mergers and Acquisitions
- Structural changes – centralising/decentralising
- Reward changes
- Skills shortages
- Downsizing

- Partnerships
- Outsourcing
- Diversity
- Absenteeism.

To name but a few!

It also wouldn't be a surprise if you are reading this list and thinking, "all of these and more!". So if Business Partners are working on many of these issues, it is critical that the function as a whole creates some definition of the key strategic objectives and prioritises the business needs, as discussed in Chapter 2.

Many tools exist to help define key strategic objectives for organisations, such as McKinseys 7 S model (1980) as well as SWOT and PEST (Figure 11.2) analyses.

McKinsey's model helps to review whether the individual strategies for different areas of the business are mutually supportive. For example, do the systems in place relate to the structure and values the organisation is seeking to achieve? Do the style of managers reflect the needs of the business?

Turbo-Charging the HR function (Mooney, 2001) also has a useful "Strategic Clarity Quiz" for assessing whether you are as clear as you think you are on the business strategy. The book also suggests you ask yourself whether you would

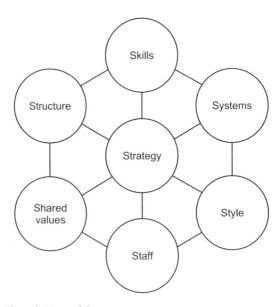

**Figure 11.2** McKinsey's 7s model.

**Table 11.2** HR Priorities Linked to the Stage of Organisational Development

|  | Staffing | Rewards | Training | Employee relations | Goals cultural |
|---|---|---|---|---|---|
| Start up | Key skills | Salary Equity | Key skills | Philosophy | Flexibility |
| Growth | Skills mix | Salary Bonuses | Skill building | Commitment | Growth |
| Maturity | Retention of key players | Focus on efficiency | Management skills | Involvement | Efficiency Motivation |
| Decline | Redeployment | Focus on cost saving | Retraining | Flexibility | Cost reduction |

feel capable of giving a talk to new recruits on the organisational strategy, which is a good indicator of your understanding.

However, one model, which can be particularly useful for reviewing priorities, is to link the HR activity to the business lifecycle and stage of organisational development. Table 11.2 illustrates the stages of business development linked to the key HR challenges.

It may be that in large corporations, different business areas have very different priorities as they are at differing stages of development. Business Partners, in *Marconi* for example, are largely focused on initiatives aimed at cost reduction and effective redeployment of staff as some of the areas of their business move into decline. Other developing areas, however, require a focus on building new skills.

If the priorities of the Business Partner function are not clearly defined, it will be virtually impossible to evaluate success.

## What models of evaluation might apply to business partnerships?

HR working as Business Partners is a relatively new discipline, and as such, there are few established models for evaluating success. In drawing together approaches which are talked about for this chapter, it became apparent that the models used stem from a number of different areas, each of which have a value to bring to the process. Figure 11.3 highlights some of the key models in existence, each of which will be discussed in turn.

**Figure 11.3** Evaluation models.

## Traditional HR approaches

Historically, as HR has focused more on transactional activities such as hiring, firing and administering rewards, the common approach to measuring the value of HR has focused on evaluating HR as a profit centre. The tools most useful for this type of evaluation are:

- Benchmarking
- Balanced scorecard
- Satisfaction surveys
- Activity tracking.

Whilst these methods may still have their uses, if HR is working as a true Business Partner then the focus needs to move away from analysing HR transactions to measuring improvements in business results.

### Employee satisfaction surveys

Opinion or satisfaction surveys provide a measurable trend on HR issues and are commonplace in large organisations. Research shows that levels of employee satisfaction have a direct correlation with business performance, so monitoring changes in the level of satisfaction can be a useful indicator.

Surveys can also be important for Business Partners as a way of tracking cultural change in areas such as communication, employee issues and perceptions of customer service. The possible disadvantage of focusing on survey improvements as a way of measuring success for HR is that what employees rate poorly becomes the focus for HR projects, rather than necessarily focussing on what adds value to the business.

## The balanced scorecard

The balanced scorecard model, developed by Kaplan and Norton (1996), provides a means of measuring and tracking the impact of employee-related initiatives on the bottom line. It has been widely adopted in organisations, including *BNFL, Royal and Sun Alliance* and the *CAA*.

Typically, it looks at results from the perspective of:

- Finance (e.g. revenue growth and cost improvements)
- Customer (e.g. satisfaction measures, market share)
- Internal business processes (e.g. operational efficiency)
- Learning and growth (e.g. employee satisfaction, skill levels).

The specific measures an organisation includes in its scorecard vary depending on the nature of the business and its strategic approach, but are intended to give a more holistic sense of how the business is performing. Typical HR measures include compensation and benefits, recruitment, absenteeism, turnover, training and development and health and safety.

## External benchmarking

A benchmark is a standard against which items can be compared. It helps to determine how the company or function is performing compared to other organisations in similar sectors as well as providing models of best practice. Benchmarking is ideally an ongoing process of measuring practices and procedures against competitors or those considered best in class in order to give an indication of where improvements can be made.

In terms of HR, benchmarking data is often gathered on:

- Ratio of HR to managers in the organisation
- Board membership and levels of HR staff
- HR processes
- HR structure and functions
- Turnover rates
- Use of technology by HR
- Training provision
- Evaluation practices.

Benchmarking Business Partnership functions may also lead to gathering data on:

- the perceived image of the department or section;
- the cost charging mechanism;

- the ratio of partners to managers in the organisation;
- qualification levels of Business Partners; and
- added value data.

One of the difficulties with benchmarking is that it can be hard to identify appropriate companies as comparators and each company will place a different emphasis on particular aspects of HR depending on how they connect to the business. It is important that when looking for benchmarking data checks are made on whether the data is current and whether it measures the same things you want to measure.

In large, diverse organisations, internal benchmarking may also be appropriate, in order to compare the success of the partnership function in different areas. This can help to improve internal best practice and make knowledge transfer more effective. The Partnership function within the *Inland Revenue* for example came up against barriers within the business over whether they added value. They chose to use benchmarking across organisations to help to show their worth.

### Activity tracking/HR costing

In this method, the value of the HR function is determined by the level of activity, such as the number of new employees recruited in a period of time. The cost of each activity is measured and tracked as a way of identifying areas where savings can be made. This type of process is more appropriate for transactional HR and is less applicable for Business Partnership models as it assumes that HR activity adds value, without establishing links to the business results.

## OD evaluation models

Many of the processes for evaluating internal consultancy are drawn from models used for training and development. Highlighted below are some of the key models in existence which are seen to have application to Business Partnerships projects. More detail on these and other OD methods can be found in Tamkin, Yarnall, and Kerrin (2002). These models indicate that there is a need to focus more clearly on the different types of outcomes sought by the interventions and to tailor the technique to the organisation in order to ensure that the approach suits the culture and values. In addition, there is an increased emphasis on non-financial measures and a suggestion that a more rounded picture needs to be developed to show the indirect returns on all aspects of the business.

## The four-level approach – Kirkpatrick

The best-known and most widely used framework for classifying evaluation is the Kirkpatrick (1996) model. Benchmarking forums have shown that Kirkpatrick's model of evaluation is still the predominant means of evaluating OD. Where this model is used, more and more companies, such as *BT*, are also attempting to evaluate certain key activities at the higher levels of application of learning and impact on the organisation. Although Kirkpatrick's model has come under some criticisms in recent years, the strengths of the model lie in its simplicity and pragmatic way of helping practitioners think about interventions.

The model consists of four stages, described more recently by Kirkpatrick as levels. Each of these four levels are examined critically below:

**Level 1: Reaction**
This assesses what the participants thought of a particular intervention, and is normally assessed by the use of reaction questionnaires.

Gathering data at a reaction level can help to assess the initial impact of an intervention and can have real value in terms of encouraging a positive message and giving an indication of teething problems either in terms of method or content. A recentstudy by the Industrial Society found that 84% of companies evaluate reactions to training and development using reaction questionnaires or "reactionnaires" (Industrial Society, 2000). Yet despite this, there is considerable evidence to suggest that reaction-level evaluation has little value in terms of determining business impact.

In a training context it has been found that participant reactions were generally unrelated to subsequent job behaviour (Warr, Allan, & Birdi, 1999) and this finding is backed up by other researchers who also found negative relationships between reactions and learning, i.e. if the participants found the intervention uncomfortable and unsettling, it may have had more impact on them than they were prepared to admit (Alliger & Janak, 1989).

One reason for this may be that learners often mistake good presentation style as good learning and difficult messages may lead to poor ratings. Psychologists have argued that people are not good at reporting their experiences and many people argue against participants evaluating training instructors for this reason, as the evaluation data may lead to inappropriate changes to the training programme.

This would also be relevant to Business Partners choosing to evaluate the reactions to interventions they make.

As a result, if Business Partners choose to use reaction-level measures to assess their intervention, they need to analyse quite carefully the types of reactions they are assessing and be clear about the purpose of the data. The evidence suggests that if organisations are seeking to evaluate the *value* of the intervention rather than aiming to improve on its content, then reaction data may not be appropriate. In addition, even when there is an interest in improving effectiveness by validating the intervention in terms of content and process, the literature suggests that data generated need to be treated with caution due to the inability of raters to distinguish impact from style or approach.

## Level 2: Learning
Level 2 measures the changes in knowledge, skills or attitude with respect to the objectives of the intervention.

Where a partnership intervention is aimed at changing knowledge, skills or attitude, this is normally assessed using some type of performance rating, or by participant and line manager giving feedback on the extent of the change taking place. There is a high level of agreement in the literature that ideally measures of performance need to be taken both before and after the intervention to be able to assess the change. Control groups are commonly suggested as a good way of countering the effects of other factors which may effect the performance levels. Often, however, testing prior to an event taking place and establishing control groups are not practical for organisations due to the numbers involved and organisational constraints. As a result the measures used are often less scientific.

360-Degree assessment is growing in popularity in organisations and is one way of the assessing competency gains over time. *Motorola* for example used 360-degree performance appraisal to measure leadership behaviours and looked at how this related to training the leaders had received (Blanchard, Thacker, & Way, 2000).

## Level 3: Behaviour and the transfer of learning
Level 3 measures changes in job behaviour resulting from an intervention and seeks to identify whether the learning is being applied. Assessment methods typically include observation, self- and manager-assessments and productivity data.

Organisational culture and the degree of management support for change have been shown to have a significant effect on the transfer of learning from behavioural change programmes to changed behaviour in the workplace.

Research indicates that when supervisors and peers encourage and reward the application of new approaches, the intervention is likely to achieve more positive results. Business Partners can therefore take active steps to encourage management support and cultural change in line with projects being implemented.

Some of the important cultural elements which effect success at this level are an individual's "self-efficacy", or the degree to which employees have confidence in their own ability to cope with new tasks, as well as employees' motivation to learn and their willingness to put any new skills and knowledge into practice.

**Level 4: Results**

Level 4 measures the bottom-line contribution of interventions. Methods used for evaluation include measuring costs, quality and return on investment.

## Are "Hard" measures always possible?

Certainly the premise of Business Partnership is based on the belief that interventions not linked to organisational mission, strategy and goals are unlikely to produce results that are valued by the organisation and that it should be possible to forecast the financial benefits before a project begins.

However, the process of linking HR interventions to business results is highly interpretive, especially in complex business environments. Pulley (1994) argues that what is needed is "responsive evaluation" which pays attention to both hard and soft issues and provides both quantitative and qualitative measures. She states that relying too heavily on either type of data can result in misleading conclusions. She draws on research which shows that people's actions tend to be more affected by stories and anecdotes than statistical results and argues that although senior managers may request hard data, they are more influenced by qualitative measures.

The ability of "hard" measures to become visible in an appropriate time frame is also questioned. Many researchers argue that organisational constraints impact on the rigor of evaluation and that whilst some measures and cross-validation can be achieved, the "worth" of a project is not just about cost-benefit. Often it can take 12–18 months to establish evaluation data that proves the effectiveness of a particular intervention and the time lag needs to be taken account of when relating results to the bottom line. Kaplan and Norton (1996) go further than this and argue that financial measures are inadequate for guiding and evaluating organisations. "They are lagging indicators that fail to capture much of the value that has been created or destroyed by manager's actions in the accounting period".

In addition, some transformational programmes aimed at shifting culture can often happen before the organisation is ready for them and consequently the benefits are not visible for some time after. Rough (1994) argues that progress sometimes needs to be based upon trust, mutual involvement and facilitation. The Ministry of Defence (July 2001) evaluation toolkit appears to take this approach and states that evidence of results can be direct, indirect, quantifiable or qualitative, as long as managers have a sufficient range of information with which to make a decision.

However, there is an increasing concern in organisations to justify investment in terms of improved organisational performance, such as increased productivity, profit or safety, reduced error and enhanced market share and there are a number of supporters of the view that results can and should be analysed using numerical "hard" data. Many researchers in this area believe that all results can be turned into numerical measures and that every business has numerous hard indicators of organisational effectiveness at their disposal, such as manufacturing efficiency, inventory levels, accidents, order-entry accuracy, abandoned calls, defect rates and cycle times. Plenty of guidance is also available for practitioners for measuring productivity, cost-effectiveness and return on investment. More recently the Watson Wyatt Human Capital Index has also established exactly which human-capital practices have the greatest impact on shareholder value (see Pfau & Cundiff, 2002).

## The KPMT model – Kearns and Miller (1997)

Kearns and Miller argue that clear objectives are an essential component of an evaluation model. They have developed a useful "toolkit" to help evaluators work through the process of identifying bottom-line objectives through questioning techniques; evaluating existing deliverables and using process mapping to identify the added value to organisations.

They argue that interventions can only bring added value to an organisation if the business is not performing effectively or there is a market opportunity which can be exploited. There is a heavy emphasis on establishing measures up front and clarifying objectives from a business perspective rather than that of the participants.

The key elements cited prior to the start of the process involve a broader analysis of the organisational context – its values, practices and current situation. Following this, there is a more explicit focus on the needs of the business and how these tie to the development of objectives and the design of the most appropriate solution. Whilst not forming part of the assessment process, it is argued that these contextual steps inform the future evaluation strategy and as such need to be included in any evaluation model.

The process they suggest to achieve this is:

Step 1: Discuss the needs of the business
Step 2: Design some proposed training and development solutions
Step 3: Decide on the real training issues and get buy-in to this
Step 4: Deliver
Step 5: Evaluate
Step 6: Feedback the results.

Where Kearns and Miller differ from some of the other models is that they believe that return on investment can only be looked at in hard terms. As an example, they argue that even if an intervention is aimed at bringing about greater awareness (e.g. of customers) then it should still only be measured by the eventual effect on hard measures such as customer spend and number of customers.

Applying their model to Business Partnership, the percentage return on investment (ROI) for a particular project would be calculated as:

$$\frac{\text{Benefits from intervention (\$)} - \text{Costs of intervention (\$)}}{\text{Costs of Intervention (\$)}}$$

To combat the difficulties of attributing long term financial gains directly to a particular intervention, they suggest the use of simple process flow maps so that the causal connections can be made explicit.

Business Partners interested in this approach are recommended to read Paul Kearn's forthcoming book on evaluation and ROI.

## Responsive evaluation – pulley (1994)

Responsive evaluation is a tool for communicating evaluation results more effectively by tailoring it to the needs of the decision-makers. Pulley argues that the objective of the evaluation should be to provide evidence so that key decision-makers can determine what they want to know. The stages involved are:

1. Identify the decision-makers so as to ascertain who will be using the information and what their stake in it is.
2. Identify the information needs of the decision-makers – what do they need to know and how will it influence their decisions?

3. Systematically collect both quantitative and qualitative data. Pulley argues that the qualitative data is normally relayed in the form of stories or anecdotes and "gives life to the numbers".
4. Translate the data into meaningful information.
5. Involve and inform decision-makers on an on-going basis.

This technique may have a lot of relevance to the work of Business Partners, particularly where their role is less project related. The approach would be to find out what your internal customers want in terms of success measures and then collect the data that will answer those questions, rather than be defined by a pre-existing framework.

## Business partnership models

The aim of Business Partnership is to move away from operational delivery to impacting the business at a strategic level. By definition this means that evaluating HR activity or planned interventions are unlikely to provide an accurate picture of the impact Business Partners are having. Whilst there are a few studies that have shown that moving to a more strategic role in HR does impact firm performance (Becker & Huselid, 1998), there is little evidence of the particular activities that add value, or of how to assess the value added.

Cabrera (2003) argues that evaluation needs to move away from traditional measures of HR and focus on the extent to which employee behaviours are contributing towards the organisation's strategic objectives and the extent to which existing HR practices are encouraging or discouraging the desired behaviours. For example, a high-tech company pursuing a strategy of innovation and speed of delivery to market, will be seeking staff who are highly committed, creative, work in self-managed teams and are empowered to take risks. The Business Partner role should be focused in this instance, on ensuring that the culture and nature of the employees are in line with this. Evaluating the success of the role is therefore focused on the links between what the Business Partner does, employee behaviours and the business results. Three relatively new models have emerged in the literature to support this role and each of these is examined below.

### Herring (2001)

Herring discusses how HR can determine their "market-value" as a five-step process. Once again, this approach has its basis in identifying up front what the key issues are and getting a good understanding of the impact of these issues on the business. The five stages are:

1. Determine the key issues: Work with the business to determine the issues of most concern, regardless of whether they have any obvious links to HR
2. Determine the impact on the business: This entails digging deeper into the consequences of unresolved problems in the business. For example, what is the result of decisions being avoided?
3. Develop collaborative solutions: Working in partnership with the client group to determine how HR can help.
4. Establish measurable outcomes: If the impact on the business is clear, then it should be possible to identify key business information that should be improved.
5. Assess effectiveness: This needs to be done on an on-going basis, re-tuning and reshaping the problem as it emerges in partnership with the client group.

## Boudreau and Ramstad (1997)

This model separates out the impact that HR practices have on the efficiency of internal processes from the impact on employee's behaviours and strategic business results. The model is simple and has three levels of evaluation:

1. What HR does;
2. What HR makes happen; and
3. Business Success.

This has a lot of similarities with the balanced scorecard approach, highlighted earlier in this chapter. The model links measures through a cause and effect chain, which helps managers to understand how different measures are related and how they ultimately contribute to the business results.

## Cabrera (2003)

Cabrera has built on the earlier model by Boudreau and Ramstad and has developed a framework for evaluation which classifies HR measures into five distinct types.

1. Traditional HR operational measures – efficiency, cost, ratios, e.g. speed of offer letters; hours of training per employee;
2. Organisational capability measures, where HR should have impact, e.g. employee behaviours, skills and attitudes;
3. Measures of the impact of HR practices on organisational capabilities;

4. Measures of the impact of organisational capabilities on strategic business results; and
5. Direct measures of the impact of HR practices on strategic business results.

She stresses that any evaluation model must incorporate an assessment of the causal links between the different levels. More complex analysis in this field would require predictive validity or utility analysis techniques, normally beyond the scope of most HR functions. Many researchers in the HR field, however, are trying to establish causal links and the recent work of Guest, Michie, Shhhan, and Conway (2000) is aimed at gaining a better understanding of how HR affects performance.

## Summary

The evidence suggests that few Business Partnerships are engaged in comprehensive evaluation processes. However, Business Partners are under increasing pressure to show that they are adding value to the business. To do this they need to work effectively with their clients to determine the best way to help the organisation progress and to set in place appropriate measures of success. At the start of any project it is essential that the Business Partner and the client collaborate on the bottom-line measures. It is also likely that the impact of any partnership will need to be measured in both quantitative and qualitative ways, in order to show a more enriched picture of the value being added.

Depending on the nature of the intervention being evaluated, existing HR and OD models may provide an appropriate framework for evaluation. However, to evaluate the Business Partnership Function as a whole, it is likely that the framework will need to draw on an initial understanding of the strategic aims and contribution the partner is seeking to make. The newly emerging partnership models provide a good basis for this analysis.

The selection of a particular framework for evaluation is a complex one and does not have a simple answer. Effective evaluation is about thinking through the purposes of the intervention and its intended outcome on the business; the purposes of the evaluation and how the data will be used; the audiences for the results of the evaluation; the points at which measurements can be taken; the difficulties in accessing the necessary data; the time and resources available and the overall framework which is to be utilised. Ideally, Business Partners should seek to conduct the most informative evaluation possible, given these differing needs and the constraints of each situation.

Reviewing the Business Partnership Function as a whole is also critical, not only in ensuring that Business Partners are working in a coordinated way and are sharing knowledge and skills, but also to ensure the right business focus. Establishing clear priorities for the function based on the business needs is imperative, if Business Partners are to stay focused on work that adds value rather than just pleasing their clients. The HR priorities need to be aligned to the strategic and cultural objectives of the organisation, as well as the stage of development the company has reached.

## Checklist

- Are you clear on what you are trying to achieve?
- Have you established an adequate focus on evaluation up front?
- Have you involved your client in establishing a framework for evaluation?
- What does a successful evaluation look like to your client?
- Are the measures you have selected appropriate, given the time scales?
- Are the measures you have selected both accessible and relevant?
- Have you separated out validation of the process from evaluation of the impact?
- Are you committed to carrying out the evaluation?
- Are you clear on how you will use the evaluation data?
- What processes are in place for reviewing the effectiveness of the Business Partnership Function as a whole?
- How well are the priorities of the Partnership Function aligned with the business needs?
- Where do the Business Partners sit on the value triangle?
- Are there existing HR evaluation models which can be utilised?
- Is there a clear requirement for either hard or soft measures?
- What depth and level of analysis is appropriate, given the work being evaluated?
- What links can be drawn between the work being undertaken and the predicted impact on the business?

## References

Abernathy, D. J. (February 1999). Thinking outside the evaluation box. *Training and Development, 53*(2), 18–23.

Alliger, G. M., & Janak, E. A. (1989). Kirkpatrick's levels of training criteria: thirty years later. *Personnel Psychology, 42*(2), 331–342.

Becker, B.E., & Huselid, M.A. (1998). High performance work systems and firm performance: a synthesis of research and managerial implications. In G. Ferris (Ed.), *Research in personnel and human resource management, Vol. 16.* pp. 53–101.

Blanchard, P. N., Thacker, J. W., & Way, S. A. (2000). Training evaluation: perspectives and evidence from Canada. *International Journal of Training and Development, 4*(4), 295–304.

Boudreau, J., & Ramstad, P. M. (1997). Measuring intellectual capital: Learning from financial history. *Human Resource Management, 36*(3), 343–356.

Brocket, S. (January/February 2004). Becoming a business partner: HR at Coca-Cola enterprises. *Strategic HR Review, 3*(2).

Cabrera, E. F. (2003). Strategic human resource evaluation. *Human Resource Planning, 26*(1), 41–50.

Corporate Leadership Council. (2006). Web report at www.corporateleader-shipcouncil.com.

Guest, D., Michie, J., Sheehan, M., & Conway, N. Getting inside the HRM-performance relationship. Paper Presented at the 60th Annual Meeting of the Academy of Management, Toronto, 2000.

Herring, K. (October 2001). HR takes a hands-on approach to business and delivers results. *Workforce*.

Industrial Society. (April 2000). Managing best practice. *Training evaluation, 70*.

Ingham, J. (2006). *Strategic human capital management – Creating value through people*. Oxford: Butterworth Heinemann.

Kaplan, R. S., & Norton, D. P. (Jan–Feb 1996). Using the balanced scorecard as a strategic management system. *Harvard Business Review*. 75–85.

Kearns, P., & Miller, T. (1997). *Measuring the impact of training and development on the bottom line*. FT Management Briefings. London: Pitman Publishing.

Kearns, P. (1998). Moving up the HR ROI scale. *Financial Times*.

Kirkpatrick, D. L. (January 1996). Great ideas revisited: revisiting Kirkpatrick's four level mode 1. *Training & Development, 50*(1), 54–57.

Ministry of Defence. (July 2001). *Training and evaluation toolkit*.

Mooney. (2001). *Turbo charging the HR function*. CIPD Developing Practice Series, Wimbledon.

Pfau, B. N., & Cundiff, B. B. (November 2002). 7 Steps before strategy. *Workforce, 81*(12), 40–44.

Pulley, M. L. (September 1994). Navigating the evaluation rapids. *Training and Development, 48*(9), 19–24.

Rough, J. (1994). Measuring training from a new science perspective. *Journal for Quality and Participation, 17*(6), 12–16.

Tamkin, P., Yarnall, J., & Kerrin, M. (2002). *Kirkpatrick and beyond: A review of models of training evaluation*. Institute of Employment Studies. Report 392.

Warr, P. B., Allan, C., & Birdi, K. (1999). Predicting three levels of training outcome. *Journal of Occupational and Organisational Psychology, 72*, 351–375.

Waterman, R. H., Peters, T. J., & Phillips, J. R. (1980). *Structure is not organisation*. McKinsey Quarterly in-house journal. New York: McKinsey & Co.

# 12

# Case Studies

This section is another new addition to this book. We have left examples, stemming from our discussions with Business Partners in a range of organisations, scattered throughout the main text. In particular, you will find illustrations of Business Partner structures from *Barclays*, *the Immigration Office* and the *National Trust* in Chapter 3, as well as a small marketing case study from the *Body Shop* in Chapter 2. However, we decided to add some more comprehensive case studies to give our readers some real perspectives on the role of the Business Partner. We have tried to include a range of organisations in terms of size and complexity and highlight different aspects of the function and role from the practitioner's point of view.

A summary of the case studies is shown below:

1. DSGi Business – widening out the partnering principles

   Roy Mark is the HR and IT Director at DSGi Business, part of the Dixons Stores group responsible for business-to-business (B2B), IT sales and services. With many years in a variety of HR roles, Roy provides his view on what it takes for successful Business Partnering and how he has transferred some of the key principles into other service areas such as IT and Security.

2. NHS Wirral – moving from an operational to Partnering role

   Gemma Mcardle is a Business Partner in the Wirral NHS. She has recently moved from working in an operational role in HR to that of a Business Partner and reflects on the challenges of the transition and the particular skills which have become critical in the new role. Her ability to re-position herself in the business with her key clients is explored.

3. English Heritage – a gradual approach to introducing a Business Partnership
   Sarah Aston is HR Director for English Heritage and over the last three years has been aiming to more closely align the HR department to some of the Business Partner principles. She describes her vision for the department and some of the learning points along the journey.

4. A High Street Retailer – Skilling the Business Partners
   This anonymous case study of a high street retail business, tells of how they developed the awareness and skills of their HR team through a series of training and development interventions. The case study discusses the challenges the HR team faced, particularly in raising their credibility in the business, and how they sought to overcome them.

5. Cargill – an established and successful multinational Business Partnership
   In this short case study, Karin Braanker, HR Director for Europe and Africa, looks back on nine years of Business Partnering, reflecting on how far they have come and the skills that have been developed to help them get there.

6, 7 and 8 – Value added interventions: short case studies from Chevron Texaco, the Home Office and Severn Trent Water
   The final three case studies were in our original book published in 2005 and we decided to keep them in this revised edition for the interest of our readers. They all relate to examples of Business Partners (in name or behaviour) being able to influence and/or lead change through their focus and intention.

## Case study 1: DSGi business – Widening out the partnering principles

Roy Mark is the HR and IT Director at DSGi Business, part of the Dixons Stores group responsible for business-to-business, IT sales and services. He is a Board Director of DSGi Business where his responsibilities have evolved from purely HR and Training & Development, to now including diverse other business services such as IT, e-Commerce, Facilities, Security, innovation and Health & Safety.

### Background

Roy talked to us about the transition within his own role over the past five years and with the HR services offered, driven by a need for cutting costs, improving business performance and closer alignment with customers and their business needs.

With a staff of approximately 700 and a small (downsized) HR structure, DSGi Business operates within the broad policies of the parent Dixons group, but is able to implement business-focused policies more applicable for a B2B than a retail operation when necessary. This means that DSGi Business has the flexibility to use either the structure of a shared service centre for basic HR administration provided by the parent group, or the local HR service when a more bespoke and customer-focused service is required. Roy has a role in relation to HR Business Partnering with approximately 30% of his time focused on providing this service to senior managers. His two Senior Business Partners support him and their partners in the business and four HR Consultants provide core services such as reward, recruitment and training. He also has responsibility for a number of other key services where the partnering principles can be applied with good results. Five years ago, Roy recognised that the basics around HR still needed attention but since an emphasis has been placed on a greater understanding of business needs and building up knowledge and understanding of the customer, things have improved.

## The challenge – getting the right people

In Roy's view there is a big step between someone with experience of HR only or a graduate who has been trained in HR and someone with a good understanding of commercial reality and business needs. "I do not look for purely an HR background when recruiting; that I consider to be a 'given'. What will differentiate one candidate from another and what I look for (in terms of a Business Partner) is: have they worked in a role other than HR?" For example, from the last two Senior HR Business Partners (HRBPs) who Roy recruited, one had worked as a retail store manager and the other as a recruitment consultant with an agency background. Both had full commercial responsibilities which allowed them to "talk at the same level and in the same language as their managers". A track record and reputation of working successfully with the business can be developed but it is easier and quicker if there is a base of business knowledge there to start with.

## Widening out the principles

Roy talked about the links between HR and other services such as IT, Finance and Security, who all have to understand the concept of the customer and what the business is there to do. Knowing your customers is key, as is building their trust and confidence. In the IT section, for example, the quip would be about a stock answer of "computer says no!" when people asked for help. Specialists in this area had previously based their advice primarily on technical aspects rather than any real understanding of the customer's needs and business advantage. Some basics needed to be transferred from partnering principles including:

- To stop calling customers "users" and refer to them as customers – this represents a mindset shift and goes beyond a change in name
- To start analysing customer problems and explain either why their request was flawed or how a more advantageous solution was possible at no greater or even less cost, rather than just delivering the initial request
- To stop doing the technical aspects of the work they enjoyed and concentrate on a service that delivered the "customers" needs (no "fluffy" projects)
- Evaluating proposals to make sure that there was a business advantage and not just a technical solution
- Being more proactive – not waiting for problems to surface but identifying potential areas for performance improvement continually

Another example in Roy's area is that of security. Here again, the principle of the customer has been embedded and the importance of being mindful of costs. "Security staff now see that they are a supplier of services to their customers and are encouraged to come up with ideas on how to improve services." For example, the Security staff identified that they could undertake grounds maintenance work themselves, rather than the business contracting this out. Roy used the example of a previous M.D. (from a retail background) who used to say when presented with a new proposal "how many more dresses will it sell?" In other words, was there a clear commercial reason for doing things and how did it fit into the business plan and strategic objectives?

According to Roy, key to partnering in all the service areas including HR are the following principles:

- Everyone can save money if they have an eye on cost and understand the business
- Always look for a way to be proactive – don't wait to be asked, what they ask for may not be the real need (as Henry Ford said "If I had asked people what they wanted, they would have said faster horses")
- The culture of the organisation has to support innovation and proactive behaviour
- Be patient and think about timing for making changes, there needs to be an appetite in the business and you may need to nurture this over time
- Always be thinking about the business benefit – is it commercially viable rather than fashionable HR?
- Talk the language of the business, not HR terminology (or IT, Finance, etc.)
- It's the Business Partners' job to make their customers look good to their boss not make themselves look good to theirs

Roy advises up-skilling the HR team first including their understanding of the business to make sure you have something to offer. "If you are selling your services, make sure you have something to sell"

HR can now become a role model of good practice in building relationships and business credibility which other service areas can learn from and this perhaps provides the best opportunity yet to change the old impression of HR as being stuck in an Ivory Tower.

Roy has two other pieces of advice to HR Business Partners – "if you don't want to be outsourced – you have to continually prove you are of more value than an outsourced service" and "throw away the HR operational guide and replace it with the business strategy and budget forecast".

Martin Dorchester is the Managing Director of DSGi Business and he was asked for his views on the following two questions:

(1) What would you say are the behaviours and competencies you value most in an HR Business Partner?

"Commercial awareness rather than commerciality. I want the best they can give me but not filtered before it reaches me, the filtering comes afterwards. Rather than 'can do' I prefer 'will do' and more often than not 'have done'.

I want them to have challenge in their DNA structure and then know when to go into facilitate mode. I want them to have a broad range of HR knowledge, or be very adept at accessing it.

Personally I would also like them to have covered emotional intelligence, neuro linguistic programming or something of that nature."

(2) How can HR Business Partners best support you and other senior managers?

"For me it's about engaging and involvement. Back to the floor exercises, running a department for a while, covering holiday roles, taking on projects outside the comfort zone and being subsumed into the business while retaining a holistic view."

## Case study 2: NHS Wirral – Moving from an operational to partnering Role: Reflections from Gemma Mcardle, HR business partner

### Background

The two key drivers for the move to Business Partnership were a change in the Director of HR and changing Business needs. Back in 2007 *a new Director of HR* was appointed, who undertook a review of the resources needed to provide a modern and fit for purpose Human Resources service to the organisation. In undertaking this review she met with senior members of the HR team to review their current roles and identify pressures, as well as meeting with senior managers across the organisation to gain an appreciation of the level of satisfaction with the previous service.

The previous structure (Figure 12.1) had a traditional split between operational HR services, headed by the Deputy Director of HR, and Training & Development, headed by the Head of Workforce Modernisation, and delivered through the Learning and Development team. There were three HR Managers providing support to Directorates on HR issues, although one of these also headed up the recruitment team, meaning there was little opportunity to address other areas. These managers mainly dealt with employee relations issues.

Feedback from managers within the organisation was that the previous service was very much appreciated and was extremely responsive when issues arose. Managers felt supported in dealing with employee relations cases and the advice given was professional and sound. The common area of criticism related to delays in the recruitment process. There was also a gap in strategic, proactive support for Directorates or teams, and managers indicated that this would be a welcome development.

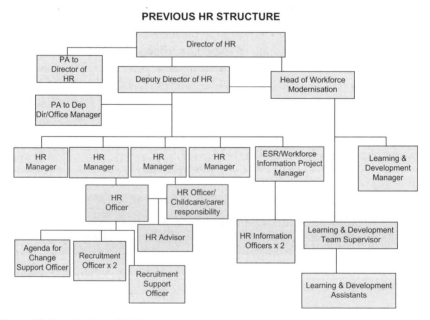

**Figure 12.1**   Previous HR Structure.

Members of the HR team felt they were constantly "fire-fighting" and were unable to proactively address the areas where they knew there were management and HR issues, due to capacity. There was particular pressure on the Deputy Director of HR and the Head of Workforce Modernisation as the next layer in the organisational structure was two bands lower, creating a significant gap in skills and experience. This resulted in the entire senior managerial and strategic workload falling to two individuals and a disproportionate amount of their time was spent resolving relatively low-level operational issues. These two members of staff were well-respected in the organisation and they were also routinely contacted by senior managers to lead on complex change management and organisational development issues.

Training was delivered with a very operational focus – mandatory training. There was little resource to identify organisational learning needs and develop and commission appropriate interventions, developing links with professional leads, education institutions and developing vocational as well as educational learning. There was also a lack of strategic focus within the Directorate, with little or no workforce planning activity and policy development being done as an "add on" to existing roles.

The **_business drivers for change_** stemmed from the Commissioning Plan in 2008, which set the direction for the commissioning and provision of services for the next five years. The implications of the plan for the organisation's workforce were significant:

- Service and role re-design was a key feature to enable providers of services to respond to the need for value for money, high-quality service tenders, and to meet targets.
- Workforce planning was a key feature of both service provision and commissioning.

In addition:

- The operating framework placed an increasing focus on the importance of effective enabling strategies, including HR processes.
- The operating framework also required an increased focus on staff satisfaction and engagement, with assessment at regional and national levels.
- It included the development of World Class Commissioning competencies which required significant organisational development.
- The post-implementation stage of an Electronic Staff Record offered the opportunity to realise significant benefits in terms of workforce reporting and increased managerial capability and control, but this needed project managing.

- HR was consistently required to play a significant part in organisational-wide projects
- There was no strategic support to Directorates in planning services.
- There was limited use of workforce information to drive improvement and performance management.

It was anticipated that by developing the HR function to enable it to develop high performance work practices, there would be performance benefits for the PCT in terms of:

- improved leadership
- increased individual and team performance
- increased staff engagement and commitment
- reduced turnover
- improved attendance
- increased workforce skills

## The new structure

Given the size of the organisation, it was clear that there were benefits in retaining centralised core HR functions, where expertise could be developed. By effectively retaining an "internal shared service model" covering the essential transactional HR functions (recruitment, staff records, employee relations management, administration of training), we hoped to avoid localisation of practice, diminishing of HR expertise and achieve economies of scale.

By grouping the transactional functions together, there was an opportunity to develop the "transformational" part of the HR function to provide a service that was lacking. We introduced HR Business Partners based on the Ulrich model. The Business Partners were set up to be aligned to specific Business Units, and work within or alongside them contributing to decision-making and providing a strategic HR perspective on the unit's work. By introducing such roles to the organisation, we hoped to develop a detailed understanding of the HR issues affecting directorates (effectively our Business Units), and ensure that the HR implications of decisions were considered at the earliest stage. The Business Partner's purpose was to drive workforce planning, support organisational change and facilitate organisational development and also lead on specific areas of policy development.

The current structure is set out in Figure 12.2.

The new Business Partner vacancies were advertised internally in the first instance and it was anticipated that the previous HR Managers would apply. Two internal HR Managers applied and I was one of them and both of us were successful. The other vacancies were put out to external advert and two were filled by

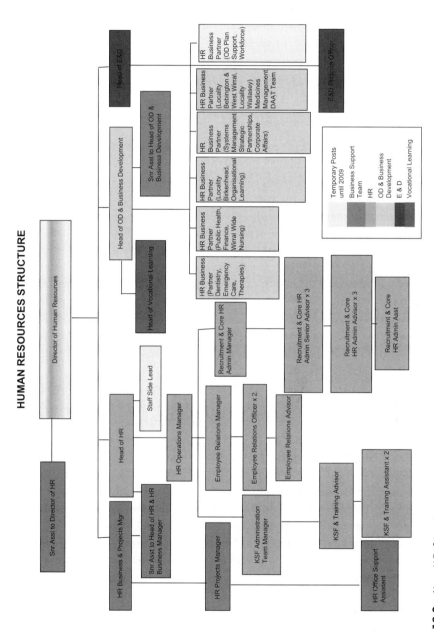

**Figure 12.2** New HR Structure.

candidates with private sector Business Partner and consultancy experience, and one was filled by another public sector employee with previous Business Partner experience in another public sector organisation.

The selection process consisted of an interview and presentation to the Director of HR, Head of Organisational and Business Development and a very senior manager from within the organisation outside of HR. Critical verbal and numerical reasoning tests were also used to support the selection process.

## Reflections on the change in role

I commenced as a Business Partner in June 2008 and quite literally one day I was an HR Manager operating at an operational transactional level and the next I was a Business Partner who would provide transformational and strategic HR support. My location didn't change in any way, I was sat at the same desk and my contact details remained the same.

I had a number of transferable skills in relation to negotiation, influencing, change management, policy development and implementation to name but a few as these were deployed in various situations with both line managers and staff as an HR Manager, however, it soon became apparent that there was a greater need in this role for coaching and project management skills. It is these two main elements of being a Business Partner that are not developed skills to any formal extent in the HR Manager role and in particular, the level of project management required is significant in that it can become a specific job in itself just to manage one project.

The briefing I had in relation to the role was focused not only on the Ulrich model, but also the organisational greatness model developed by Franklin Covey in order to set the objectives for the role. I understood the principles of Business Partnering and how this is different from being a transactional HR Manager but I found it very difficult applying this in practice within the areas I was working.

The biggest challenge of moving from being operational to strategic was managing the new relationship with line managers. They really struggled to understand the concept of Business Partnering and how what I am now offering was different but of additional value to what I was offering them before. Even when I was asking them about their workforce plans or asking them to articulate future activity in relation to workforce planning and/or change management they would focus on the operational issue that they were experiencing as a result of this activity and were reluctant to engage in discussions on how I could get involved and add strategic value to the process or project.

Although the consultation process with managers within the business identified that they desired more strategic input from HR, in reality and practice they began to perceive the new structure as a withdrawal of the level of transactional support they were used to, despite the fact that this was still being provided by another part of the HR structure.

I had been an HR Advisor and then an HR Manager in the same organisation for nearly six years; so the legacy of giving day-to-day advice on annual leave calculations, flexible working requests, sickness absence management and disciplinary and grievance procedures was a hard and long one to shake off.

For the first six months, I went through many highs and lows almost daily; it really was like a roller coaster ride. It became apparent very quickly that until these roles were bedded in and some of the key HR Business Partner works had been undertaken to establish both credibility for the role and understanding it would be necessary to do both roles, i.e. that of a transactional and transformational nature.

This was incredibly difficult and stressful and at times, there were conflicting priorities not just with the line managers but also within the HR team at all levels and particularly from my own senior managers as they were wanting to delegate the strategic project work that they had been struggling with for such a long time. However, the old issues of capacity were still there as I was still involved with disciplinary investigations and sickness absence management as well as some long standing and on-going capability and performance management issues.

I think this is unavoidable for those HR practitioners who are moving from a previous operational role into a more strategic role from within the same organisation. Nearly 12 months on things have got better and we are continually developing the role within our organisation and awareness amongst line managers is starting to dawn especially with those who have gone through a difficult or complex change management programme where the Business Partner has been key in helping them drive through that change in the areas of consultation and workforce implication planning and resolution. However, we are not completely there yet and we are constantly re-framing ourselves as individuals and as a Business Partner team in response to the changing environment of the NHS and also to the needs of our business.

Going forward for me I have recognised that I need to develop formal project management and coaching skills in order to be as effective as I can be in this role. I have determined this by benchmarking myself against my colleagues who have consultancy Business Partnering experience as they clearly demonstrate this knowledge and skill base with tangible results and as a previous HR Manager these skills aren't necessarily there at an operational level.

I consider myself to still be developing in this role but despite the teething problems, I am still fully committed to the Business Partner model and feel that this is ultimately the best option for our organisation in order to help it achieve its strategic aspirations.

## Case study 3: English heritage from Sarah Aston, HR director

### Background information

Sarah joined English Heritage as HR Director in 2006. At that time, the existing Personnel Department had a somewhat traditional "tears and tissues" approach and was rule bound and risk averse in its management of casework. Despite the organisation being very diverse, the way that it was supported through HR structure, policies, procedures and processes was very "one size fits all". Within the organisation there was a low level of understanding of the potential contribution of HR and little respect for the function. The general management population was very variable and often lacking in its people management ability, largely due to the specialist nature of their skills.

   Whilst it was apparent that some of the existing HR teams would never fit into the HR Business Partnership model, Sarah was keen to align HR to the diverse elements of the organisation and to give them some dedicated support and indeed challenge. In particular, she wanted to introduce the behavioural elements of the HR Business Partnership model so that HR could be a significant part of the organisation's modernisation agenda through both support and challenge.

### The approach

The approach taken was not to introduce all three elements of the typical Ulrich model, but to focus on creating a small central team of HR specialists and to develop the HRBP "mindset" in all members of the new team. Part of this involved regionally dispersed HR teams reporting into HR as a cohesive unit for the first time. The introduction of HR Business Partners was a gradual one, starting small with trusted colleagues and acting almost covertly along the journey towards Business Partnership. To support this strategy, a very clear vision was put in place to drive decision-making and to guide day-to-day practice. This vision was to:

- Support English Heritage to be a well-managed, high-performing organisation in terms of its resources as well as its output;
- Helpline managers to be confident, enabled and empowered;

- Encourage open, adult, mutually constructive dialogue between employees, their representative bodies, managers and leaders;
- Ensure that basic HR admin processes are so user friendly and reliable that HR, managers and staff use them effectively and are confident in them;
- Help make English Heritage a great place to work for both current and prospective employees;
- Give professional specialist advice which is pragmatic, fit for purpose, trusted and valued.

The main challenge was to acknowledge that the journey to Business Partnership was just that and would not be something which would happen overnight. The process involved a series of interventions, ranging from simple conversations, through to training and development interventions for both the personnel team and the wider management population. Over a period of 18 months through restructuring, recruitment and relocation, a very different team was built.

It was important to the credibility of the department that they did not go public with the strategy and have a big roll-out plan until they had gained some evidence, from anecdotes and key stakeholders, that the approach was working.

## Lessons learnt

Sarah recognised quite early on in the process that the new role of HR Advisors, who reported to the Business Partners, was quite instrumental in the process. They needed to "up their game" in order to support the Partners and as such, needed to be involved from the start of the strategy.

People transitioning from operational HR to the new Business Partner role had quite a challenge in weaning clients away from black and white answers to questions. Whilst they needed to provide pragmatic and constructive options and input, they also needed to support clients to make their own decisions and as a result found themselves pivoting between supporting and challenging clients. They also needed to adopt a "mantra" for every intervention, which involved simple advices, such as:

- Count to 10 before saying "yes" (which had been the natural default position)
- When you say no explain why
- Answer each request with a question "what would YOU like to do?"
- Hold your nerve!
- Have a "doorstep" speech at your disposal meaning: be able to communicate the vision of the new function quickly and naturally as if your life depended on it!

One of the greatest challenges has been balancing the individual interests of clients with organisational interests. Sarah reflects that there are rarely right or wrong answers in the field of HR and that the 80:20 approach where you are working in the spirit of the approach rather than the letter, has been a useful technique, also vital is knowing the exact context within which you are operating.

The political dimension of the role, working with different agendas; dealing with competing interests and balancing personal, functional and organisational needs, has emerged quite strongly. The Business Partners have found that the role can be a power struggle at times and people's positions are constantly shifting. Sarah stresses the importance of "authentic networking" and informal communication channels as a means of tuning into the "intelligence".

## Case study 4: A high street retailer – the initial transition to business partnership

### Background

This high street retailer had team of 30 HR Advisors located UK wide. They reported to a small team of Human Resource Managers (HRMs) who were located at the main regions. The company had an established service centre to deal with transactional HR issues.

This company is typical of many that we have worked with in that it was seeking to change the existing HR Advisor role to be more strategic and act more as Business Partners. There was no intention to change the structure or people in the role to do this, although it was recognised that some of the existing HR staff may not be suited to the new role.

Existing strengths came from the fact that the HR Advisors had strong relationships with their Area Managers and that the company had established procedures for monitoring performance and ensuring that HR tasks were focused on business needs. In addition, the HR team had regular communication across the business and worked well as a function.

### The challenge

Due to the strong, and in some cases long service, relationships that existed between HR Advisors and their Business Unit, there was a strong desire to please the Area Manager. As a consequence, despite the service centre, there was still considerable hand-holding of managers with transactional HR issues. The more senior Regional Managers perceived HR as supporting rather than driving the business.

It was unclear to the Head of HR whether some of the HR Advisors really understood what they were trying to achieve with the new Business Partner role, and if so, whether they had the ability to take a more challenging and strategic stance with the business.

## The approach taken

As a first step in the transition, the company held a facilitated one-day workshop with all of the HR team. The objectives and content of the day is shown in Figure 12.3.

---

The objectives of the workshop are to:

- Increase your understanding of what it means to be a Business Partner;
- Explore some of the challenges in transitioning to the new role;
- Develop an action plan to move the HR function further towards Business Partnership

**Programme Outline:**

Introductions and Objectives
Outline of the programme

What is a successful Business Partnership?

- The role of the Business Partner
- Core knowledge, skills and attitudes
- Creating value for the business

Exploring the options

- What are the options?
- How do these link to different structural models?
- Assessing client readiness and capability

Lunch

Exploring the client perspective

- Developing your role to suit the client
- Overcoming resistance

Influencing Change

- Developing a business case
- Marketing the function as a whole
- How do you measure success?

Mapping personal challenges and developing action plans

---

**Figure 12.3**  HR business partner workshop.

Whilst the over-riding objective was to increase understanding of the role, there was also a need to explore some of the barriers to success and give people the opportunity to self-assess whether the Business Partner role was really for them.

The day was incredibly well received, but inevitably raised more questions than it answered. Particular issues which were of relevance to this organisation were:

- The question of whether Area Managers were ready and committed to the change;
- Concerns over whether the service centre could deal effectively with all of the transactional issues;
- Personal concerns over the ability to "say no" to managers and hold back on providing expertise to encourage their development;
- A general recognition that most HR Advisors were not operating as strategic Business Partners.

## Ongoing actions

As a result of the workshop, a couple of key actions took place. Firstly, a core team from HR took the lead on establishing the move to Business Partnership as a strategic change project. The team decided that they needed to model their new approach to working by engaging stakeholders more effectively and developing a joint understanding of the model in order to get active support for the business case. In doing this, they hoped to get a real sense of where the value would come to the business through operating more strategically and get buy-in to the business change process. They are in the early stages of this process, but have already found that this has led to some challenging debates about the role of HR in the business and an increased awareness by operational managers of the changes proposed.

Secondly, the team recognised that they needed more personal development to assist them in their own progression to Business Partners. With our help, they developed a modular programme of development covering many of the core skills and behaviours. This programme is shown in outline in Figure 12.4.

Whilst it is early days in their transition, the company now feels better equipped to respond to the challenges of Business Partnership and more confident in the value of their approach.

**Figure 12.4**  Modular HR Business Partner Programme

## Case study 5: Cargill – an established and successful multinational business partnership from Karin Braanker, HR director for Europe and Africa

Cargill is an international producer and marketer of food, agricultural, financial and industrial products and services. It is a privately held company, founded in 1865, employing 160,000 people in 67 countries. In 2008 Cargill had $120 billion in sales and revenue. The company provides animal nutrition, consulting services, as well as feed and ingredients for livestock producers.

Nine years ago, Cargill restructured its HR function as a Business Partnership model. The HR function is currently split into three broad areas:

1. Shared service provision
2. Business Unit HR Partners
3. Specialists

251

The Shared service provision is a global unit with a regional head based in Europe. The HR Partners are embedded in the business and work on the strategic business agenda. They are supported by specialists, who provide expertise in areas such as compensation, learning and development, leadership and talent management.

Cargill has several Business Units that are grouped on seven platforms. The platforms were set up around common customers or common business capabilities such as trading and food. The job level of the BU HR Partners varies depending on the size and complexity of the Business Unit. Some businesses are small, positioned in one country and one location, compared to others that have multiple plants and offices across several countries.

Prior to the structure being introduced the company was working on a country basis. When the structure was first introduced, nine years ago, some countries still had a country HR person, but they found that they were not driving into key HR issues and provided more of the day-to-day shared service functions. Although initially turnover was high, over the last three years turnover has been low and the HR organisation structure has stabilised. The expertise of HR is now used well. There is now a true partnership between HR Partners and the business, and a structure which also works in partnership with the specialist HR providers. The shared services partnership was slowest to become established but has now improved and is still mostly staffed by personnel professionals as the business is keen to know what value they are bringing.

In terms of the skills needed for the role, Karin told us that most of the Business Unit HR Partners have to work across Europe to do their job. Therefore, they need to have a good generalist experience in sourcing and selection, compensation, employment law, performance management and development. They also need to develop facilitation skills so that they can help to lead strategic HR issues with the business.

To develop these skills, Cargill undertakes a range of training and development activities, including:

- Giving real responsibilities in the Business Units
- Using the London Business School
- Visiting sites, e.g. in Germany to get close to the customers
- Young people are brought in and trained on new assignments
- Appointing a coach or mentor outside the own area, e.g. across shared services and HR Business Units.
- Attending internal Cargill leadership programmes.

## Case studies 6, 7 and 8: value added interventions

When we published the original book in 2005, we asked a number of people in the role of Business Partner (although not necessarily with that title), for examples of what they felt were "value added interventions" for HR working more strategically within their organisation, and we have included their responses again here for the interest of our readers.

### Case study 6: Chevron Texaco upstream Europe from Howard Kewney, HR manager

Influencing leadership was discussed as an important area for the Business Partners to impact.

The role of the supervisor in performance management, employee development and pay determination is critical in an organisation that rewards for performance yet the linkage between performance measurement and pay is little understood by the workforce.

The processes within the organisation are well defined, and well established yet the understanding among employees is very limited. There is a lack of appreciation of the role that the supervisor plays in determining an individual's pay and overall a mistrust of the system.

This year the HR function has taken the initiative to design and roll out a series of workshops to all employees to help them understand the process and remove any mystery that may previously have existed.

These workshops were run by department/team in groups of around 15–20 with the supervisor present. Prior to the employee workshops, supervisor workshops were held to ensure that supervisors understood and supported the process, and were able to assist with questions from their group, and re-enforce the messages about the process. This gave them the opportunity to role model leadership behaviours and take on the responsibility of ownership rather than allowing it to be seen purely as an HR activity.

Key learnings and outcomes can be summarised as follows:

- The box has been opened, leading to a greater understanding among employees
- The importance of clear objectives and constructive discussion on achievements between employee and supervisor and how this impacts pay has become clearer
- For employees, the recognition that their supervisor plays a critical role in representing them in the employee ranking sessions.

- For supervisors, the increased understanding that their employees place a greater responsibility on them to ensure that they get it right.
- An enlightened workforce will constructively challenge the processes with more knowledge of the system and ensure that management continues to improve them.

The key message from this for Howard is that influencing can come in many forms and shades. This intervention was not primarily intended to change management attitudes or behaviours, but the process will encourage employees to influence upwards which in turn will influence supervisor's behaviour.

Other aspects of influencing change include:

- Determining how much time you are spending on operational issues against the more strategic work
- Keeping the ratio of time spent on influencing management by asking them how things are going, and keeping a regular connection with them
- Supporting managers to think about the business long term – for example, what the business demands will be in 2010.

In Howard's view all of these require a high level of interpersonal skill with coaching being a key part of the role.

## Case study 7: home office, human resources directorate from Tracey McGee, HR business partner

Tracey was involved in a TUPE-like transfer (TUPE – Transfer of Undertakings [Protection of Employment] Regulation 1981) of approximately 250 staff from the Department for Education and Skills (DFES) to the Home Office.

The staff in the Work Permits UK area were required to transfer under Government legislation and Tracey's role as the senior HR Advisor at the time was to ensure their smooth transition.

Challenges included providing the same or improved terms and conditions for the transferred staff whose grades ranged from Director to the more junior levels in the organisation.

The perceived difference in values and culture of the two organisations was a potential barrier to a smooth transition. There was a lack of clarity about the ability to preserve terms and conditions for the new staff and DFES staff were concerned about issues surrounding immigration and asylum. Building trust and understanding were therefore key.

The change strategy for helping smooth the transition included:

- Getting a seat on the Senior Management Team of UK Work Permits
- Working out the terms and conditions so that staff would face no detriment in joining the Home Office

- Working alongside the DFES and maintaining good relationships with the HR team there
- Ensuring that access to benefits such as health and welfare met the staff needs
- Reconciling recruitment practices between the two organisations
- Spending time with the new staff in Sheffield
- Making sure that managers had access to seminars on any new procedures
- Arranging for "drop in" surgeries for managers and junior staff
- Being available on a week-by-week basis
- Selling the benefits – for example, improved promotion opportunities
- Ensuring that the HR team were kept up to date on events.

A key point in the transition seemed to be the move of one of the Senior Directors to Sheffield where the DFES staff were based. This signalled a positive move towards integration.

The TUS were also instrumental (both within the Home Office and DFES) in helping to get the changes pushed through.

Key learning and outcomes can be summarised as follows:

- Keeping a visible presence and maintaining communication channels
- Building up relationships and trust
- Delivering on what you say you can
- Providing dedicated teams on specific queries – for example pay
- Never assume that you know the issues
- Getting your face know
- Working in partnership, particularly around recruitment
- DFES staff are now more integrated within the Immigration and Nationality Directorate and also with regions outside Sheffield.

## Case study 8: Severn trent water from Jane Miller, learning and development manager

Developing and delivering a pay system which linked performance to salary was a huge scale change where Jane felt Business Partners had to influence behavioural change in the organisation.

The new pay system meant line managers were in a position to influence people's individual pay rewards and so the strategy for introducing the change needed careful consideration.

The range of interventions which was part of this change strategy included:

- Joint implementation teams working at both strategic and operational levels across HR and management

- Communication and updates – particularly, monthly team briefings including reminders of the impending new process, so that this could be cascaded down the line
- Articles in company magazines, to give the big picture view of what was happening
- Newsletters were issued every couple of months which were e-mailed to managers (approx. 160) with suggestions to print these out and put them on notice boards
- Staff were invited to a workshop to help them understand how pay would link to performance in the future.
- Training delivered by both HR and senior managers
- Frequently asked questions on the intranet which could be accessed by HR and managers

As a minimum people were invited to a workshop and they were all issued a handbook on pay, performance and rewards. The same booklet was issued for managers and staff, modelling an intention of transparency and openness.

Extra training programmes in performance management were planned throughout the implementation period to ensure that there was sufficient opportunity for those who needed to improve their skills to be able to do so.

Managers attended workshops in the early part of the appraisal year so that they understood the implications of the revised system. Subsequent briefings meant they knew how to measure performance success and outcomes. At the end of the year they also had briefing sessions so that they were clear on how to give performance ratings to their staff. A half-day workshop supported the managers in communicating the subsequent pay awards to their staff. Letters would be personally delivered to individuals by their line managers and so needed careful handling.

The managers, according to Jane, mostly wanted to get involved in the process so that they had some control over pay and rewards. They wanted more flexibility in the pay awards and to have some say in pay differentials. Having more say in pay differentials went hand in hand with the sometimes difficult messages that managers would also have to give to certain staff.

Key learning and outcomes can be summarised as follows:

- Keeping the communication going alongside actions
- Training workshops were tailored to specific work groups
- Departments took the opportunity to integrate the introduction of this new system with other changes they wanted to make – this ensured consistency and a more holistic approach
- Securing and maintaining the ownership of the process by line managers is critical

- The HR team needed to keep in touch regularly to share thoughts on how and what to communicate
- Not feeling like you have to have all the answers
- Keeping open to an evolving and iterative process
- All pay changes were made on time
- From an audit of 500 staff (48% returned the questionnaire) 92% of respondents understand what their manager expects of them
- 93% felt their appraiser's expectations of them were fair
- 91% felt they can have an open and honest discussion with their appraiser about their performance and behaviour
- 93% agree that their appraiser listens to their views about their job and performance.

# 13

# Conclusions

In the last edition of this book, this final chapter provided us with an opportunity to reflect back on some of our learning about the role of the Business Partner and consider how it was evolving in the reality of the different organisational contexts. At the time, it was not easy to neatly summarise where the role of the Business Partner ought to be or how we think it should look in practice, as it was in the early stages of implementation in many organisations.

What was clear was that the Business Partner role needed to be dependent on the market you were in, the services you provided, what your client needs were and the resources you had available. Three years on, this still holds true, although the challenges of the role and the skills required by Business Partners taking on the task are now somewhat clearer.

The chapters in themselves provide a framework, which is worth holding in mind for developing the Business Partner function. If time and attention is paid to the purpose for setting up a strategic HR role, which sits alongside senior managers in the business, it is more likely that the function will be successful. Working through the checklists at the end of each chapter will also provide a useful basis for reviewing your effectiveness.

What we have tried to pull together here are some practical elements, as well as highlighting the less tangible aspects of the role. For us, building good relationships within the HR function as well as with your internal clients is an essential part of the success of the role. Having the ability to develop managerial capacity in the organisation to deal with the business challenges and move forward in the right direction for the company, taking people with you. This requires caring, competent, connected and challenging Business Partners who can enable the organisation to see what is missing as well as what is enabling within the present culture. We have called this the 4C approach to Business Partnership.

## The 4c approach to business partnership

### Caring

Caring means being attuned to the human aspects of the role: paying attention to process as well as content issues; understanding the human condition and how people might react in times of change; paying attention to your own needs and drivers as well as those of others. Caring also means paying attention to the little things – sitting down and having a cup of tea with someone, spending time on small talk as well as business-focused conversations.

### Competent

Competent means making sure you have the necessary knowledge about the business and organisations more widely; the ability to look ahead and anticipate what the business might need for the future; committing to continuous professional development; getting skilled in the areas in which you have less competence and using others both within the HR team and from outside the organisation who can meet the needs more effectively.

### Connected

Connected means developing excellent relationships with all your stakeholders; understanding their needs and goals; understanding the politics of the organisation and how to work with integrity within the system; connected to issues of corporate social responsibility and what this might mean for your organisation. Above all, working to keep connected with yourself.

### Challenging

Challenging means constantly pushing the boundaries of possibility within the business, challenging people and processes to deliver added value to the organisation.

This also means challenging yourselves on a daily basis, to ensure that the partnership is focused on the right issues.

Business Partners need to be constantly questioning themselves to achieve the best. Listed below are some of the questions that can help to provide a focus for the work of Business Partners in your organisation:

- Why do we want to work with our internal clients in this way?
- What are the drivers for setting up an internal Business Partnership function?

- What's in it for our internal clients?
- What are some of the options around structuring the function?
- How will that structure best suit our client needs?
- What services will be needed?
- At what level?
- Who will our primary customers be?
- What are our options for resourcing the function?
- What existing skills and capabilities do we have?
- Where are the gaps?
- How can we attract the right people for the roles?
- What training and development might people need to equip them for the roles successfully?
- What will their continuing professional development look like?
- How can we develop their capacity to think strategically, get alongside our internal clients and provide a value-added service to the business?
- What differences will this mean for our clients?
- What skills and resources will our clients need if we are to make a successful transition into a more strategic role?
- How do we support our client's needs around operational issues as well as the more strategic goals?
- How do we market our services and clarify what role we are now taking on?
- How can we continually monitor our services at both a content and process level?
- Do we know what our clients think about the service now?
- How can we capture their needs for the short, medium and longer terms?
- What measures do we need to put in place for evaluating the success of our service?

## Lessons from best practice

When we first wrote this book we were initially seeking to find a model of Best Practice from the companies we spoke to and drew examples from. What became increasingly clear as we progressed in the research was that the wide variety of examples of Business Partnership in operation meant that the findings were too diverse and organisational specific to make this possible. Even within one organisation, there were often examples of effective and less effective Business Partners, depending on the nature of the individual and the stage of development of the business unit.

This time around, we have thrown our net wider and sought even more examples of what is happening in practice. Over the years, we have also worked with numerous HR teams to help them establish themselves as Business Partners, or indeed, to explore whether the Business Partner route is the one for them. It was particularly striking that a number of common themes emerged from the case studies and people we spoke to, despite the diverse nature of the businesses contributing. Particular points to note are highlighted here.

## The importance of getting the basic, transactional, HR delivery right

Whatever the business, Business Partners appear unanimous in their opinion that their success hinges on the effectiveness of the operational HR delivery. Be this in a service centre, outsourced or sitting alongside the Business Partners, there has been a strong trend towards improving standards of the transactional HR service, to help free up the Business Partners to operate at a more strategic level.

## There is a growing trend towards recruiting HR business partners with wider business experience and not necessarily an HR background

Many companies are recognising that the skills and competencies required by Business Partners differ considerably from that of operational HR professionals. This book has focused on some of these core skills, including process consulting skills; project management; strategic business thinking; change management and greater influencing and political capability. Many of the case studies allude to a shift in their recruitment strategy, focusing more on these skills and business awareness than on a knowledge and experience of HR practices. This has obvious implications for HR, not only in how to transition across roles within the overall function from a career perspective, but also in the potential danger of the Business Partners losing their valuable people perspective as they strive to align more closely with the business.

## Business partners often need to prove the benefit of the approach in small steps in order to build their credibility

Where Business Partners have made the transition from operational HR roles, there is a strong pressure from the business to continue to field the transactional issues, as described in the NHS case study in the previous chapter. Their personal credibility often comes from solving these day-to-day problems, rather than engaging in more strategic activities. The case studies indicate that this challenge is best overcome by building stronger relationships where they can start to take more risks and challenge preconceived perceptions. They describe the need to prove the value of the approach by a series of smaller interventions, rather than a big bang approach.

## The business partnering approach is helping to streamline HR processes and ensure greater cross-organisational consistency in delivery

There is a strong indication from the case studies that despite the difficulties of transition, the Business Partnering approach is starting to pay dividends for organisations. Companies are reporting more streamlined and professional delivery of the transactional processes, with clear service-level agreements with the business. Clarifying roles and process mapping activities has also meant that there is much greater consistency of delivery across companies. The economic downturn has also meant that Business Partners have a strong role to play in the future strategic direction of the business including restructuring projects and changing business models.

## The shift from supporting to driving the business requires a re-education and often a re-skilling of the management population

The transition to Business Partnership often raises the question "to what extent does what our clients want, match what they need?" Many companies provided examples of managers who only wanted the transactional service from HR and were keen to have an individual to personally support them in dealing with transactional issues. The shift to Business Partnering therefore often left managers feeling unsupported and under-confident in dealing with such issues. In addition to this, they were faced with Business Partners who wanted to talk about their future business needs, but who they felt had no expertise to bring to the table. Quite a challenge!

As a consequence, companies are starting to realise the amount of work that needs to be put into both educating and preparing the management population for the change in approach and have undertaken both communication and marketing campaigns, as well as leadership and management training.

## Business partners are starting to strip away the "nice to haves" and proactively focusing on aspects that add value to the business

In the time since the first edition of this book, Business Partners are noticeably focusing more on the value that they bring to the business. They are becoming more proactive in their activities and as a consequence are able to choose to operate only in areas that add, or create, value for the business. As this continues, they will increasingly build their credibility and instil this new operating model in the business.

## Tensions invariably exist between what the client wants and what the client needs, with the ability to "say no" diplomatically becoming critical

As a consequence of refocusing on high value work and varying management capabilities, Business Partners often find themselves having to "say no" to

263

requests that are made of them. Virtually all of the case study companies commented on the need to develop the skill to challenge requests diplomatically and to have the assertiveness to maintain a position.

## Guiding principles for the business partner role

While this book and the examples we have used to illustrate aspects of the Business Partner role will never apply wholesale to every organisation, what we think can be pulled together are some guiding principles for good practice. These guidelines and principles will then need to be interpreted and tailored to meet the needs of the specific organisational context.

These principles encapsulate for us the essence of the Business Partner role.

- Clear purpose and strategic intent
- Working collaboratively and assertively with internal clients
- Helping to improve the business and quality of people's working lives
- Open to learning and sharing learning with others
- Adding value by clarifying what's needed and evaluating outcomes
- Working with integrity for the greater good
- Supporting each other as well as our internal clients
- Committed to continuous professional development

# Resources and Recommended Reading

There are a multitude of different resources available to support and develop business partners and aid implementation of the concept in organisations. We have picked out here just a few of the texts and resources we have found particularly useful and would recommend as essential reading for those in or aspiring to the Business Partner role:-

For a general overview of the role:

- Griffin, E., Finney, L., Hennessey, J., & Boury, D. (2009). *Maximising the value of HR Business Partnering* – Roffey Park Institute, Horsham.
- Ulrich, D., & Brockbank, W. (2007). *The HR Value Proposition*. Harvard Business School Press, Harvard.
- Evans, C. CIPD (2009). *Understanding and attracting strategic HR talent: A focus on the business partner role*. Research Insight: C Evans.
- Ingham, J. (2006). *Strategic human capital management – creating value through people*. Oxford: Butterworth Heinemann.
- Hirsh, W., Carter, A., Gifford, J., Strebler, M., & Baldwin, S. (2008). *What customers want from HR: The views of line managers, senior managers and employees on HR services and the HR function*. Report 453, Institute for Employment Studies.
- Reilly, P. (2000). *HR Shared Services and the Realignment of HR*. Report 368, Institute for Employment Studies, July.

To develop consultancy and project management skills:

- Block, P. (2001). *Flawless Consulting,* 2nd ed., San Francisco: Jossey-Bass/Pfeiffer.
- Cockman, P., Evans, B., & Reynolds, P. (1992). *Client-centred consulting: A practical guide for internal advisors and trainers*. London: McGraw-Hill.
- Cannon, J. A. (2006). *Making the business case*. London: CIPD.

- Harvard Business School. (2006). *Essentials of project management*. Harvard Business School Press, Harvard.

To develop influencing and thinking styles:

- Laborde, G. Z. (2000). *Influencing with integrity*. Wales: Crown House Publishing.
- De Bono, E. (2000). *Six thinking hats*. Harmondsworth: Penguin Books.
- O'Connor, J. (2001). *NLP workbook*. London: Thorsons.
- Goleman, D. (1996). *Emotional intelligence*. London: Bloomsbury Publishing.

To develop change management skills:

- Stacey, R. D. (1996). *Complexity and creativity in organisations*. San Francisco: Berrett-Koehler Publishers.
- Senge, P., et al. (1994). *The fifth discipline fieldbook*. London: Nicholas Brealey Publishing Ltd.
- Ackerman Anderson, L., & Anderson, D. (2001). *The change leader's roadmap: How to navigate your organisation's transformation*. San Francisco: Pfeiffer.
- Barger, N. J., & Kirby, L. K. (1995). *The challenge of change in organisations*. California: Davies Black Publishing.

To develop relationship skills:

- Sheth, J., & Sobel, A. (2000). *Clients for life*. New York: Fireside.
- Maister, D., Green, C., & Galford, R. (2002). *The trusted advisor*. London: Simon and Schuster.
- Pemberton, C. (2006). *Coaching to solutions*. Elsevier, Oxford.
- Networking web sites such as www.linkedin.com (Accessed 1st sept 2009-09-03)
- Coaching accreditation (various suppliers can be found on the web)

Training organisations and consultancies providing HR Business Partner training and development:

- Dr J M Yarnall. Skills Evolution Ltd. www.skillsevolution.co.uk (Accessed 1st sept 2009-09-03)
- Miss B Kenton. *The change and conflict consultancy*. WHooSH. www.whoosh. uk.com (Accessed 1st sept 2009-09-03)
- Roffey Park Institute: www.roffeypark.com (Accessed 1st sept 2009-09-03)

- Chartered Institute of Personnel and Development: www.cipd.co.uk (Accessed 1st sept 2009-09-03)
- Institute of Employment Studies: www.employment-studies.co.uk (Accessed 1st sept 2009-09-03)

Organisations providing HR process mapping: www.skillsevolution.co.uk (Accessed 1st sept 2009-09-03)

# Appendix

## Guidelines for completion

Review the following list of skills and behaviours to identify your current performance as a Business Partner. Having completed the questionnaire, review the aspects you have rated as needing more attention and use this to focus on your key development needs.

## Section 1: Delivering to the business

| | I do this well | I need to do more of this | This is not relevant |
|---|:---:|:---:|:---:|
| **Holistic overview** | | | |
| 1. I understand systems thinking and use this to consider the impact of interventions | ☐ | ☐ | ☐ |
| 2. I understand the bigger organisational context and future vision and strategy of the company | ☐ | ☐ | ☐ |
| 3. I demonstrate a good understanding of the business environment | ☐ | ☐ | ☐ |
| 4. I encourage discussions which help identify things stopping the organisation from moving forward | ☐ | ☐ | ☐ |
| 5. I am a strategic thinker – taking a helicopter view on business needs | ☐ | ☐ | ☐ |

| | I do this well | I need to do more of this | This is not relevant |
|---|---|---|---|
| *Plays many roles successfully*<br>6. I am able to flex my skill and experience to suit a wide variety of business needs | ☐ | ☐ | ☐ |
| 7. I am able to provide both expert advice and support and guidance appropriately | ☐ | ☐ | ☐ |
| 8. I identify and use appropriate specialists where boundaries of the role end | ☐ | ☐ | ☐ |
| *Long-term perspective*<br>9. I avoid getting bogged down in the operational side of HR work | ☐ | ☐ | ☐ |
| 10. I delegate appropriately to others | ☐ | ☐ | ☐ |
| 11. I keep up to date with trends inside and outside the sector which may have business implications | ☐ | ☐ | ☐ |
| 12. I help to shape the direction of the business in line with strategic priorities | ☐ | ☐ | ☐ |

*My overall sense of my performance in Section 1:*

_____

_____

_____

## Section 2: Working alongside managers in the business

|  | I do this well | I need to do more of this | This is not relevant |
|---|---|---|---|
| *Collaboration and empowerment* | | | |
| 1. I develop good internal networks across my defined area of the business | ☐ | ☐ | ☐ |
| 2. I build and maintain effective relationships with people outside my functional area | ☐ | ☐ | ☐ |
| 3. I engage relevant key stakeholders and sponsors | ☐ | ☐ | ☐ |
| 4. I actively involve others in the decision-making process | ☐ | ☐ | ☐ |
| 5. I ensure that clients are confident and competent to carry on after any intervention | ☐ | ☐ | ☐ |
| *People-oriented* | | | |
| 6. I build strong relationships with clients quickly | ☐ | ☐ | ☐ |
| 7. I am able to build and maintain rapport with a wide range of people | ☐ | ☐ | ☐ |
| 8. I demonstrate empathy and understanding in challenging times | ☐ | ☐ | ☐ |
| 9. I build trust by getting to know clients and their needs well | ☐ | ☐ | ☐ |
| 10. I identify and work with the strengths of others in the team | ☐ | ☐ | ☐ |
| 11. I share knowledge and information with others | ☐ | ☐ | ☐ |
| *Towards 'win'* | | | |
| 12. I ensure that contracts are in place for specific areas of work which meet the needs of the client and the business | ☐ | ☐ | ☐ |

| | I do this well | I need to do more of this | This is not relevant |
|---|:---:|:---:|:---:|
| 13. I monitor contracts at both the content and the process level | ☐ | ☐ | ☐ |
| 14. I clarify the boundaries of both my role and the work to be carried out | ☐ | ☐ | ☐ |
| 15. I avoid creating unrealistic expectations by my clients | ☐ | ☐ | ☐ |
| 16. I act with political sensitivity towards 'win' situations for individuals and the business | ☐ | ☐ | ☐ |

*My overall sense of my performance in Section 2*:

_____

_____

_____

## Section 3: Self-awareness and impact

| | I do this well | I need to do more of this | This is not relevant |
|---|:---:|:---:|:---:|
| *Focused on learning* | | | |
| 1. I question basic assumptions about self and others in order to heighten learning | ☐ | ☐ | ☐ |
| 2. I continually seek self-improvement | ☐ | ☐ | ☐ |
| 3. I demonstrate a good awareness of strengths and areas for development | ☐ | ☐ | ☐ |
| 4. I use learning as a basis for future development | ☐ | ☐ | ☐ |
| 5. I seek opportunities to move out of my comfort zone | ☐ | ☐ | ☐ |

| | I do this well | I need to do more of this | This is not relevant |
|---|---|---|---|
| 6. I share learning about the organisation and business issues with others | ☐ | ☐ | ☐ |
| 7. I choose self-development opportunities which are appropriate to needs | ☐ | ☐ | ☐ |
| *Self-expression* | | | |
| 8. I actively promote the business of the organisation through deeds and words | ☐ | ☐ | ☐ |
| 9. I demonstrate credibility by understanding the business and the range of issues facing managers | ☐ | ☐ | ☐ |
| 10. I am resilient – able to cope with the day-to-day pressures | ☐ | ☐ | ☐ |
| 11. I am able to maintain an appropriate work–life balance | ☐ | ☐ | ☐ |
| 12. I present information in a confident and clear way which meets the needs of the audience | ☐ | ☐ | ☐ |
| *Dynamism* | | | |
| 13. I am regarded as someone who 'walks the talk' | ☐ | ☐ | ☐ |
| 14. I act as a role model for others in the organisation | ☐ | ☐ | ☐ |
| 15. I engage others by showing a real interest in them as individuals | ☐ | ☐ | ☐ |
| 16. I am approachable and visible | ☐ | ☐ | ☐ |
| 17. I bring visible energy and drive to the role | ☐ | ☐ | ☐ |

*My overall sense of my performance in Section 3*:

_____

_____

_____

## Section 4: Creating and leading change

| | *I do this well* | *I need to do more of this* | *This is not relevant* |
|---|---|---|---|
| *Proactive and preventive* | | | |
| 1. I am proactive in seeking opportunities within the business to support strategy | ☐ | ☐ | ☐ |
| 2. I anticipate likely obstacles to implementing business change | ☐ | ☐ | ☐ |
| 3. I apply knowledge and understanding of change theory to implement changes successfully | ☐ | ☐ | ☐ |
| 4. I strike an appropriate balance between achieving the business goals and managing emotional reactions to change | ☐ | ☐ | ☐ |
| 5. I use influence to engage others in the change process | ☐ | ☐ | ☐ |
| *Innovation and entrepreneurship* | | | |
| 6. I find creative ways to work with managers, drawing on a range of methodologies to support business needs | ☐ | ☐ | ☐ |
| 7. I am able to work independently and make strategic decisions aimed at business improvement | ☐ | ☐ | ☐ |
| 8. I look for and identify solutions beyond the obvious | ☐ | ☐ | ☐ |

| | I do this well | I need to do more of this | This is not relevant |
|---|---|---|---|
| *Pathfinding* | | | |
| 9. I am able to cope with ambiguity and complexity | ☐ | ☐ | ☐ |
| 10. I work on the edge of my own comfort zones | ☐ | ☐ | ☐ |
| 11. I identify new possibilities to take the business forward and create competitive advantage | ☐ | ☐ | ☐ |

*My overall sense of my performance in Section 4:*

_____

_____

_____

## Section 5: Maintaining a business focus

| | I do this well | I need to do more of this | This is not relevant |
|---|---|---|---|
| *Prioritising* | | | |
| 1. I place the right priority on business needs in the light of longer-term goals | ☐ | ☐ | ☐ |
| 2. I recognise the need to withdraw from a piece of work and move on without impacting relationships | ☐ | ☐ | ☐ |
| 3. I demonstrate an understanding of the difference between urgent and important | ☐ | ☐ | ☐ |
| 4. I utilise business data to help shape the direction of the business | ☐ | ☐ | ☐ |
| 5. I am able to challenge appropriately and say no when necessary | ☐ | ☐ | ☐ |

| | I do this well | I need to do more of this | This is not relevant |
|---|---|---|---|
| *Utilising feedback* | | | |
| 6. I actively seek and review feedback as the basis for insight and learning | ☐ | ☐ | ☐ |
| 7. I demonstrate learning from feedback by applying new ways of working | ☐ | ☐ | ☐ |
| 8. I look for ways to improve the service of the Business Partner provision | ☐ | ☐ | ☐ |
| 9. I seek to enhance relationships and actions by thorough questioning during reviews | ☐ | ☐ | ☐ |
| *Demonstrating effectiveness* | | | |
| 10. I set appropriate measures at the start of any project | ☐ | ☐ | ☐ |
| 11. I ensure buy-in from the business to the evaluation process | ☐ | ☐ | ☐ |
| 12. I utilise evaluation data to demonstrate the added value of interventions and the impact on business strategy | ☐ | ☐ | ☐ |

*My overall sense of my performance in Section 5*:

_____

_____

_____

# Index